Holocaust Education

Holocaust Education

Contemporary challenges and controversies

Edited by
Stuart Foster, Andy Pearce and Alice Pettigrew

UCLPRESS

First published in 2020 by
UCL Press
University College London
Gower Street
London WC1E 6BT

Available to download free: www.uclpress.co.uk

A CIP catalogue record for this book is available from The British Library.

ISBN: 978-1-78735-797-6 (Hbk)
ISBN: 978-1-78735-796-9 (Pbk)
ISBN: 978-1-78735-569-9 (PDF)
ISBN: 978-1-78735-798-3 (epub)
ISBN: 978-1-78735-799-0 (mobi)
DOI: https://doi.org/10.14324/111.9781787355699

Contents

List of figures

About the contributors

Stuart Foster is Professor of History in Education at the UCL Institute of Education and Executive Director of the UCL Centre for Holocaust Education. He has provided strategic leadership for the Centre since its inception in 2008. He was a co-author of the Centre's two landmark national studies (2009 and 2016), focused on teaching and learning about the Holocaust. Stuart also served as Executive Director of the British government's flagship First World War Centenary Battlefield Tours Programme. He has written more than fifty scholarly articles and book chapters focused on history education and has authored or co-authored six books.

Andy Pearce is Associate Professor in Holocaust and History Education at the UCL Centre for Holocaust Education, with over a decade of experience in the field. He is involved in delivering the Centre's CPD programme and its educational research. Previously he has collaborated with the Imperial War Museum, the Wiener Holocaust Library and OSCE. He is the author of *Holocaust Consciousness in Contemporary Britain* (Routledge 2014), editor of *Remembering the Holocaust in Educational Settings* (Routledge 2018), and co-editor of *The Palgrave Handbook on Britain and the Holocaust* (Palgrave 2020). He serves on various advisory boards and has provided consultancy for the UK Government.

Alice Pettigrew is Head of Research at the UCL Centre for Holocaust Education and was one of the principal authors of the Centre's 2009 and 2016 research studies *Teaching About the Holocaust in England's Secondary Schools* and *What Do Students Know About the Holocaust?* She is also the co-author of two education studies texts, *Learning in Contemporary Culture* and *Education Studies: A reflective reader* (Sage 2009 and 2010) and has acted in an advisory capacity for the International Holocaust Remembrance Alliance (IHRA) Education Working Group.

Arthur Chapman is Associate Professor in History Education at the UCL Institute of Education. He taught history, sociology and related subjects for 12 years and has worked in higher education since 2005, at the universities of Cumbria, London and Edge Hill. He is editor of the *History Education Research Journal*, the series editor of *The International Review of History Education* and edited *Teaching History* for seven years. He has edited five books in history and Holocaust education and currently has a further two edited collections in press. His core research interest is in how children think and learn about the past.

Rebecca Hale is a Senior Research Associate at the UCL Centre for Holocaust Education and one of the principal authors of *What Do Students Know and Understand about the Holocaust?* (2016). She leads the Centre's evaluation activity, studying the impact of its professional development and Beacon School programmes. She began her career as a secondary school teacher before completing a Masters and PhD in psychology, and has been based at UCL since 2013. She has worked as a researcher on a number of projects in the fields of psychology and education.

Tom Haward is a Lecturer in History and Holocaust Education at the UCL Centre for Holocaust Education. After a career spanning more than twenty years teaching in secondary schools in Sussex, London, Zimbabwe and Brazil, he started working in higher education at Sussex University and joined UCL in 2015. His specialism is in understanding how students learn visually, which formed the basis of his doctoral research, and he is the published author of *Seeing History*, a teacher's guide to using visual historical sources. His most recent article about visual learning was published in the *British Educational Research Journal* in October 2019.

Darius Jackson is an Education Consultant specialising in Primary History. He taught for 19 years in secondary schools in Gloucestershire and Birmingham. From 2003 he worked at the University of Birmingham as Lecturer in History and Citizenship Education and then at UCL as Lecturer in Holocaust and History Education. He is interested in how young children make sense of the past; the ideas that frame their understanding and how this understanding relates to historical knowledge. He writes for both academic and professional audiences and has presented his research at conferences in Britain, Austria, Germany and Switzerland in recent years.

Eleni Karayianni works as a Research and Evaluation Officer at the UCL Centre for Holocaust Education. She is involved in the Centre's research into teachers' practices and students' understandings of the Holocaust, and has recently edited the publication of a series of briefings that disseminate the research findings to educational practitioners. She trained as a primary school teacher and later received her PhD in History Education from the UCL Institute of Education. Before joining the Centre, she worked as a teaching fellow at the University of Cyprus and as a primary school teacher in Cyprus and the UK.

Ruth-Anne Lenga is Programme Director at the UCL Centre for Holocaust Education. A leading figure at the Centre since its establishment in 2008, Ruth-Anne directs the educational vision and strategy, oversees programme delivery, drives the Beacon School Programme and created its MA offer. Ruth-Anne has over twenty-five years' experience in Holocaust education, serving as a Lecturer at the UCL Institute of Education and as Learning Director at London's Jewish Museum. Ruth-Anne leads the Centre's engagement with Holocaust survivors and has played a pivotal role in national and international projects, including Belsen75 and the Centre's work with OSCE to address antisemitism.

Preface

Research that informed this book: Landmark studies with teachers and students

The chapters in this book were written by colleagues at the UCL Centre for Holocaust Education (CHE). All of the Centre's educational programmes and courses are informed by academic scholarship, practical classroom experience and empirical research. Distinctively, however, the Centre is the only Holocaust education institution in the world which explicitly employs applied research to develop and improve classroom practice.

In service of its distinctive mission, the Centre has a small team of researchers who work closely with members of the Centre's pedagogic team to ensure its work is research-informed and evidence led. The research is ongoing and systematic and for almost a decade has explored a wide range of issues and topics. Notwithstanding this body of important research and scholarship, the Centre's programme is primarily informed by the results of two major national studies, published in 2009 and 2016 respectively. Throughout this book authors will consistently refer to these two landmark studies. This preface provides a brief overview of these two national studies and hopefully offers readers a point of reference as they explore the challenges and controversies identified by the authors.

The Centre's first national study, *Teaching About the Holocaust in English Secondary Schools*, was published in 2009 (Pettigrew *et al.* 2009). The Holocaust had been a mandated element of England's National Curriculum for history since 1991, but very little was known about how the Holocaust was taught in schools during the previous two decades. The research, therefore, sought to address this significant gap in understanding and, on the basis of the findings, to offer ways to improve teaching in learning. Thus, the 2009 research had two important aims. First, to examine when, where, how and why the Holocaust was taught in state-maintained secondary schools in England. Second, to inform the design and delivery of a continuing professional development (CPD) programme for teachers who taught about the Holocaust. Essentially, therefore, the research provided the catalyst for the original development of an educational programme for teachers which later became the UCL Centre for Holocaust Education.

The research was both the first of its kind to be produced in England and the largest in terms of scope and scale. It employed a two-phase mixed methodology. The first phase was based on responses to a detailed online survey (comprising 54 sections) completed by 2,108 teachers. The second phase focused on follow-up interviews with 68 teachers in 24 different schools across England. In overview, the 132-page research report provided a more comprehensive empirical portrait of Holocaust education in England's secondary schools than had ever existed before. The research exposed a number of key concerns and challenges and in many respects served as a call to action in the quest to improve Holocaust education.

Whereas the 2009 study primarily focused on the perspectives and practice of teachers who taught about the Holocaust, the 2016 study explicitly focused on students. The landmark 2016 publication, *What Do Students Know and Understand About the Holocaust? Evidence from English secondary schools* (Foster *et al.* 2016),was the result of an intensive three-year study. The first aim of the research was to provide a detailed national portrait of students' knowledge and understanding of the Holocaust. It also explored students' attitudes to this history and their encounters with it, both in and outside school. The second aim was to establish an empirical basis from which considerations of the most effective ways to improve teaching and learning about the Holocaust could be made.

The 2016 research also adopted a two-phased mixed methodology. The first phase was underpinned by responses to a detailed online survey (comprising 91 sections) completed by 7,952 students. The second phase featured focus-group interviews with 244 students in schools across England. Participating students came from all years of state-maintained secondary schools in England (i.e. 11–18-year-olds). In total, including those who had participated in pilot studies, more than 9,500 students contributed to the research. It represented the world's largest ever study of its kind in terms of scope and scale.

In particular, the study identified significant gaps in students' knowledge and limitations in their understandings of the Holocaust. It also evidenced the existence of common myths and misconceptions among many young people about the causes, conduct and consequences of the Holocaust. Accordingly, the findings of the 2016 study offer many challenges and issues for those working in the field of Holocaust education. As a result of the chapters in this book and the research that underpins them, it is hoped that readers will acquire a greater sense of the challenges and controversies that exist and, most importantly, consider how they can be effectively addressed and overcome.

Throughout the book, we refer to these research projects as the 'IOE teacher study' (Pettigrew *et al.* 2009) and the 'UCL student study' (Foster *et al.* 2016) or with similar identifying words.

Acknowledgements

The research in which the essays contained in this volume are grounded was made possible by the funding of the Department for Education and Pears Foundation. The editors and contributors gratefully acknowledge the continued support of these funders.

1

Challenges, issues and controversies: The shapes of 'Holocaust education' in the early twenty-first century

Andy Pearce

Introduction

On Thursday, 12 April 2018, as media channels speculated how Western governments would respond to allegations of the Syrian President Bashar al-Assad using chemical weapons against rebels in Douma, a striking article appeared in the *New York Times* (NYT). With the Chairman of Yad Vashem, Avner Shalev, having already claimed that events in Syria indicated 'the mechanisms and international bodies developed after the Holocaust to prevent the recurrence of crimes against humanity are failing' (see Aderet 2018), the NYT article ran with the headline 'Holocaust is Fading From Memory' (Astor 2018).

The article reported the findings of a survey conducted by the Claims Conference. Foremost among these was the discovery that 'many adults lack basic knowledge of what happened', with the 'millennial' generation of 18–34-year-olds identified as being especially ignorant. Overall, a third of respondents dramatically underestimated the number of Jews killed, over 40 per cent 'cannot say what Auschwitz was' and more than 52 per cent 'wrongly think Hitler came to power through force' (Astor 2018). The full research report – the 'Holocaust Knowledge and Awareness Study' – featured other notable findings, like 'seven-out-of-ten Americans say fewer people seem to care about the Holocaust than they used to and [that] a majority (58%) believe something like the Holocaust could happen again' (Schoen Consulting 2018). The only rays of light in an otherwise dank and depressing picture was 'an overwhelming consensus . . . that all students should learn about the Holocaust in school' and that 'Holocaust denial remains very rare' (Astor 2018).

It was not only events in Syria that provided a foreboding backdrop to the NYT article. By being published on Yom Hashoah, the annual day of Holocaust commemoration in Israel and the diaspora, the survey had symbolic potency: it purportedly highlighted, in the words of the Executive Vice President of the Claims Conference, Greg Schneider (2018a), that the 'issue' was the Holocaust was 'receding from memory'. More pointedly, 'this lack of knowledge while there are still survivors alive' brought forth the spectre of what might come to pass in decades to come (Schneider 2018b). For its sponsors, the survey's findings were a clarion call – one that 'underscores the importance of Holocaust education in our schools' and placed an urgency on finding new ways to bring young people into contact with survivors after their passing (Schneider 2018c).

On the face of it, the research findings were indeed arresting. As much as they had to be seen and understood in a longer-term context of levels of public knowledge and understanding, it was true to claim, as one commentator did, that 'creeping ambient fascism and antisemitism' in contemporary society meant 'things today *feel* worse' (Onion 2018), and thus made the trajectory of travel projected by the survey all the more frightening. However, what seemed to pass without comment was how findings such as these could exist at a time when teaching, learning and remembering the Holocaust are key issues of concern around the globe.

In the American context of course, the decentralised nature of the education system means there is no national mandate to teach the Holocaust – something which some commenting on the survey findings pointed to as potential explanation (Markowicz 2018). Meanwhile, the discovery that 80 per cent of those surveyed by the Claims Conference had not visited a Holocaust museum indicated the mere existence of institutions dedicated to commemoration and education is no guarantor of levels of knowledge and understanding. Nevertheless, even with these caveats, the position of the Holocaust in American historical culture – like that of much of the Western world – has deeper foundations than many other histories.

If it is the case that, in spite of these footings, significant numbers harbour troubling knowledge gaps and misconceptions, then this poses elemental questions to existing activities around teaching, learning and remembering. As it happens, certain aspects of the Claims Conference findings echo findings of the ground-breaking 2016 student study conducted by the UCL Centre for Holocaust Education (CHE). On account of substantial differences in aims, scope and detail, like-for-like comparison with these studies is not possible. Nevertheless, the UCL finding that 'student knowledge and conceptual understanding is often limited and based on inaccuracies and misconceptions' (Foster *et al.* 2016, 1) clearly has relation with conclusions drawn from the Claims Conference survey.

In this chapter, I want to take the occasion of the NYT article and the Claims Conference survey to reflect upon some of the challenges, issues and controversies around 'Holocaust education'. One of these, as the remarks above indicate, is the need to recognise and accept that some of our precepts, presumptions and practices in and around Holocaust education may themselves require review and, potentially, revision. There are others, of course – a number of which are taken up and discussed during the course of this volume. This introduction thus functions to orient the reader to the directions explored and examined in this book, outlining some of the key themes and threads the reader will encounter in subsequent pages.

Memory and knowledge

> We live with such easy assumptions, don't we? For instance, that memory equals events plus time. But it's all much odder than this. Who was it said that memory is what we thought we'd forgotten? And it ought to be obvious to us that time doesn't act as a fixative, rather as a solvent. But it's not convenient – it's not useful – to believe this; it doesn't help us to get on with our lives; so we ignore it.
>
> (Barnes 2011a, 63)

In his short novel *The Sense of an Ending*, Julian Barnes presents the story of how a retired man, Tony Webster, has to confront the ways in which history, memory and time imprint themselves in and on the present. In the process, Webster becomes increasingly meditative on what memory is and is not, its nature and purpose, and its centrality to our functioning. The fruits of this enterprise, as the above quotation illustrates, is a realisation that much of our thinking and understanding of memory is determined less by what memory is, than driven by what we want memory to be and enable us to do.

Webster's ruminations chime with the insights brought by the development of Memory Studies as an interdisciplinary field of academic research and investigation. It is one which, as is now commonly recognised, is synergetic with the growth and expansion of Holocaust consciousness in the latter quarter of the twentieth century (Olick *et al.* 2011, 29–30). Moreover, through this scholarly endeavour, not only do we today possess vastly enriched and diversified understandings of the multiple and myriad ways in which the past acquires presence in the present through human actions; fundamentally, we also now know more about 'the workings of contemporary culture and society' in terms of how the past is used and for what ends (Reading 2003, 69).

How far contemporary culture and society is willing to take on board the insights we now have and revise embedded public understandings of memory is a different matter. The reality that memory – in Barnes's words – is 'not only faulty but sometimes over-reliant on the imagination' (2011b) is an unpalatable one precisely because it carries with it the potential to undermine the certainties on which we construct identities, erect belief systems and sustain power relations. Instead, it can be preferable – necessary, even – to see memory as something pure, unsoiled and authentic. Preserving and perpetuating memory – remembering – thus becomes more than just an exercise in defying the passage of time and takes on connotations of securing and guaranteeing truth in the face of tyrannical oblivion.

To return to the NYT report and Claims Conference survey, the proclamation the 'Holocaust is Fading From Memory' can be seen from one perspective as a perfectly correct statement of fact: an 'alethic truth' (Bhaskar 2012, 30), if you will, encapsulating the reality that those men and women who *can* personally recall and remember are sadly but unavoidably experiencing some degree of mnemonic atrophy – either through sheer old age or by their very mortality. But for those concerned by the survey the issue is not with the loss of individuals' memories; the frame of reference is rather the collective: the Holocaust fading from *our* memory. Notably, the explanation offered for this is not necessarily the passage of the survivor generation, though this is of much concern. Rather, history is presented as receding from memory not because 'forgetting is the normality of personal and cultural life' (Assmann 2008, 98), but as a result of 'critical gaps both in awareness of basic facts as well as detailed knowledge of the Holocaust' (Claims Conference 2018). The disappearance of memory is therefore presented as a failure of epistemology, meaning the correction of this trend is relatively straightforward; a simple matter of more people acquiring more knowledge.

These are powerful explanations and persuasive answers to the perturbing prospect of the Holocaust vanishing from our memory. All the same, they are also open to contestation. Generations of memory scholarship has enlightened us to how, for example, forgetting in a collective context is 'mainly deliberate, purposeful and regulated' (Lowenthal 1999, xi). This does not mean collective knowledge is irrelevant, but highlights knowledge alone is no guarantor of memory. Then there is the matter of knowledge itself: by this do we mean what is called substantive knowledge in history education, or something more experiential and existential – what Shoshana Felman and Dori Laub (1992, 64) frame as 'the knowledge of the trauma, the knowledge of facing it and living in its shadow'? Then there is the question of how knowledge is to be encountered: is it to be transmitted from teacher to learner, to be duly absorbed and assimilated? Is the learner to be left to their own devices and construct knowledge for themselves? Or, something in between? And, finally, what is to be *done* with knowledge: is it knowledge for knowledge's sake, knowledge to affect attitudinal or behavioural change, or knowledge for action? Knowing to remember still leaves unanswered what the ultimate purpose of remembering is.

These very brief remarks illustrate that the nature, operation and intersection of memory and knowledge in teaching and learning about the Holocaust is of a complexity rarely evident in much popular discourse around Holocaust education. Elsewhere I have argued this is the product of 'a general lack of theorisation of how Holocaust education and memory relate to one another, and an underwhelming amount of analysis of projects which actively combine the two' (Pearce 2018a, 2); it may also be because, at root, 'we' as collectives do not wish to call into question the orthodoxies and axioms that have calcified around the Holocaust, for these have enabled us to domesticate it.

The state of the field

Since Holocaust education has become a principal conduit for the transmission of its memory and the object of numerous national and transnational initiatives in recent decades, it would be reasonable to presume there is clarity and consensus around elemental issues. This is, however, far from the case. Following Oliver Plessow, Holocaust education can, indeed, be viewed as a 'field' when field is taken to mean

> a relatively autonomous social system with certain practices, rules, and institutions, which is constituted by a system of relative

positions created by competitive interaction between different agents and thus prone to constant reorganization.

(Plessow 2017, 317)

Even so, because it is 'part of the wider discourse on the overall significance of the Holocaust', Plessow suggests Holocaust education 'is also subject to the conflicts that are being waged around the globe to determine the Shoah's discursive position in memory and history'. Accordingly, 'struggles between competing "memory frames" mirror in the debates about suitable pedagogies of the Shoah' (Plessow 2017, 317).

A perception of the field of Holocaust education as one characterised by fracture and fragmentation has been borne out by a number of studies conducted in recent years. Research by the Georg Eckert Institute (Carrier *et al.* 2015, 13–14) on the position of the Holocaust in curricula and its representation in textbooks around the world uncovered '*general* convergent and divergent tendencies' and 'evidence of *regional* convergent and divergent trends'. Accordingly, its authors described 'an overlapping multipolar pattern which is partly global, partly regional and partly national', prompting them to forward the notion of 'education about Holocausts'.

Meanwhile, a major 'meta-analysis of existing studies' on 'teaching and learning about the Holocaust (TLH)' (Eckmann and Stevick 2017a, 19) conducted under the auspices of the International Holocaust Remembrance Alliance (IHRA) found 'the field remains in quite different states of development in different linguistic communities of scholars, and it lacks mature exchanges between those language communities' (Eckmann and Stevick 2017a, 21). Tellingly, among the general conclusions forwarded by the authors of this research was the assertion 'TLH itself is a broad umbrella with many different approaches and areas of focus. Terms such as "Holocaust education" and "teaching and learning about the Holocaust" encompass such a wide range of content and practices that it is problematic to conceive of them as a single entity' (Eckmann and Stevick 2017b, 287).

Such claims pose particular challenges for an organisation which describes itself as 'promoting Holocaust education, research and remembrance since 1998' (International Holocaust Remembrance Alliance 2019). Yet, according to a recent policy guide produced by UNESCO (2017, 18), 'the expression "Teaching and Learning about the Holocaust" is used by the International Holocaust Remembrance Alliance' and 'addresses didactics and learning, under the larger umbrella of education about the Holocaust, which also comprises curricula and textbook studies'. Holocaust education, meanwhile, is defined by UNESCO as 'efforts, in formal and non-formal settings, to teach about the Holocaust'.

One could well be forgiven for finding these developments disorienting. The phrase 'Holocaust education' has indeed long been problematic, suffering from the ailments of insufficient conceptualisation, lack of clarity, and imprecision. Despite this, the term has been institutionalised in a number of countries and become currency in international Holocaust politics. This does not mean, of course, that we are obliged to using 'Holocaust education' indefinitely; in refocusing attention on pedagogy, the phrase 'teaching and learning about the Holocaust' has much to commend it and is arguably preferable. However, because 'Holocaust education' has acquired normative dimensions – partly through transnational initiatives promoted by organisations like the IHRA – it seems unlikely that a change in discursive frames will get good traction very quickly.

Ultimately, umbrella phrases are – by their nature – characterised by breadth and variety. They cease to be useful when they create confusion and handicap common understanding. In making sense of the growing questions around 'Holocaust education' it is worth reiterating that it has, for some time, been 'largely under theorized' (Eckmann and Stevick 2017a, 21). On this Doyle Stevick (2017, 155) notes, 'a field requires a certain critical mass of data and research studies to enable the development of well-supported theory, and teaching and learning about the Holocaust is not yet in that position'. This would suggest that whether we call it 'Holocaust education' or 'Teaching and Learning about the Holocaust', we are talking about a collection of practices, principles adorned with the garbs associated with a field, but bound together by belief, conviction, and resolution rather than being housed within clear conceptual or empirical frameworks. As Eckmann and Stevick (2017a, 30) have written, 'there is much more consensus about the importance of addressing the Holocaust than about "why, what and how to teach" it, and about how to know if those goals have been achieved'.

The coexistence of, on the one hand, consensus around addressing the Holocaust and, on the other, inability to determine what this looks like pedagogically, is both a product and cause of reductive understandings of memory, knowledge and education – as well as the blurring of lines of separation between mnemonic and educational activity. Changes may be slowly occurring, but it remains to be seen how far new research into teaching and learning about the Holocaust, and new ways of theorising these enterprises, will affect practice in classrooms and at a policy-making level. As the IHRA study revealed, for all the diversity, certain trajectories and prevailing issues can be observed. These include the reality that teachers and students are products of their cultural milieu, the deleterious consequences that follow insufficient specialist training, and the potentially problematic ways in which memory is used to teach history, such as a 'pedagogy of reverence' (Tyaglyy 2017, 149). In an ideal world, advances in research and changes in pedagogical approaches would exist in a reciprocal relationship. However, certain long-term trends have combined with more recent unforeseeable developments to add new immediacy and new pressures.

Contemporary contexts

Of these trends, four contexts merit particular mention. The first is what Joanna Michlic (2017, xxvii) calls 'the growing awareness of the inevitable encroachment of the "postsurvivor" era'. This 'evolving temporal and ethical framework' (Popescu 2015, 4) is not new; rather, it was a central dynamo in driving efforts to institutionalise the Holocaust in national cultures during the final quarter of the last century. Nonetheless, Michlic (2017, xxvii) is right to intimate that the 'passing of the first decade of the twenty-first century' has served to focus a growing number of minds on the future of both Holocaust memory and Holocaust education.

For some, this creates an existential challenge: as Thomas Harding (2014) puts it, 'who is going to educate young people about the Holocaust when the survivors are no longer with us?' In shining a light on the formative contributions survivors have made to the evolution of Holocaust education, Harding's question is important. As Michael Gray (2014, 82) records, 'across the globe, survivors have played a key role in Holocaust education, playing an important part in its development and delivery'. Still, Harding's question also carries with it a number of presumptions. One of these is that it is survivors alone who have taught generations about the Holocaust; another that survivors are, by their status as witnesses, not only well-positioned to 'educate' but also the best qualified; and another still is that the absence of survivors from young people's educational encounters will necessarily impoverish their learning.

All of these notions can be contested without undermining or denying the invaluable contribution made by survivors. For some time, survivors were indeed in the vanguard of teaching about the Holocaust – compensating for the lack of classroom resources and teaching materials, as well as teachers' own insufficient subject knowledge. But with the emergence of state-sponsored initiatives this began to change. As to whether survivors are the most-suited (and most able) to educate about the subject, such a notion must be measured against their own reliance on memory, the partiality of their personal experience vis-à-vis their capacity to comprehend the totality of the event, and the reality that the majority of survivors are not professionally trained teachers. And, whilst students are profoundly impacted by first-hand engagements with survivors, for most a personal encounter with a survivor is the exception and not the norm. Thanks to technology and pedagogical innovation this means the majority of young people can engage with survivors, and though the nature of this experience will be unavoidably different, there is no existing evidence to say young people who hear directly from survivors necessarily 'know more' or have better understandings of the Holocaust than those who do not.

The continued passing of the survivor generation has acquired greater poignancy when set against the second context, that being the recent increase of antisemitism in contemporary culture, society and politics. While antisemitism has persisted throughout the post-1945 epoch, a distinguishing feature of this particular period has been the entwinement of antisemitism with the politics of the Middle East. Accordingly, the particular turbulence and turmoil which occurred in the region in the early twenty-first century – thanks, in no small part, to Anglo-American foreign policy – contributed to a sharp rise in antisemitic sentiment and incidents across many Western nations. The 'resurgence' of antisemitism, its reappearance 'in new ways and in unexpected strength' (Penslar *et al.* 2005, vii), was characterised by a shift in some of its foundational precepts. As Alvin H. Rosenfeld (2013, 2) observes, 'in contrast to past antisemitisms, which drew largely on religious and racial biases against Judaism and the Jews, much of today's anti-Jewish animus is driven by ideological and political biases. The older forms of Jew-hatred are not altogether gone, but among most enlightened people in the West they are no longer considered respectable or persuasive'.

Antisemitism has never been entirely removed from politics and ideology, of course, but in the opening decades of the millennium it has found new forms of expression and new degrees of intensity – particularly, and paradoxically, within circles of Islamic extremism and 'in social spaces which think of themselves as antiracist and democratic' (Hirsh 2018, 1). While all variants of antisemitism pose threat and carry danger, David Hirsh offers food for thought when he suggests that what makes certain contemporary strains so pernicious is they do 'not come dressed in a Nazi uniform' or 'openly proclaim . . . hatred or fear of Jews'. Rather, antisemitism currently found on the left of the political spectrum 'says it has learnt the lessons of Jew-hatred *better* than most Jews have, and it says that, unlike them, it stands in the antiracist tradition' (Hirsh 2018, 7).

The historic ties between Holocaust education, antiracism and the Left in many Western countries makes the growing prominence of this particular brand of antisemitism all the more challenging, and raises questions about the politics of teaching, learning and remembering the Holocaust. Yet it is the upsurge in antisemitic violence that has blighted the West over the last decade which gives the continued passing of survivors an obsidian and ominous tone; especially when its witnesses speak of antisemitism being 'no longer' taboo (Echikson 2017) and warn that civilisation is 'but a thin veneer, very easily torn away' (Sherwood 2017).

The sense of a breakdown in consensus over what is and what is not deemed offensive or unacceptable is inseparably connected with the third contemporary context – what the journalist Matthew D'Ancona (2017) terms 'the new war on truth'. As it is, the notion of 'post-truth' currently so much in vogue may, as James Ball (2017) has pointedly suggested, be better understood as 'how bullshit conquered the world', but regardless of the moniker there remains a palpable sense 'that facts and truth are endangered in today's political arena' (Mcintyre 2018, xiii). For Lee Mcintyre, this is something distinctive, for it is 'not just that truth is being challenged, but that it is being challenged as a mechanism for asserting political dominance' (Mcintyre 2018, xiv).

For those who care for the history and the memory of the Holocaust, assaults on truth and actuality are – ostensibly – nothing new. Holocaust denial, conceived and born in the midst of the events themselves, was a clear and present danger for the majority of the post-war period and more recently has found succour from pronouncements made by the Iranian regime and the unregulated spaces of the internet. Whilst outright denial is now discredited in mainstream society, attempts to revise, distort or trivialise continue unabated. Meanwhile, within intellectual circles, the advent of postmodernism in the last quarter of the twentieth century had a particular impact on Holocaust consciousness, with the Holocaust often 'invoked as a "test case" for postmodern ideas' (Eaglestone 2004, 3).

These experiences and trends have not inoculated the Holocaust against contests over truth, but they have helped to enrich scholarly thought and endeavour, forcing academics, advocates and public intellectuals to be more rigorous and robust in their assertions. Still, if the institutionalisation of the Holocaust – the creation of cultural memories, the establishment of educational programmes – has in some regards helped to reinforce it against malignant forces, it has not meant it is impervious to the zeitgeist of our age. Indeed, it is hard to disagree with Deborah Lipstadt's clarion call (2017) that 'now more than ever those who value truth, irrespective of their political opinions, must do the legwork necessary to expose those for whom facts are but a suggestion'.

Such legwork exerts particular demands on teaching and learning, requiring approaches that move beyond merely transmitting 'facts' towards developing critical understanding. The urgency to do so stems from the fourth and final context, itself directly related to the third. In the spring of 2017, with both eyes firmly on the new incumbents in the White House, Timothy Snyder (2017) announced that 'post-truth is pre-fascism'. Snyder's remarks were purposely pointed, with his fuller explanation worth quoting at length:

> This whole idea we're dealing with now about alternative facts and post-factuality is pretty familiar to the 1920s. It's a vision that's very similar to the central premise of the fascist vision. It's important because if you don't have the facts, you don't have the rule of law. If you don't have the rule of law, you can't have democracy. And people who want to get rid of democracy and the rule of law understand this because they actively promote an alternative vision. The everyday is boring, they say. Forget about the facts. Experts are boring. Let's instead attach ourselves to a much more attractive and basically fictional world. So I'm not saying that Trump is just like the fascists of 1920s, but I am saying this isn't new.
>
> (Snyder 2017)

Snyder's remarks may have been focused on Trumpian America, but they had a transnational quality given the renaissance of the political right and populist politics in Europe. Whilst we can loosely benchmark this development against the economic crises of 2008, David Goodhart (2017, 51–2) offers the salient reminder that 'populism is a socio-cultural and identity phenomenon more than a socio-economic one, which is why so many conventional politicians, especially on the left, do not know how to respond to it'. Most potently, Goodhart suggests 'it is in cultural matters, not economic ones, that the consensus in liberal democracies is most broken'.

Adopting this perspective casts the very real and tangible gains made by right-wing movements across Europe in recent years in an even more uncomfortable light. For it suggests that the reappearance of parties with fascist tendencies and extremist views, not to mention their renewed confidence, cannot be fixed simply through such mechanisms as the redistribution of wealth or provision of contemporary equivalents of bread and work. At issue are matters of culture and identity, issues made all the more acute by the demographic changes and social upheavals brought by the movement of people – many of whom have been forced to move in order to escape wars and conflicts that show no sign of conclusion in the near future. The recourse of right-wing populists to age-old techniques of othering and exclusion in the face of these developments only finds new dimensions and danger in a 'post-truth', 'post-survivor' age.

Volume overview

The four contemporary contexts briefly mentioned above all have, in differing ways, implications for how the Holocaust is taught and how it is learnt. As such, they provide a useful backcloth against which to consider in greater detail some of the key challenges, issues and controversies that currently surround Holocaust education.

The essays contained in this volume work towards this objective. Clearly, no single publication – however large – could hope to cover all questions currently circulating within and around teaching and learning about the Holocaust, and this book does not claim to be comprehensive. Similarly, because education of all and any description is dynamic and multidimensional, challenges, issues and controversies can – and do – emerge and recede in different ways at different moments in time. Thus, the essays in this volume do not profess to be the final word on these matters; instead, as much as being reflections of their particular context, they are intended to raise awareness, stimulate thought and provoke debate.

Rationale, aims and objectives

Arguably one of the most long-standing issues in Holocaust education – certainly in the United Kingdom – relates to rationale. Two pressing questions flow from this: why is the Holocaust part of school curricula, and why should young people learn about the Holocaust? Whilst interrelated, these questions also exist as discrete enquiries in their own right. To answer the first, for example, one must consider what curriculum is and how it operates – that is, its relationship to and with broader culture, and the intractable truth that curricula are inseparable from matters of power and influence. It is also prudent to understand how curriculum functions, in terms of the ways it constructs parameters in which teachers and learners move and interact, and its capacity to contribute to the formation and perpetuation of norms. Finally, if we are to truly comprehend the presence of the Holocaust in the school curriculum, we must be cognisant of how this position came to pass, and the trajectories of curriculum development since.

All of the above can (and, arguably, should) inform how one answers why students should learn about the Holocaust. But this question is equally entwined with issues of history, educational philosophy and ontology. It requires, for instance, identification of what the Holocaust as a historical entity was – or, at the very least, an unambiguous articulation of what 'the Holocaust' is being taken to refer to; it demands clarity about and around what is intended to be achieved and how this will occur; and, underlining all of these, it insists on a clear sense of purpose about why it is necessary for valuable curriculum time to be devoted to learning about this subject. What makes the task complex and challenging, of course, is that none of these queries lend themselves to simple, straightforward resolutions. Instead, they remain – perhaps for perpetuity – open to competing and contrasting interpretations. Where some will see this to be liberating in terms of the opportunities it opens up for Holocaust education to continually renew and develop, it is equally experienced by many at the chalkface as confusing, overwhelming and debilitating.

In his contribution, **Stuart Foster** broaches questions of rationale by considering the position of historical knowledge in teaching and learning about the Holocaust. Focusing on the history classroom, Foster's point of departure is that different perspectives on how much (or how little) students need to 'know' about the Holocaust are driven by judgements about the usefulness – and, ultimately, the value – such knowledge is believed to have. Foster suggests that for those who see Holocaust education as a utilitarian exercise, one ultimately aimed at young people learning the so-called 'lessons' of the Holocaust, knowledge is only relevant in the pursuit of this goal; others – particularly those who believe that learning history is about the transmission of an official narrative – regard knowledge acquisition alone as the principal reason for historical study.

Foster argues for a third way, maintaining 'that in order to derive true meaning from the Holocaust, it is essential that students have an informed understanding of its specific and contingent historical context'. He is clear that 'to argue for the value of historical knowledge is unequivocally not to suggest that knowledge needs to be acquired for knowledge's sake'; instead, it is to make the case for the foundational role of epistemology in allowing students to move towards understandings which reflect historical actuality and enabling them to, in turn, 'critically evaluate the way the Holocaust is presented in modern culture'. To exemplify his argument, Foster draws on the UCL student study (Foster *et al.* 2016) and convincingly shows how limits and absences in knowledge either prohibited understandings or actually nurtured problematic misunderstandings.

Like Foster, **Arthur Chapman** is also concerned with issues related to knowledge and its usage. In his chapter, Chapman trains his sights specifically on the matter of Holocaust 'lessons'. As Chapman shows in his review of existing literature, it is fair to say that the notion such lessons exist and can be learnt has been a point of considerable and long-standing debate. However, despite the impassioned claims and appeals of advocates and opponents alike, less attention has been given to constructing theoretical frames of analysis through which one can capture and conceptualise how 'lessons' operate and what they are understood to do.

Chapman's chapter is a much-needed contribution to addressing this lacuna. Through a systematic and diligent approach, Chapman deconstructs the constituent parts of much discourse around Holocaust lessons, to schematise the elemental features of the two distinct processes related to this endeavour: namely, 'learning about' and 'learning from'. In so doing, Chapman underlines the complexities of these particular operations by emphasising how these enterprises are necessarily filtered and experienced differently in various contexts. From here, Chapman forwards a typology in which we can posit 'lessons' and see with greater clarity the type of work they are being asked to do. Chapman's typology reinforces two of his core arguments: first, that 'purely historical approaches to the Holocaust' are limited on account of not being able 'to answer the compelling ontological questions that often arise'; and second that attempts at fashioning or drawing 'lessons' must be duly cognisant of how understanding necessarily entails 'the contestation of stereotypes and presentism and a focus on context and specificity'.

Taken together, the chapters by Foster and Chapman are welcome interventions for how they refocus attention on elemental questions of praxis and pedagogy. How we as practitioners and educators choose to answer these questions – or if we opt to avoid them altogether either because we do not want to consider them, or because we presume they do not warrant consideration – can have critical consequences for students' learning. It is worth remembering, however, that while a development of knowledge and sophistication of understanding will certainly mean students are better positioned to approach the complexities of the Holocaust, this does not mean answering the questions it poses is any more straightforward.

This truth is especially palpable when it comes to the task of explaining not just how, but *why* people chose to actively participate in the murder of other human beings. **Rebecca Hale** approaches this territory in her chapter by way of reflecting on how A-level psychology students conceptualise perpetration. Drawing on previously unpublished research, Hale examines the degree to which students have been influenced by what they know and (think they) understand about Stanley Milgram's famous obedience experiments. As Hale explains, A-level psychology students do not formally study the Holocaust as part of their course – though they are likely to have studied the topic at an earlier age as part of their formal schooling. At this advanced level, students do commonly encounter Milgram's work, and they are aware that he linked his research to the Holocaust. Moreover, when presented with Milgram's studies in their textbooks, they are provided with cursory information on the Holocaust, shorn of any detail.

Hale's new research uncovered some troubling tendencies. Beyond an absence of any critical representation of Milgram in textbooks, students were found to believe that people participated in murder 'because they were following the orders of an authority figure' but that this was not 'thoughtless obedience'; rather, the students explained perpetrators' actions as being driven by fear for their own lives. Intriguingly, this sense of perpetrators being driven by human impulses extended into a wider tendency 'to believe the majority of perpetrators were essentially normal people who had been put in a "life or death" situation and had no choice but to kill the Jews'. Hale notes this overriding sense of normality corresponds with national trends in what young people know and understand about the Holocaust, but suggests the particular strength of these ideas amongst these older A-level students indicates how pervasive Milgram's impact has been – not just in schools and colleges, but in wider culture as well. Hale's conclusions echo remarks made by Foster and Chapman on the integral role of historical knowledge, but also highlight a sense of missed opportunity: at this age, at this level of study, Hale argues, these particular students 'are especially well placed' to contemplate some of the most complicated and challenging issues of the Holocaust. That this does not occur is the result of a confluence of reasons related to resources, teaching, and the very endurance of deeply ingrained misconceptions about this period in history.

Where do misconceptions about the Holocaust originate from, and at what point do they start to take root? Identifying the point of genesis holds out the prospect of being able to make meaningful interventions, but any search for a defining moment or juncture is inherently futile. This is because, as was repeatedly emphasised in the UCL student study (Foster *et al.* 2016), young people's misconceptions are the product of multiple forces – many of which are located in the cultural hinterland beyond the classroom. However, this is not to say that what occurs within formal educational settings is inconsequential; far from it – understanding the forms and shapes that teaching takes in conjunction with the knowledge and understandings that students develop is critical for the development of effective teaching and learning. This, therefore, is the power and the potential of educational research, and what research-informed practice can look like.

One area where our awareness of what is taking place on the ground is currently underdeveloped is how the Holocaust is being taught and learnt by those at the lowest ends of the age range. Over ten years ago, Simone Schweber (2008, 2075) coined the prescient phrase 'curricular creep' to refer to how a critical mass of teachers of 'younger and younger grades', in 'seek[ing] out personally meaningful topics', were making the Holocaust an increasingly common topic in the curricula of the youngest students. Where Schweber's observations were based on trends in America, this has been a transnational development. In the UK, this process has been driven not just by teachers but also by organisations such as the Holocaust Memorial Day Trust (HMDT), the National Holocaust Centre, and the Holocaust Educational Trust (HET), all of whom have created resources for use in primary schools where children are 5–11 years of age. The result has been a discernible 'curricular creep', despite the inclusion of the Holocaust in primary curricula remaining a highly contentious issue (Hale 2018, 222).

In the absence of any large-scale empirical research into Holocaust education in the primary sector, **Eleni Karayianni** uses her chapter to explore potential relationships between children's encounters with the Holocaust in their primary education and attitudes they may hold to 'others'. Karayianni begins by showing how many of the claims made in favour of teaching the Holocaust to young students are handicapped either by a lack of empirical foundation or 'small and unrepresentative samples'. From here she moves to 'further problematize' prevailing assumptions by analysing data produced by a sub-sample of Year 7 students (11–12 years of age) gathered in the UCL student study (Foster *et al.* 2016). Having divided the sub-sample into those who say they have and those who say they have not studied the Holocaust, Karayianni finds some elemental problems with claims that are commonly made regarding the capacity of Holocaust education to advance primary students' civic attitudes. Critically, Karayianni argues, the available evidence calls into question assertions that learning about the Holocaust in primary school can help foster positive attitudes towards immigrants or diversity.

In addition to exploring attitudes, Karayianni also touches on issues related to knowledge. Where some have sought to justify teaching the Holocaust to younger students on the grounds that it lays the foundations of a knowledge-base which can then be built upon in the secondary system (Cowan and Maitles 2017, 102), Karayianni's analysis suggests that in fact the reality may be far more problematic. Pointing to responses to questions about antisemitism, who Jewish people were, and who they thought was responsible for the Holocaust, Karayianni concludes there is evidence students already 'hold misconceptions and inaccuracies' even before learning about the Holocaust in their secondary education. This is not to levy blame or responsibility on primary teachers, but it is clear – as Karayianni suggests – that 'these findings . . . raise important questions about the purpose and value of including the Holocaust in the primary curriculum'.

Curricula issues: Content, approaches, resources

Issues of curricula are, of course, not limited to matters of purpose and value. They also include considerations related to content. In England, teaching the Holocaust in state-maintained schools has – since the introduction of the National Curriculum in 1991 – been a statutory requirement. However, the rationale for doing so has never been made explicit within the curriculum stipulations, and no government has ever outlined what content they believe should be delivered. This open-endedness has afforded teachers a degree of freedom, but has equally caused uncertainty and confusion (Pettigrew *et al.* 2009, 89) and brought forth questions relating to why teachers have chosen to focus on certain topics and particular themes (Pearce 2014, 208). Given the cultural dynamics of school curricula, part of the answer lies in the world beyond the classroom and how the Holocaust is treated and perceived in wider society.

It is with this in mind that **Tom Haward** suggests we understand Britain's relationship with the Holocaust as 'a complex and problematic history': that is, as a challenging and difficult past with which Britain has not, as yet, fully reckoned. Noting how recent years have seen the Holocaust being used politically to demonstrate (and, to some extent, validate) notions of British 'values', Haward argues this has seen official narratives become increasingly removed from the historical record. In the process, distorted understandings and erroneous perceptions have been fostered – evidence of which can be seen in the UCL student study (Foster *et al.* 2016), and the misconceptions students held about Britain's knowledge of the Holocaust and response to it.

Haward's chapter recounts his attempts to challenge this state of affairs through new classroom materials. Underpinned by a social constructivist pedagogy and drawing on archival material from a variety of institutions, Haward outlines the development of his resource *British Responses to the Holocaust*. As he explains, when the material was piloted with students it exposed 'a complex interaction between notions of identity and identification with the nation, ways of explaining British responses in light of archival records, and affective reactions'. Rather than buttress official narratives, students were instead finding their encounters with different historical sources were disrupting and disturbing existing ideas and assumptions about not just Britain and the Holocaust, but Britain and Britishness per se. This did not always culminate in students completing a wholesale revision of their thinking, but it did lead many to experience dissonance and assume a new-found criticality towards what they thought they knew and understood. Haward shows that a similar shifting could be observed among teachers using the material, albeit that in some cases this conflicted with a palpable 'sense of needing to frame British responses in a more benign light'.

Haward's contribution is valuable in illustrating how resources can 'open a landscape and dialogue that aims to rethink dominant political and cultural narratives'. The inherent impulse among students and teachers to 'paint a more benign picture of British policy' towards the events of the Holocaust exemplifies the overall tenor of Holocaust consciousness in contemporary Britain, but it also underlines the power and potency that selective cultural memories of the past exert on how we construct our identities and the ways we see the world. Because of this, it is not easy or straightforward to overhaul existing ideas about what the Holocaust was, the dramatis personae involved, and its meaning(s) for us today. That does not mean we should not try, of course, and resources such as Haward's are critical vehicles for doing so.

An insight into the size of this task is provided by **Darius Jackson**'s chapter on *The Boy in the Striped Pyjamas*. 'We have a generation of children who are introduced to the Holocaust by this novel', writes Jackson, 'and their understanding of the Holocaust is moulded by many of its ideas and assumptions'. Keen to position the novel into contexts it is commonly divorced from, Jackson explains how and why all literary works which take the Holocaust as their subject are 'prone to controversy' – though he emphasises that 'the relationship between literatures set in a specific historical context and historical understanding is complicated'. As he explains, 'historical literature seeps into historical understanding' and 'cultural events' serve to 'provide the frameworks through which we construct our understanding of the past'. This may go some way to explaining the influence that John Boyne's novel has come to exert, but Jackson argues it is also necessary to recognise how its core ideas 'become tools used to construct meaning from studying the Holocaust'.

For Jackson, this only amplifies the significance of the story's historical inaccuracies. Through cross-referencing remarks made by students during the UCL study (Foster *et al.* 2016), Jackson illustrates the impact of *The Boy in the Striped Pyjamas* on how young people conceive entities like concentration camps, conceptualise victimhood, and construct understandings of agency and responsibility. This may not have been Boyne's intention, but Jackson suggests this is the price paid for the book's specified aims and objectives. As he argues, 'the historical inaccuracies and anachronisms are less to do with mistakes than the need to show Bruno to be an absolute innocent in the harshest of realities'. In asserting this, Jackson thus gestures to a broader point which connects with arguments forwarded by Haward and others – namely, that in some instances, what we want the Holocaust to do, to be, or to show us, determines how we choose to represent or to teach it.

One can arguably observe the principle in action when we examine a particular discourse which has emerged in recent years around Holocaust education and antisemitism. As **Andy Pearce, Stuart Foster and Alice Pettigrew** note at the beginning of their chapter, antisemitism has become a 'persistent presence' across the West, finding visible expression in the form of articulated opinions and actions and in initiatives designed to try and combat these. Importantly, Pearce *et al.* highlight how within certain quarters there is a growing consensus which argues the most effective way to address antisemitism is through teaching and learning about the Holocaust. Whilst the authors do not dispute the potential contribution Holocaust education can make to understanding antisemitism, they suggest the underlying notion that learning about the Holocaust will necessarily act as panacea is both presumptuous and naïve.

Part of the problem, Pearce and his colleagues suggest, is that research shows most young people do not have a developed understanding of what antisemitism is. As they demonstrate, without a conceptual framework in which to posit their knowledge, students' ability to 'name' and identify phenomena is necessarily impeded. In this particular context, students are unable to grasp how historic anti-Jewish prejudice relates to and departs from the more modern, secular brand of antisemitism; similarly, they are also limited in how far they can both relate anti-Jewish sentiments to other forms of prejudice and discrimination, and distinguish it from these.

The consequences, they argue, are multiple. In the context of the Holocaust, not only do students find it difficult to appreciate the specific place occupied by Jewry in the Nazi worldview; they are also unable to recognise how and *why* Nazi policies towards the Jews were different to those enacted against other groups. With these existing tendencies and shortcomings in mind, Pearce and his colleagues show it is problematic to see learning about the Holocaust as a shortcut for antisemitism education. Moreover, the authors argue this belief lacks nuance and simplifies historical complexity since no singular, uniform type or brand of antisemitism existed in the 1930s and 1940s. Finally, while deepening knowledge about antisemitism in Europe during these years can serve various purposes, the authors argue it cannot necessarily substantially advance understanding of the new shapes and forms antisemitism assumes in our contemporary present.

Complicating assumptions

An underlying issue raised by Pearce and colleagues is how, for a long time, much Holocaust education has been predicated on presumptions and assumptions. In the absence of extensive empirical fieldwork or research-informed theorisation, educators and campaigners have tended to either overlook the mechanics of pedagogy and/or act on instinct and good intention. As a result many pedagogical orthodoxies have emerged in abstentia of a secure evidence base. However, as what we know and understand about the body of practice expands and extends, 'spaces are opening up for more sophisticated ways of conceptualising teaching and learning about the Holocaust' (Pearce 2018b). Clearly this does not mean that everything we thought we knew and understood is now thrown in doubt. But, as we acquire new insights, what we are obliged to do is revisit long-standing tenets and existing conventions and ask whether they require revision or amendment.

Alice Pettigrew's chapter embodies this process. Pettigrew's objective is to offer a 'critical questioning' of the tendency for teaching the Holocaust to Muslim students to be 'presented as a challenge and most commonly framed in terms of controversy'. To do so, Pettigrew employs a number of conceptual instruments from the toolbox of cultural studies and applies them to the dominant discourse about Muslim students and Holocaust education. She traces the genesis of concern – in the UK at least – back to 2007, and particular (mis)interpretations of the Historical Association's Teaching Emotive and Controversial History (TEACH) report of 2007 that rapidly acquired cultural currency. As Pettigrew shows, unfounded claims that teachers were avoiding the Holocaust for fear of how Muslim students would respond found traction because prevailing winds in wider culture had seen Muslims 'increasingly positioned as the pre-eminent contemporary "folk-devil"'. In this manner, Pettigrew argues, the 'moral panic' which quickly emerged in 2007 assumed the properties of a '*constructed* controversy' – one that, at the time, could lay no claim to evidenced reality.

Though focused on the UK context, Pettigrew shows how the development of issues around Muslims and Holocaust education tracked similar trajectories in other European and Western nations. Importantly, she also demonstrates that despite this matter being highly charged, it did not spawn large or sustained research initiatives; instead, though a number of projects were conducted over the following years, they remained small-scale and self-contained. Furthermore, because of this their findings were invariably inconclusive and open to interpretation.

Pettigrew inserts her own analysis of data gathered in the UCL teacher and student studies (Pettigrew *et al.* 2009; Foster *et al.* 2016) into this mix. Though acknowledging the limits of this research, she nevertheless offers persuasive evidence that 'Muslimness' was not a determining factor in how teachers or students approached Holocaust education. Nor was it found that Muslim students were more likely than others to display reluctance or negativity towards learning about the subject. In interviews, some Muslim students did demonstrate a critical questioning of the 'prominence given to the Holocaust' and 'ventured criticism of the celebratory British national narrative within which they felt this history was framed'. But Pettigrew emphasises such 'sentiments and potential provocations' were equally found among non-Muslims.

Pettigrew's chapter – which ends, notably, with a call for 'further, more nuanced, reflexive and responsible research and classroom reflection' – exemplifies the important contribution that educational research into how the Holocaust is taught and learnt can make to practice. The need for the field to recurrently engage in self-evaluation and assessment is a theme taken up by **Ruth-Anne Lenga** in her chapter. Lenga's principal concern is to take 'a disruptive perspective on the prevailing position among leading Holocaust education organisations: that atrocity images have very limited, if any, place in the classroom'. According to Lenga, this axiom comes from various sources and is often born out of concerns about potentially traumatising students, 'objectify[ing] the photographed subjects', and benumbing young people to horror. As much as she is sympathetic to these views, Lenga suggests they are in tension with other objectives: 'protecting' or 'shielding' students from atrocity images in the classroom risks diminishing the 'power' of student knowledge of the Holocaust, shutting down opportunities for important, complex conversations.

Lenga observes further complications. These include the ways in which the internet has made atrocity images 'widely accessible' to young people 'without filter, context or careful pedagogic framing': something further compounded by how digital advances more generally have significantly altered our and our students' relationship with visual culture, with effects on ways of seeing. Then there is the philosophical matter of just what an atrocity image *is*; after all, Lenga argues, beyond the visibly graphic, the 'atrocity element' of an image 'can be deceptive, its disturbing elements obscured' meaning context and contextualisation are vital factors that can determine if, and how, just what makes a particular image atrocious comes to the fore. And, of course, atrocity can be surfaced not only in the visual, but 'witnessed' in various other sources, too.

Lenga's chapter explores the implications of these developments for our thinking about atrocity images in Holocaust education. For her, the critical issue is whether 'the common presence of atrocity images' from the Holocaust, and the inherent horror of these visual traces, necessitates 'a blanket ban on their use' in the classroom. In Lenga's view, there can be 'profound educational value' in working with these sources – not least because the inquiries they can provoke are 'vital if young people are to engage seriously with the reality of this genocide'. Moreover, whilst there is unavoidable 'risk' in handling these images, Lenga believes this can and must be embraced within 'a supportive school environment' where respect is shown to both the victims of the past and the students of the present.

To the future

In recent years two significant commemorative events related to the Holocaust have occurred. The first, occurring in September 2019, was the 80th anniversary of the outbreak of the Second World War. With the start of that conflict Nazi anti-Jewish policy entered a new phase, bringing hitherto unseen levels of violence, brutality, and repression to the Jews of German-occupied Poland and Greater Germany. Though mass murder remained far beyond even the imagination of its later perpetrators, forces which would leave an indelible mark on European history had been unleashed. The second event, in May 2020, was the 75th anniversary of the end of the Second World War. While that milestone carried with it the relief – in multiple senses of the word – which came with the end of war in Europe, the development of Holocaust consciousness in the Western world has been such that it necessarily drew attention to the devastation and destruction wrought by the Holocaust. Moreover, such is the position of the Holocaust in our contemporary cultures, that a commemorative event such as the 75th anniversary unavoidably cast a blue light on the accelerating loss of the survivor generation.

In 'our broad present' (Gumbrecht 2014), moments such as these anniversaries occasion a patterned, almost pre-packaged response. Public events are staged, words of solemnity and lamentation from public figures are intoned, various forms of cultural activity occur. This is, by all accounts, unobjectionable and composite with the forms and functions of commemorations in the modern world (Gillis 1994). Yet the unique and unusual constellation of these two particular occurrences – representing, as they do, the respective bookends of the most lethal conflict currently known to man – is especially peculiar for how they symbolically condense and compress memorialisation of six years of war and genocide into an eight-month period. In so doing, they speak much to how the ways we perceive, sense and structure time (Nowotny 1996, 10) have undergone upheaval in the last 50 years, and how 'the present has turned into a dimension of expanding simultaneities' (Gumbrecht 2014, xiii). If this has brought fundamental change to how we relate the past, present and future to one another – highlighting 'the existence of different sediments of time' rather than simple 'linear or cyclical temporal processes' (Koselleck 2018, 9) – it has also contributed to our 'contemporary obsession with memory' (Huyssen 2000, 28); a fixation in which, and through which, the Holocaust and memories of it have come to the fore.

A quarter of a century ago Andreas Huyssen (2000, 28) contended 'the more we are asked to remember in the wake of the information explosion and the marketing of memory, the more we seem in danger of forgetting and the stronger the need to forget. At issue is the distinction between usable pasts and disposable data.' Determining what we regard to be of use and what we see as superfluous is not just a criteria for the content of our memories. It has broad applicability to our education systems as well. Moreover, we can bring these two realms closer to one another and our discussion here when we acknowledge that the relationship between teaching, learning and remembering has become a critical one for the spread and maintenance of Holocaust consciousness in many nation-states (Pearce 2018c).

Given the existing condition of Holocaust culture in the Western world, there is little to suggest that the importance accorded to teaching, learning and remembering by statesmen, lobbyists and others will abate any time soon. On the contrary, one could well imagine this will continue to increase in the coming years. Yet if this sounds all well and good in principle, it nevertheless leaves a number of questions unanswered. Some of these concern issues raised in this volume, while others relate to as-yet unseen developments.

Though it is true that 'of the future we have no knowledge' (Larrain 2015), its potential colours and contours do not lie beyond our imagination. Indeed, it is increasingly pertinent that we do not just imagine the future of Holocaust education but actually undertake exercises in modelling it. This need not be pie in the sky or wholly divorced from reality; by analysing historic trends and developments, and reflecting on present trajectories, it is feasible to construct informed pictures of what the future – what Michael Young and Johan Muller call 'possible educational futures' (2010, 11) – and consider available options for action accordingly.

What, then, can we say about the future? Whilst many await with baited breath for the supposed arrival of the post-survivor era, in truth this reality is already with us – as is only made more apparent with the passing of each survivor. We can also anticipate a continued utilisation of technology in teaching practice, with its perceived benefits articulated in terms of responding to the void created by the loss of the survivor generation. Cutting across both of these elements will be the ongoing receding of the Holocaust into history – bringing with it issues of relevance, memory and epistemology – as well as unforeseen developments in culture, politics and society which can (and will) impact the position of the Holocaust in our contemporary world in myriad ways.

At present, a significant number of countries within the Western world are confronted with a number of particularly acute challenges. These include a political mainstreaming of right-wing ideologies, the presence of a number of authoritarian governments, a revival of ethno-nationalism, and rising levels of intolerance and discrimination. Critically, in a number of cases, this has occurred in nations which have long and much-celebrated histories of liberalism and democratic rule – prompting the emergence of a cottage industry of commentaries on how to foresee and forestall the death of democracy (Levitsky and Ziblatt

2018; Mounk 2018; Runciman 2018). Given how far Holocaust memory and education have been institutionalised within many of these countries, long-standing beliefs that teaching, learning, and remembering the Holocaust are hallmarks of enlightened societies which act as bulwarks to man's basest behaviours presently appear hopeful at best.

If the field of Holocaust education is to continue to exist, to meet these and other challenges and to fulfil its potential, then it will be essential for substantive changes to be made in the very near future. Whilst this centres on practice and pedagogy, it also extends to how the field speaks of and sees itself. Beginning such a process starts with open and honest dialogue: about what 'Holocaust education' has achieved over the course of its life-span, but also the challenges, controversies and issues it continues to face. The contents of this book are offered in pursuit of that conversation.

References

All online material last accessed 24 July 2019 unless indicated otherwise.

Aderet, O. 2018. 'Yad Vashem: Syria shows mechanisms developed after the Holocaust to prevent crimes against humanity are failing', *Haaretz*, 10 April. Online. https://www.haaretz.com/israel-news/yad-vashem-syria-shows-post-holocaust-mechanisms-are-failing-1.5990403 (accessed 14 January 2020).

Assmann, A. 2008. 'Canon and archive'. In *Companion to Cultural Memory Studies: An international and interdisciplinary handbook*, edited by Astrid Erll and Ansgar Nünning, 97–108. Berlin and New York: Walter de Gruyter.

Astor, M. 2018. 'Holocaust is fading from memory, survey finds', *New York Times*, 12 April.

Ball, J. 2017. *Post-Truth: How bullshit conquered the world*. London: Biteback Publishing.

Barnes, J. 2011a. *The Sense of an Ending*. London: Jonathan Cape.

Barnes, J. 2011b. 'Speak, Memory: "An Ending" that uncovers the past', *NPR, Weekend Edition Saturday*, 19 November. Online. https://www.npr.org/2011/11/19/142468838/speak-memory-an-ending-that-uncovers-the-past.

Bhaskar, R. 2012. *From Science to Emancipation: Alienation and the actuality of enlightenment*. London: Routledge.

Carrier, P., Fuchs, E. and Messinger, T. 2015. *The International Status of Education about the Holocaust: A global mapping of textbooks and curricula*. Paris: UNESCO.

Claims Conference. 2018. 'New survey by Claims Conference finds significant lack of Holocaust knowledge in the United States'. Online. http://www.claimscon.org/study.

Cowan, P. and Maitles, H. 2017. *Understanding and Teaching Holocaust Education*. London: Sage.

D'Ancona, M. 2017. *Post-Truth: The new war on truth and how to fight back*. London: Ebury Press.

Eaglestone, R. 2004. *The Holocaust and the Postmodern*. Oxford: Oxford University Press.

Echikson, W. 2017. '"Their message is urgent": The Holocaust survivor and his 7,000 pieces of antisemitic propaganda', *The Guardian*, 27 March.

Eckmann, M. and Stevick, D. 2017a. 'General introduction'. In *Research in Teaching and Learning about the Holocaust: A dialogue beyond borders*, edited by Monique Eckmann, Doyle E. Stevick and Jolanta Ambrosewicz-Jacobs, 17–32. Berlin: Metropol Verlag.

Eckmann, M. and Stevick, D. 2017b. 'General conclusions'. In *Research in Teaching and Learning about the Holocaust: A dialogue beyond borders*, edited by Monique Eckmann, Doyle E. Stevick and Jolanta Ambrosewicz-Jacobs, 285–300. Berlin: Metropol Verlag.

Felman, S. and Laub, D. 1992. *Testimony: Crises of witnessing in literature, psychoanalysis, and history*. New York: Routledge.

Foster, S., Pettigrew, A., Pearce, A., Hale, R., Burgess, A., Salmons, P. and Lenga, R.-A. 2016. *What Do Students Know and Understand about the Holocaust? Evidence from English secondary schools*. London: UCL Institute of Education.

Gillis, J.R. ed. 1994. *Commemorations: The politics of national identity*. Princeton, NJ: Princeton University Press.

Goodhart, D. 2017. *The Road to Somewhere: The populist revolt and the future of politics*. London: C. Hurst.

Gray, M. 2014. *Contemporary Debates in Holocaust Education*. Basingstoke: Palgrave Macmillan.

Gumbrecht, H.U. 2014. *Our Broad Present: Time and contemporary culture*. New York: Columbia University Press.

Hale, R. 2018. 'Reflections on what year 7 students know and understand about the Holocaust: An argument for empirical research in English primary schools'. In *Holocaust Education in Primary Schools in the Twenty-First Century: Current practices, potentials and ways forward*, edited by C.W. Szejnmann, Paula Cowan and James Griffiths, 221–37. Basingstoke: Palgrave Macmillan.

Harding, T. 2014. 'Teaching the Holocaust in the "Post-Survivor Era"', *Huffington Post*, 26 January.

Hirsh, D. 2018. *Contemporary Left Antisemitism*. London: Routledge.

Huyssen, A. 2000. 'Present pasts: Media, politics, amnesia', *Public Culture* 12 (1): 21–38.

International Holocaust Remembrance Alliance (IHRA). 2019. 'About us'. Online. https://www.holocaustremembrance.com/about-us.

Koselleck, R. 2018. *Sediments of Time: On possible histories*. Trans and ed. Franzel, S. and Hoffmann, S.-L. Stanford, CA: Stanford University Press.

Larrain, B. 2015. 'El pasado no sirve, el futuro no lo conocemos: Aceleración y Presente Extendido en la publicidad chilena', *Cuadernos.info* 36: 173–89.

Levitsky, S. and Ziblatt, D. 2018. *How Democracies Die: What history reveals about our future*. New York: Penguin Random House.

Lipstadt, D. 2017. 'In the post-truth era we must fight the deniers even harder', *The Times*, 23 January.

Lowenthal, D. 1999. 'Preface'. In *The Art of Forgetting*, edited by Adrian Forty and Susan Küchler, xi–xiii. Oxford: Berg.

Markowicz, K. 2018. 'Why we're forgetting the Holocaust', *New York Post*, 15 April. Online. https://nypost.com/2018/04/15/why-were-forgetting-the-holocaust/.

Mcintyre, L. 2018. *Post-Truth*. Cambridge: Massachusetts Institute of Technology Press.

Michlic, J. 2017. 'Jewish families in Europe, 1939–present: History, representation and memory, an Introduction'. In *Jewish Families in Europe, 1939–Present: History, representation, memory*, edited by Joanna Michlic, xv–xxxiv. Waltham, MA: Brandeis University Press.

Mounk, Y. 2018. *The People vs. Democracy: Why our freedom is in danger and how to save it*. Cambridge, MA: Harvard University Press.

Nowotny, H. 1996. *Time: The modern and postmodern experience*. Cambridge: Polity.

Olick, J., Vinitzky-Seroussi, V. and Levy, D. 2011. 'Introduction'. In *The Collective Memory Reader*, edited by Jeffrey Olick, Vered Vinitzky-Seroussi and David Levy, 3–62. Oxford: Oxford University Press.

Onion, R. 2018. 'The NYT says we're forgetting about the Holocaust: History suggests otherwise', *Slate.com*, 13 April. Online. https://slate.com/human-interest/2018/04/the-nyt-says-were-forgetting-about-the-holocaust-but-history-suggests-otherwise.html.

Pearce, A. 2014. *Holocaust Consciousness in Contemporary Britain*. New York: Routledge.

Pearce, A. 2018a. 'Introduction: Education, remembrance and the Holocaust – towards pedagogic memory-work'. In *Remembering the Holocaust in Educational Settings*, edited by Andy Pearce, 1–21. London: Routledge.

Pearce, A. 2018b. 'Holocaust education at Australian universities: Reflections on a roundtable', *Australian Humanities Review*, 63: 167–71.

Pearce, A. ed. 2018c. *Remembering the Holocaust in Educational Settings*. London: Routledge.

Penslar, D., Marrus, M. and Gross Stein, J. 2005. 'Preface'. In *Contemporary Antisemitism: Canada and the world*, edited by Derek Penslar, Michael Marrus and Janice Gross Stein, vii–viii. Toronto: University of Toronto Press.

Pettigrew, A., Foster, S., Howson, J., Salmons, P., Lenga, R.-A. and Andrews, K. 2009. *Teaching about the Holocaust in English Secondary Schools: An empirical study of national trends, perspectives and practice*. London: Institute of Education.

Plessow, O. 2017. 'Agents of transnationalization in the field of "Holocaust Education": An introduction'. In *Entangled Memories: Remembering the Holocaust in a global age*, edited by Marius Henderson and Julia Lange, 315–52. Heidelberg: Universitätsverlag Winter.

Popescu, D. 2015. 'Introduction: Memory and imagination in the post-witness era'. In *Revisiting Holocaust Representation in the Post-Witness Era*, edited by Diana Popescu and Tanja Schult, 1–7. Basingstoke: Palgrave Macmillan.

Reading, A. (2003) 'Digital interactivity in public memory institutions: The uses of new technologies in Holocaust museums', *Media, Culture and Society* 25 (1): 67–85.

Rosenfeld, A.H. 2013. 'Introduction'. In *Resurgent Antisemitism: Global perspectives*, edited by Alvin H. Rosenfeld, 1–7. Bloomington: Indiana University Press.

Runciman, D. 2018. *How Democracy Ends*. London: Profile Books.

Schneider, G. cited. 2018a. 'Two-thirds of US millennials "do not know what Auschwitz was"', *The Week*, 12 April. Online. http://www.theweek.co.uk/92886/two-thirds-of-us-millennials-do-not-know-what-auschwitz-was

Schneider, G. cited. 2018b. 'Survey reveals gaps in knowledge of Holocaust history – and that most Americans believe it could happen again', *Time*, 12 April. Online. http://time.com/5235725/holocaust-history-survey/

Schneider, G. cited. 2018c. 'New survey by Claims Conference finds significant lack of Holocaust knowledge in the United States', Claims Conference. Online. http://www.claimscon.org/study

Schoen Consulting. 2018. *The Holocaust Knowledge and Awareness Survey*, 1. Online. http://www.claimscon.org/wp-content/uploads/2018/04/Holocaust-Knowledge-Awareness-Study_Executive-Summary-2018.pdf (accessed 15 February 2020).

Schweber, S. 2008. '"What happened to their pets?" Third Graders encounter the Holocaust', *Teachers College Record* 110 (10): 2073–115.

Sherwood, H. 2017. 'UK's "social splintering" risks repeating past, say Holocaust survivors', *The Guardian*, 1 August.

Snyder, T. 2017. Cited in Illing, S. '"Post-truth is pre-fascism": A Holocaust historian on the Trump era', *Vox*, 9 March.

Stevick, D. 2017. 'Research in English'. In *Research in Teaching and Learning about the Holocaust: A dialogue beyond borders*, edited by Monique Eckmann, Doyle E. Stevick and Jolanta Ambrosewicz-Jacobs, 153–67. Berlin: Metropol Verlag.

Tyaglyy, M. 2017. 'Research in the East-Slavic linguistic region'. In *Research in Teaching and Learning about the Holocaust: A dialogue beyond borders*, edited by Monique Eckmann, Doyle E. Stevick and Jolanta Ambrosewicz-Jacobs, 121–51. Berlin: Metropol Verlag.

UNESCO. 2017. *Education about the Holocaust and Preventing Genocide: A policy guide*. Paris: UNESCO.

Young, M. and Muller, J. 2010. 'Three educational scenarios for the future: Lessons from the sociology of knowledge', *European Journal of Education* 45 (1): 11–27.

2
To what extent does the acquisition of historical knowledge really matter when studying the Holocaust?

Stuart Foster

Introduction

The UCL student study (Foster *et al.* 2016) provided intriguing insights into what young people know and understand about the Holocaust and the extent to which they are able to make meaning from it. In broad overview, although the vast majority of students thought learning about the Holocaust was important and interesting, the research also starkly demonstrated that students often lacked core historical knowledge and typically harboured an array of troubling misconceptions. This chapter further explores the implications for these findings. In particular, it examines conflicting views about the relative importance of historical knowledge in understanding the Holocaust.

On the one hand, for example, it can be argued that it is not the specific historical knowledge of the Holocaust that is of essential educational importance, but rather the broader 'lessons' it provides for contemporary society. From this perspective it is assumed that a cursory overview of the Holocaust is sufficient for students to appreciate that this was a deeply troubling episode in modern history and one which sharply illustrates where prejudice and discrimination might lead if left unchallenged. Developing this argument further it is, therefore, claimed that the key educational focus should be on considering the implications of the Holocaust for the present, not on a detailed exploration of the past.

On the other hand, an alternative position exists which argues that in order to derive true meaning from the Holocaust, it is essential that students have an informed understanding of its specific and contingent historical context. This perspective claims that unless the *historical* Holocaust is more fully understood, there is a danger that students might acquire simplistic moral and universal lessons which, though well intentioned, typically will be ill-informed and fuel the prevalence of troubling myths and misconceptions.

Although it is recognised that the complexity of any educational enterprise can never be distilled into a crude binary choice of two possible alternatives, to provide some clarity the primary focus of this chapter will be to argue strongly for the second position (i.e., on the importance of students' acquiring and developing key historical knowledge of the Holocaust in order for them to develop deeper understandings). As will be explained later in this chapter, the principal reason for adopting this position is because the UCL study clearly demonstrated that limitations in students' historical knowledge proved a barrier to deeper and more profound understandings of the Holocaust and its contemporary significance.

This chapter will, therefore, briefly position the arguments advanced above into the broader educational and political landscape. It will also explore the concept of 'historical knowledge' and discuss divergent views on these important educational issues. The chapter will then summarise the key findings of the UCL study, paying particular attention to common limitations in students' historical knowledge. In advancing the core argument, specific examples from the 2016 study will be identified which illustrate how a lack of core knowledge appeared to hinder students' deeper understanding of the Holocaust and its salience for the modern world. The chapter will then conclude by arguing for an approach to teaching which encourages the development of substantive and conceptual historical knowledge so that students may acquire a more sophisticated and intelligent understanding of the Holocaust.

It is important to establish that in this chapter primary attention is given to teaching and learning about the Holocaust in *history* classrooms. In so doing, however, it is fully recognised that the Holocaust is taught in other subject areas (e.g., citizenship, English, religious education) and on occasions in whole school and cross-curricular ways. It is also recognised that many history teachers often approach the Holocaust with an emphasis on trans-disciplinary and/or civic and moral goals (Kinloch 1998; Pearce 2017; Pettigrew *et al.* 2009; Pettigrew 2017; Russell 2006; Salmons 2003; Short 1994). Nevertheless, the focus on history is warranted for three important reasons. First, the national teacher study published by the Institute of Education in 2009 demonstrated that history is by far the most likely curriculum subject in which the Holocaust is taught (Pettigrew *et al.* 2009). Second, it is the *only* subject area in which the study of the Holocaust is mandated in the current Key Stage 3 National Curriculum (DfE 2013). Third, there is a long-standing tradition in history education which recognises the important connection between the acquisition of substantive historical knowledge and distinctive disciplinary or conceptual understandings (Booth 1993; Counsell *et al.* 2016; Foster and Yeager 2001; Husbands *et al.* 2011; Lee 1999; Lee 2005; Seixas 2004; Shemilt 1987; VanSledright 2011; Wineburg 2001). This issue will be further developed later in this chapter.

Despite the focus on history education, the arguments advanced here are relevant to all curriculum areas in which the Holocaust is taught. For, if the Holocaust is to be taught in any meaningful way, it is essential that educators consider what historical and contextual knowledge and understanding is important for young people to acquire. Similarly, the issues raised in this chapter are not only relevant to educators in England but have salience for teachers in the extensive range of countries across the world in which the Holocaust is taught (Carrier *et al.* 2015).

Knowledge, historical knowledge and the current political landscape

In 1860 Herbert Spencer famously posed the essential education question: What knowledge is of most worth? (Spencer 1860). Underpinning Spencer's important question is the notion that some kinds of knowledge are more important or significant than others. A major challenge for societies across the world, therefore, always has been (and always will be) to determine what young people should learn in their formal education system. With the emergence of free compulsory education in societies across the world in the past hundred years or so, this matter has taken on greater urgency and importance and has occupied the attention of curriculum theorists, politicians, government officials, business leaders, educators and parents. The question 'what knowledge is of most worth?' is, of course, fraught with complexity and typically open to debate and dispute. The answer to the question is also inexorably value-laden and shaped by the respondent's ideological, philosophical and epistemological views. For this reason, what gets taught in schools often is contested and controversial.

Arguably, no subject has experienced more conflict and argument than school history (see, for example, Crawford 1995; Foster and Crawford 2006; Granatstein 1998; Nash *et al.* 1997; Symcox and Wilschut 2009; Taylor 2004). This is largely because in countries throughout the world, school history often is not really about understanding the past, but rather focused on serving particular agendas in the present (e.g., promoting a particular form of collective national identity). As a result, the official 'stories' that are selected to be taught to young people in history classrooms are often influenced by the ideological dispositions of those in power, and therefore they are often inherently controversial.

In England divisions over the purpose and content of school history have raged for many decades, and they were particularly vehement in the years surrounding the introduction of the National Curriculum for history in the early 1990s (Crawford 1995; Foster 1998; Phillips 1998; Slater 1989). During this period, in crude overview, two conflicting views of school history and its overarching purpose dominated. On the one hand stood those, usually from the political right, who considered the history classroom to be a place in which young people should absorb a selected version of the nation's past. Simply, their aim was to use school history as a means to instil in students a sense of unity and patriotism and a veneration for the nation's glorious accomplishments. On the other hand stood those of a more progressive political persuasion. From their perspective the historical past was open to exploration, enquiry and interpretation. It therefore demanded that students should not only encounter dominant narratives, but also critically evaluate historical evidence and appreciate how and why selected narratives or interpretations were constructed.

These contested views of school history are, of course, very much alive today. For example, in recent years, undoubtedly influenced by the work of E.D. Hirsch (1983; 1987; 2016), authoritative figures in the current government have championed the importance of 'content rich' learning and students' acquisition of core factual knowledge (see, for example, Abrams 2012; Gibb 2017; Peal 2014). As a result, they have also been critical of enquiry-based learning and the inappropriate use of historical sources in history classrooms. Furthermore, it appears that these influential political figures strongly believe that knowledge acquisition is the essential purpose of history education. In so doing, they potentially risk obscuring the vital link between knowledge acquisition and deeper conceptual understanding.

This chapter takes a very different position regarding the importance of the acquisition of historical knowledge. Compelling reasons exist for why acquiring historical knowledge is fundamentally important, but this process is significant only when it is directly linked to developing students' deeper and more profound understandings. Knowledge alone, it will be argued, is not enough. Rather, it is the acquisition of knowledge that both enables and compels young people to derive deeper meaning and understanding that is the vital goal of history education.

To appreciate the importance of historical knowledge it is essential to understand the relationship between students' substantive knowledge of the past and their conceptual, disciplinary or second-order understanding. Substantive knowledge refers to the concepts which organise and feature in any exploration of history (e.g., revolution, monarchy, dictatorship, democracy). Substantive knowledge might also include knowledge of key facts, dates, individuals and events. Second-order or disciplinary understanding of the past refers to key historical concepts such as causation, chronology, continuity and change, historical evidence and interpretation, significance and empathy. As a result of key research into students' historical understanding (see, for example, Foster and Yeager 1999; Lee and Ashby 2000; Seixas 2004; Shemilt 1987; VanSledright 2004; Wineburg 2001) it is generally accepted that students who are able to employ both key substantive knowledge and disciplinary understandings are better equipped to fully appreciate and understand the past. Accordingly, understanding this vital relationship in Holocaust education is of central importance in this chapter.

Limitations in historical knowledge and understanding

The UCL study of English secondary school students' knowledge and understanding of the Holocaust (Foster *et al.* 2016) explored a variety of issues and pursued numerous lines of enquiry. For example, it investigated students' attitudes and dispositions towards studying the Holocaust and it explored the various ways that students encountered the Holocaust, both in school and beyond. However, the primary aim of the study was to a provide a detailed portrait of students' knowledge and understanding of the Holocaust. In particular, Part III of the report (pages 99–201) focused on an in-depth exploration of students' responses to key overarching historical questions: Who were the victims? Who were the perpetrators and who was responsible? When and where did the Holocaust take place? These broad questions also encompassed other important subsidiary questions such as: What was the Holocaust? Why did it happen?

In designing and developing the study, UCL researchers were mindful that 'any empirical examination or attempt to measure "knowledge" is an inherently complex and contested enterprise' (8). Furthermore, the researchers recognised that students' 'historical knowledge is rarely fixed and inert' but typically 'socially constructed, context-dependent and complex' (102).[1] It was understood, therefore, that survey-based knowledge questions and focused interviews would 'never be able to address all the complexities of uncovering every aspect of students' knowledge and understanding of the Holocaust'. Nevertheless, a staggering array of student responses did provide an 'unprecedented and rich' body of evidence from which to draw important conclusions and identify key findings.

It is not possible to provide detailed commentary here on the full extent of UCL's 2016 study as it relates to students' historical knowledge and understanding. It is, however, potentially instructive to be reminded of some key headline findings:

- 68 per cent of students did not recognise the term 'antisemitism' and most appeared unaware of the racial dimensions of Nazi antisemitism.
- Although 90 per cent correctly identified Jews as victims, very few knew what differentiated them from other identified victim groups (e.g., gay men, disabled people, Roma and Sinti). Most students thought victims were targeted and treated in similar ways.
- 73.9 per cent overestimated the Jewish population in pre-war Germany by 15 to 30 times.
- A third massively underestimated the scale of the murder of Jewish people, with 10.3 per cent believing that no more than 100,000 Jews were killed.
- When asked 'who was responsible for the Holocaust?' 56.1 per cent of 11–14-year-olds replied simply 'Hitler' while 81.9 per cent made reference only to Hitler and/or the Nazis.
- Fewer than 10 per cent attributed any blame or responsibility to the German people and very few students appreciated broader complicity and collaboration across Europe.
- 50.7 per cent incorrectly believed that the largest number of Jews murdered during the Holocaust came from Germany and 54.9 per cent believed that mass murder occurred in Germany, not German-occupied Poland.
- Only 7.4 per cent appreciated that the German invasion of the Soviet Union was the event that primarily 'triggered the organised

mass killing of Jews', with 40.2 per cent erroneously believing that mass killing began immediately after Hitler's appointment as Chancellor in 1933.

- Only 15 per cent associated Treblinka or Bergen-Belsen with the Holocaust and only 24.3 per cent recognised the term *Einsatzgruppen*.
- 34.4 per cent incorrectly reasoned that the Holocaust triggered Britain's entry into war and 23.8 per cent incorrectly thought the British government did not know about the Holocaust until the end of the war in 1945.
- Fewer than half of all students (46.1 per cent) correctly knew the 'end' of the Holocaust (in terms of mass killing) came as a result of the Allied liberation of lands occupied by the German army.

Typically, student knowledge and understanding improved with age and it commonly proved more robust among students studying history aged 17–18. Nevertheless, as outlined above, substantial gaps in knowledge existed across all ages. For our purposes here the critical question is: to what extent does this lack of historical knowledge matter?

Why does historical knowledge matter?

In response to this question some might argue that although the possession of solid historical knowledge is useful, it is not an imperative. Indeed, if students have a broad understanding of the Holocaust (e.g., they know who the victims were, who was responsible and that it involved mass killing) it could be argued that this is a solid enough basis from which to draw important 'lessons'.

Different perspectives on whether or not teachers should pay more attention to developing students' historical knowledge, as opposed to a focus on broader moral or civic lessons, was a feature of the IOE's teacher study (Pettigrew *et al.* 2009). In fact, this tension was particularly exposed in discussions over teachers' aims. Representative of the views of many of the 2,108 teachers who participated in the study, one teacher remarked:

> I've got to be honest, I mean, the historical side of it is important, don't get me wrong, but when I'm teaching it, the moral significance of it – the human significance of it – is far more prevalent for me personally. . . . And I'd be kind of worried if there were people

> there who were just really interested in the chronology. And if I came out of my lesson thinking that pupils in the class just thought of it as just another topic, I would be a bit disappointed. In fact, I wouldn't just be disappointed, I'd be really upset.
>
> (Pettigrew *et al.* 2009, 79)

Teachers commonly argued, for example, that providing students with an elementary understanding of the history of the Holocaust allowed them to explore and understand more relevant contemporary issues such as what can happen when racism or prejudice is not challenged. In so doing, however, it appeared that classroom attention to the specific and contingent development of persecution and murder in Nazi Germany and beyond often remained disturbingly absent. In fact, what often appeared evident was classroom focus on what has been termed a 'mythic' Holocaust as opposed to an 'historical' one (Cole 1999; Bell 2003). Employing the term 'mythic' here does not mean that the Holocaust did not exist, but rather that its reality has been shaped and potentially distorted to suit contemporary agendas and broader universal aims.

The central argument advanced in this chapter is that it is vital that students acquire progressively rich and age-appropriate historical knowledge of the Holocaust in order for them to derive meaning and understanding from it. But achieving this objective has implications for pedagogy. Specifically, it challenges educators and Holocaust educational organisations to eschew *mythic* representations of the Holocaust and requires them to pay more attention to the *historical* Holocaust and its potential to develop deeper and more profound understandings. To argue for the value of historical knowledge is unequivocally not to suggest that knowledge needs to be acquired for knowledge's sake. Rather, it originates from the belief that if students are equipped with carefully considered historical knowledge they are more likely to be able to understand and make meaning from the past.

This argument also relates to the value placed upon what Michael Young and Johan Muller have termed 'powerful knowledge' (2013; 2016) which recognises that educators have a responsibility to organise specialist learning experiences which typically cannot be attained outside of school. When teaching about the Holocaust, therefore, it is important for educators to consider what particular substantive content and conceptual knowledge it is important for students to acquire. Accordingly, in the two sections that follow specific attention is paid to the issue of complicity and responsibility which illustrates how the presence, or absence, of particular historical knowledge impacts meaningful understanding.

Students' knowledge and understanding of responsibility and complicity

In articulating who they believed was responsible for the Holocaust, the vast majority of students adopted a Hitler-centric explanation. For example, 91.4 per cent of all students associated Hitler with the Holocaust, 79.4 per cent directly referenced Hitler when asked 'who was responsible for the Holocaust?' and, significantly, 56.1 per cent of 11–14-year-olds appeared to believe the Holocaust was *solely* attributable to Hitler. In a similar vein, when students were invited, in free-text responses, to 'describe what the Holocaust was' the overwhelming majority included Hitler in their descriptions:

> It was when Adolf Hitler attempted to wipe out the Jews by committing Genocide. (Year 10 student)
>
> When Hitler captured the Jews, put them in a concentration camp and gassed them. (Year 9 student)
>
> The holocaust was a period in time where the German leader Adolf Hitler discriminated against everyone who was different and tried to kill them all. (Year 10 student)

As these examples and thousands of others suggest, many students across all age ranges tended to personalise and narrate their understanding of the Holocaust through a Hilter-centric lens. His influence was seen to be ubiquitous and omnipresent. As the UCL study explained, 'For many younger students Hitler's role in the Holocaust was all encompassing and emphatic' (150). Indeed, many students appeared to believe that Hitler simply issued commands and others fulfilled his wishes. The report continues, 'Typically these acts were seen as a top-down process, with Hitler as executive director and other individuals blindly following his will' (150).[2] Of particular note in the analysis both of student survey and interview responses, was the infrequent reference to other potentially 'high profile' perpetrators. For example, in contrast to the 91.4 per cent of students who associated Hitler with the Holocaust, only 44.4 per cent stated that the SS were somehow involved in it. Similarly, only 23.2 per cent and 24.3 per cent respectively associated Adolf Eichmann and the *Einsatzgruppen* with the genocide and during interview very, very few students referenced other prominent figures such as Himmler or Goebbels. In stark contrast, Hitler dominated students' narratives and explanatory accounts.

Although students overwhelmingly identified Hitler as the agent most responsible for the Holocaust, some also ascribed responsibility to 'the Nazis'. For example, 20.6 per cent held 'Hitler and the Nazis' jointly responsible and a smaller number, 10.6 per cent, identified the Nazis as culpable, with no reference to Hitler. In an effort to more fully appreciate how younger students (i.e., 11 to 14-year-olds) perceived and understood the role of the Nazis, the UCL study uncovered a striking finding. It became apparent that most younger students did not fully grasp that the Nazis were a broad-based political party that enjoyed considerable popular support and electoral success during the early 1930s. Rather, most students appeared to view the Nazis as 'a relatively small and powerful group who ruthlessly carried out Hitler's orders' (152). Indeed, many students appeared to frame the Nazis as loyal acolytes or disciples of Hitler who did his bidding without question. Students, therefore, variously described the Nazis as 'believers', 'people who he sent to do his work', 'a disciplined core group', 'Hitler's personal hit squad' (152). Notably, one student remarked, 'I think they were like robots, because Hitler, like, controlled them. They had to do what Hitler said. They had to follow his commands really'.

Another important issue identified in the UCL study was the clear sense that very few students considered the German people responsible for the Holocaust. For example, only 3.9 per cent of 6,897 students who responded to the question 'who was responsible?' explicitly held 'Germans/Germany/German people' accountable. Furthermore, only 3.1 per cent viewed 'Hitler and the Germans/Germany' responsible and 0.9 per cent ascribed responsibility to the 'Nazis and the Germans'. Follow-up interviews attempted to further understand how students saw the relationship between the Holocaust and the German people.

What was particularly evident was most students sharply differentiated between the actions of German citizenry and the Nazis. For, whereas overwhelming numbers held strong opinions about the terrible acts committed by the Nazis against the Jews and other victim groups, very few believed the German people played a significant role in the genocide. As the UCL report explains, 'many students saw the German people as passive actors on the historical stage . . . it was [as] if the Holocaust happened around the German people, with events unfolding without their involvement or engagement' (157). Pursuing students' understanding further, the research suggested that three explanations dominated their view of the role adopted by many Germans during the Holocaust: they were brainwashed, they were scared, or they didn't know.

The UCL study offers detailed commentary on these three explanatory factors (158–66). In overview the research revealed that students believed that as a result of, for example, Nazi propaganda, charismatic speeches, and an influential education system, Hitler was able to 'control', 'manipulate' or even 'trick' the German people into supporting his actions:

> Hitler created these stereotypes about how Jews were bad and Gypsies were bad and people were bad and . . . it was drilled into their brains. (Year 9)
>
> He persuaded people obviously, like in schools. He starts teaching people how Jews are inferior to them. Brainwashing them. (Year 9)

It was clear, therefore, that many students appeared to believe that ostensibly innocent German people were 'brainwashed' by Hitler and the Nazis in the 1930s and 1940s and in this sense, they had no agency, no choice and, revealingly, no responsibility.

The second explanation for the apparent inaction of many Germans stemmed from students' common belief that they lived in a suffocating climate of fear and intimidation:

> I think if they were forced into it, it showed like that they were really, really scared of Hitler and of what he could do to them if they didn't do what he wanted. (Year 8)
>
> It speaks for how powerful Hitler must have been as a person, they must have been in absolute fear of him, they mustn't have wanted to put a foot wrong, and it shows that Hitler as a person had reached that level in Germany where if you went against him there was no going back for you. (Year 13)
>
> If the people didn't follow his orders they would be treated the same way as the Jews, forced into labour camps or shot dead. (Year 12)

Accordingly, students typically reasoned that many Germans supported or went along with the actions of the Nazi state because of the oppressive and intimidating context in which they lived. Once again, most students absolved the German people of blame or responsibility because they were perceived to have little agency or choice.

The third explanation for why students commonly believed many Germans were not culpable stems from their understanding that they 'did not know' about the brutal treatment and mass killing of Jews:

> I'm not sure that they knew the extent of what was going on as well. I think they sort of knew that Hitler was treating Jewish people badly . . . but I don't think that they knew that he was going to kill them. That wasn't really known until like after the war. (Year 10)
>
> . . . they didn't really know what was going on. They just knew that the Jews may have been a problem, but they didn't know about the concentration camps and the torture. (Year 10)
>
> Auschwitz was actually hidden from everybody in the more outskirts . . . so nobody actually knew about it. So, I guess half the population didn't know. (Year 9)

In sum, therefore, many students reasoned that due to a number of factors (including deceptive propaganda and the belief that mass killing was carried out in remote locations), the German people were unaware of Nazi crimes against the Jews. Accordingly, students commonly reasoned if the German people didn't know about the Holocaust, how could they be held responsible?

Final note should also be made of how students perceived the role of other agents and collaborators across Europe. Put simply, it was very apparent that the vast majority of students had little to no understanding of the extent to which the genocide of Jews engulfed the entire continent. For the most part, Key Stage 3 students had no sense of the role played by other collaborating regimes (e.g., the Vichy government) and most were unfamiliar with the brutal development of the 'Holocaust by bullets' in Eastern Europe which is estimated to have taken around 2 million lives (Bloxham 2009; Cesarani 2016; Desbois 2008). Typically, students framed their understanding of the Holocaust in a very German-centric way.

This was evidenced in how 50.7 per cent of students incorrectly believed that the largest number of Jews murdered during the Holocaust came from Germany, while 54.9 per cent believed that mass murder occurred in Germany, not German-occupied Poland. Many students did, however, have a limited conception of Nazi camps and the mass killing of Jews and other victim groups during the Second World War. On occasion this also led to an understanding that the Holocaust was carried out beyond Germany. But often this knowledge was sketchy and lacked meaningful detail. Certainly, it appeared the vast majority of students were profoundly unaware of the geographical scope and scale of the Holocaust and typically did not appreciate that its execution required the complicity and collaboration of tens of thousands of individuals in localities, regions and nations all across Europe.

How limitations in knowledge prevented deeper understanding of complicity and responsibility

The significant gaps in student knowledge undoubtedly hampered deeper understanding and fuelled serious misconceptions about complicity and responsibility. This deficiency poses salient educational issues and challenges, of which three will be mentioned here.

The first area of concern is students' common belief that Hitler was either solely responsible for the Holocaust and/or he orchestrated its development and execution with top-down efficiency and authority. Of course, Hitler is a central figure in the genocide of the Jews, but students' understanding of his role fails to appreciate the limitations of his power and the complex way that Nazi policy was enacted across Europe. It also exposes the repeated and ongoing issue of how students' knowledge and understanding of the Holocaust is worryingly incompatible with historical scholarship (Cesarani 2016; Lawson 2017). For most contemporary scholars of the Holocaust have moved beyond crude 'intentionalist' and 'functionalist' debates[3] over the significance of Hitler's leadership and responsibility and typically acknowledge that Hitler acted within a complex and dynamic political context which placed limitations on what one man could accomplish. As Ian Kershaw has written, most historians now eschew explicit focus of the omnipresent dictator in favour of 'the notion of polycratic rule – a multi-dimensional power structure, in which Hitler's authority was only one element (if a very important one)' (Kershaw 2000, 74).

Furthermore, the UCL research (Foster *et al.* 2016) revealed that almost no students had even a very basic understanding of the complex and often chaotic way that Nazi policy was implemented during the Holocaust. For most students, its implementation was a simple matter of top-down orders being followed by individuals almost in blind obedience to Hitler. This understanding, of course, is at odds with key historical scholarship which indicates such a simplistic interpretation is very problematic (Bankier 1992; Bloxham 2001; Bloxham 2009; Browning 1992; Cesarani, 2005; Kershaw, 2008; Marrus 1987). As Lawson (2017, 352) asserts, students' understanding is 'depressingly out of step with modern historiography ... Indeed, for many historians it was the lack of command and control, and central direction – in other words the chaotic nature of the state – that drove policy onwards.'

Of course, this is not to suggest that school students should have detailed knowledge of existing and emerging scholarship, but an urgent need exists for students to move beyond simplistic understandings of Hitler's role as an omniscient puppeteer whose every wish was carried out with clinical efficiency. Indeed, if young people are to acquire a more sophisticated understanding of how extremist ideas take root and radicalise across societies, it is imperative that students move beyond naively attributing responsibility to a single individual and consider alternative interpretations and causal factors. In this respect in the process of acquiring substantive knowledge, it is also important that students develop a more sophisticated understanding of second-order concepts such as causation and significance. For if they are to appreciate how things happened in the past, it is vital they understand causality and, crucially, have adequate substantial knowledge to inform this understanding.

The second issue of concern is directly related to the first and focuses on how many students (particularly those who had not studied the Holocaust beyond age 14) typically did not appreciate who the Nazis were and how they enjoyed popular support from people across all sectors of German society. Indeed, the UCL study strikingly revealed that many students did not appreciate that first and foremost 'Nazism' was a political movement which, for example, received the support of more than 13 million Germans in July 1932. This is of course a significant misconception. For, if students fail to appreciate the broad-based nature of the Nazi Party and the circumstances in which they rose to power, it potentially inhibits their understanding of how right-wing political extremism can develop and flourish in any society. Furthermore, in the context of the Holocaust, limitations in students' knowledge about the Nazi Party dramatically impairs their ability to understand the pivotal role played by Nazi Party members in the subsequent enactment of genocide. Once again deficiencies in both students' substantive knowledge and conceptual understanding (e.g., of causal factors) seriously undermines their ability to understand this complex history.

A third problematic issue is the common failure of many students to appreciate that the Holocaust deeply impacted societies all across Europe. This failing is troubling for many reasons. Most significantly, it suggests that few students grasp the Jewish specificity of the Holocaust in which the perpetrators determined to murder all Jews (every last man, woman and child), everywhere that they could be reached (Bauer 2002). In pursuit of this goal the Nazis and their collaborators murdered, for example, millions of Jews from Poland and the USSR, more than half a million in Hungary, in excess of 100,000 Jews in Germany, Czechoslovakia, Romania and Holland and tens of thousands in Belgium, Austria, Yugoslavia, Greece and France. In fact, few European nations escaped the brutality and destruction of the Holocaust. Typically, however, school students appeared not to know about its geographic scope and scale. As a consequence of this impoverished understanding, most students were unable to appreciate the devastating impact of the Holocaust in villages, towns, cities and nations across Europe. Furthermore, limitations in students' knowledge stood in the way of a broader appreciation of the troubling extent of widespread complicity and collaboration in nations all across Europe. Indeed, historians such as Dan Stone (2010, 32) have suggested that local participation in 'indigenous Holocausts' revealed that the genocide of the Jews was much more than a German-led project and exposed deep-seated, centuries-old prejudices commonly in existence across the European continent.

Overall, therefore, what these three examples illustrate is that students' lack of historical knowledge and conceptual understanding profoundly impaired their ability to appreciate some of the most troubling aspects of the Holocaust and, arguably, its profound significance and relevance for contemporary society. For example, most students did not grasp key causal factors. Few understood, for instance, that the persecution of the Jews did not begin with Hitler but was a feature of European history for centuries. As detailed above, in the UCL study 68 per cent of students did not recognise the term 'antisemitism' and only a tiny minority had even a rudimentary sense of its long history. As a result, therefore, most students failed to appreciate that in the particular and contingent context of the 1920s and 1930s, Hitler drew on and exploited deep-seated antisemitic prejudices already prevalent in German and European culture. Indeed, the common failure of students to appreciate how 'ordinary people' across Europe were complicit in the persecution and mass murder of Jews is, arguably, the most troubling findings from the research. For, if young people only see Hitler and a small coterie of his followers as responsible for the Holocaust, they will fail even to perceive – let alone respond to – one of the most troubling questions raised by this history: How was it that not very long ago and not very far away 'ordinary people' became complicit in the murder of their neighbours?

Unfortunately, it appeared that few students understood that the web of complicity extended across the continent and that vast numbers of Europeans willingly participated in genocide – either out of greed, peer pressure, conviction, or self-preservation. As a result, most did not have adequate knowledge and understanding of the Holocaust to consider vital questions about human agency and responsibility such as: Why did this happen? Why in the context of the times did people act as they did? In what circumstances could this happen today? Furthermore, meaningful engagement with the historical Holocaust might compel students to ask themselves what they would have done and confront the uncomfortable and 'frightening' dilemma raised by Bauman (1989, 152) not 'that *this* could be done to us, but the idea that *we* could do it'.

It was, however, clear that most students were not equipped with the historical knowledge and conceptual or second-order understanding to address such important issues. Of course, given the wealth of scholarship on the Holocaust it is unrealistic to expect students to possess encyclopaedic knowledge. It is also recognised that knowledge must be developed in age-appropriate ways. Nevertheless, at some level it is reasonable to expect that students should have relevant knowledge of the rise of the Nazi party, its membership and the development of its power structures. It is also important for students to appreciate both the extent and limitations of the power and influence of Hitler and his inner leadership circle. Additionally, students also should know something about the role played by many Germans, collaborating regimes, Axis allies and local populations. If students acquire some of this substantive knowledge alongside the development of deeper conceptual understanding (e.g., of cause and consequence, change and continuity, historical significance and human agency, and responsibility), it is highly likely that they will have a more informed and meaningful understanding of the Holocaust. Indeed, as the UCL study demonstrated, on the rare occasions when students appeared to have more robust historical knowledge and conceptual understanding, it was very evident that their broader appreciation of the Holocaust and its contemporary significance was more profound and sophisticated. This appreciation was particularly evident, for example, among students who had studied history at A Level (i.e., typically those aged 17–18). Many of these students appeared able to apply their more extensive substantive knowledge to answer deeper and more profound questions. Accordingly, a number of these older students appreciated that responsibility for the Holocaust was more widespread and diffuse than their younger counterparts believed. These students appreciated that the power structures of the Third Reich were complex and multifaceted and they typically eschewed the notion that Nazi Germany was ruled in a simplistic top-down way. Furthermore, a number of older students appreciated the limitations of Hitler's control and offered a more sophisticated appreciation that many 'ordinary' Germans were complicit in the Holocaust. As this brief example illustrates, when students were able to draw on relevant substantive knowledge, they exhibited more profound and historically accurate understandings. Unfortunately, the number of students who evidenced this more sophisticated understanding were relatively few. However, the example illustrates that with age-appropriate and thoughtful teaching it is possible to meaningfully develop students' understanding of important issues which derive from studying the Holocaust.

Thus far a detailed explanation of one important facet of the Holocaust (i.e., complicity and responsibility) has been used to illustrate how students' lack of historical and conceptual knowledge often resulted in an impoverished understanding of the Holocaust. But, of course, this finding is salient for all aspects of students' understanding of the Holocaust.

For example, another illustration of how limited substantive and conceptual knowledge typically inhibited deeper understanding relates to the victims of the Holocaust. Many students' understandings of the victims of the Holocaust were often based on crude and ill-informed generalisations. For example, although 90 per cent of students correctly identified Jews as victims, very few could precisely say what differentiated Jews from other identified victim groups (e.g., gay men, disabled people, Roma and Sinti). Typically, students erroneously assumed that all Nazi victims were targeted and treated in similar ways, chiefly because they were 'different'. This misunderstanding often led to the tendency for many students to lump all victim groups together as a faceless mass with no agency and stood in the way of a deeper understanding of the diverse experiences of ordinary people caught up in the maelstrom of history. Furthermore, it also appeared to prevent any intelligent second-order explanation of what caused the Holocaust and – without any appreciation of the vibrancy of life before the war – what was lost as a result of its devastation (i.e., its historical consequence and significance).

Another cause for concern revealed by the research was that whereas most students significantly *overestimated* the pre-war Jewish population, many also massively *underestimated* the numbers of victims murdered. Students typically appeared to accept stereotypical myths about the power, influence and size of the Jewish population in pre-war Germany and very few had any appreciation of the diversity of Jewish society and culture before the Second World War. In a similar vein, the research revealed that students' chronological and geographical knowledge of the Holocaust appeared weak and, as a consequence, their ability to identify key conceptual developments, turning points and important historical context was severely impeded. It also prevented students from understanding the process, development and radicalisation of the genocide and, by extension, their ability to assess its contemporary relevance.

Overall, therefore, an apparent lack of knowledge appeared to prevent deeper understanding of the Holocaust. Typically, students were unable to fully appreciate how, why, where and when the Holocaust happened, and the absence of this knowledge inhibited students' ability either to explain human actions in the past, or to consider the Holocaust's significance for us today. It also exposed students' weak conceptual or second-order understandings of the Holocaust which appeared to prevent intelligent exploration of, for example, cause and consequence, change and continuity, empathetic understanding and historical significance.

Conclusion

The UCL study revealed that in addition to school-based learning, most students encountered representations and narratives of the Holocaust outside of school. In fact, 85 per cent of students in Year 10 and above stated they had learned about the Holocaust outside of school. These encounters with the Holocaust took many forms and included television, literature, the internet, personal stories and museum visits. It was, however, particularly noticeable that many students were affected by representations of the Holocaust in popular films. For example, 84.4 per cent of students who said they had seen a film about the Holocaust reported they had watched *The Boy in the Striped Pyjamas*, and this experience appeared to influence their understanding of the genocide. Unfortunately, however, as numerous critics have observed, encounters with the Holocaust which occur outside of school often fuel and exacerbate common misconceptions and typically reinforce the salience of a *mythic* Holocaust (Cesarani 2008; Foster *et al.* 2016; Gray 2014a, 2014b; Pearce 2014; Pettigrew *et al.* 2009; Russell 2006). *The Boy in the Striped Pyjamas*, for example, has been heavily criticised for its historical inaccuracies and inappropriate framing. Indeed, it is potentially problematic that the mythic Holocaust represented in films and other cultural artefacts often reduces the events of the Holocaust to a simplistic morality tale of good versus evil and avoids its more profound and deeply troubling aspects (e.g., how in a modern, ostensibly educated state, could this happen?). Furthermore, the ubiquitous presence of a mythic Holocaust often obfuscates a more intelligent understanding of the substantive history of the Holocaust and its contemporary significance and leaves no room for the development of vital conceptual understandings.

Of course, the concerns raised here may not be so much of an issue if our educational system was critically challenging and addressing how the Holocaust is represented and portrayed in the broader culture. But as this chapter has shown, this seems to be far from the case. In fact, typically students' lack of historical knowledge appears to act as a significant barrier to a deeper and more meaningful understanding of the Holocaust. It also, by extension, prevents any intelligent consideration of its contemporary representation and significance and how interpretive accounts of this history are constructed. From this perspective it is potentially possible that rather than challenge prevailing misconceptions, schools may reinforce and perpetuate them. This troubling reality presents educators with a real challenge and underscores the critical importance of ensuring students acquire a robust understanding of the historical Holocaust.

As I have written elsewhere (Foster 2013; Foster *et al.* 2016; Foster 2018) an imperative exists, therefore, to ensure teachers who teach about the Holocaust are better equipped to help their students develop their knowledge and conceptual understanding in accessible, age-appropriate ways. In this respect, it is absolutely critical that teachers have access to high-quality professional development support which not only helps them consider vital pedagogical issues, but also offers insight into current and emerging historical scholarship.

The ultimate goal of course is to improve the historical knowledge and conceptual understanding of young people so that they are able both to understand the complexity of the Holocaust and address fundamental questions such as: What was the Holocaust? Who was responsible and complicit in its development and execution? Why and how did they do it? How were the actions of perpetrators, victims and bystanders affected by the context of the times? Who were the victims and how and why were they targeted? How did the victims respond? When and where did the Holocaust happen? How did the Allies and people across Europe engage with the Holocaust? How and why did it end? Ultimately, therefore, the acquisition of important historical knowledge and the development of associated conceptual understanding is of paramount importance. Indeed, developing students' substantive knowledge in conjunction with conceptual understanding is essential if students are to understand this complex history and to critically evaluate the way the Holocaust is presented in modern culture.

Notes

1. For a more detailed discussion of the study's approach to interrogating historical knowledge, see Foster *et al.*, 101–4.
2. It is important to recognise that many students who were studying history aged 17–18 had a more sophisticated understanding of Hitler's role, but this was very much an exception to the rule.
3. Historiographical debates between 'intentionalists' and 'functionalists' were particularly apparent in the 1970s and 1980s. Essentially, 'intentionalists' believe that Hitler always had a master plan to carry out the Holocaust and its execution was directed in a 'top down' manner. Functionalists oppose this theory and argue by contrast that the Holocaust resulted from the actions of those from the lower ranks of German bureaucracy and government.

References

All online material last accessed 24 July 2019 unless indicated otherwise.

Abrams, F. 2012. 'Cultural literacy: Michael Gove's school of hard facts', 25 October. Online. http://www.bbc.co.uk/news/education-20041597.

Bankier, D. 1992. *The Germans and the Final Solution: Public opinion under Nazism.* Oxford: Blackwell.

Bauer, Y. 2002. *Rethinking the Holocaust.* New Haven, CT: Yale University Press.

Bauman, Z. 1989. *Modernity and the Holocaust.* Cambridge: Polity Press.

Bell, D. 2003. 'Mythscapes: Memory, mythology, and national identity', *British Journal of Sociology* 54 (1): 63–81.

Bloxham, D. 2001. *Genocide on Trial: War crimes trials and the formation of Holocaust history and memory.* Oxford: Oxford University Press.

Bloxham, D. 2009. *The Final Solution: A genocide.* Oxford: Oxford University Press.

Booth, M. 1993. 'Students' historical thinking and the national history curriculum in England', *Theory and Research in Social Education* 21 (2): 105–27.

Browning, C. 1992. *Ordinary Men: Reserve Police Battalion 101 and the Final Solution in Poland.* New York: Harper Collins.

Carrier, P., Fuchs, E. and Messinger, T. 2015. *The International Status of Education about the Holocaust: A global mapping of textbooks and curricula.* Paris: UNESCO.

Cesarani, D. 2005. *Eichmann: His life and crimes.* London: Vintage.

Cesarani, D. 2008. 'From the pulpit: Striped Pyjamas', *Literary Review* 359: 3.

Cesarani, D. 2016. *Final Solution: The fate of the Jews 1933–1949.* London: Macmillan.

Cole, T. 1999. *Selling the Holocaust: From Auschwitz to Schindler; How history is bought and sold.* New York: Routledge.

Counsell, C., Burn, K. and Chapman, A. eds. 2016. *MasterClass in History Education: Transforming teaching and learning.* London: Bloomsbury.

Crawford, K.A. 1995. 'A history of the right: The battle for national curriculum history, 1989–1994', *British Journal of Educational Studies* 43: 433–56.

Desbois, P. 2008. *The Holocaust by Bullets: A priest's journey to uncover the truth behind the murder of 1.5 million Jews.* New York: Palgrave Macmillan.

DfE. 2013. 'History programmes of study: Key stage 3. Online. https://assets.publishing.service.gov.uk/government/uploads/system/uploads/attachment_data/file/239075/SECONDARY_national_curriculum_-_History.pdf (accessed May 2018).

Foster, S.J. 1998. 'Politics, parallels and perennial curriculum questions: The battle over school history in England and the United States', *The Curriculum Journal* 9: 153–64.

Foster, S.J. 2013. 'Teaching about the Holocaust in English schools: Challenges and possibilities', *Intercultural Education* 24: 1–2.

Foster, S.J. 2018. 'Myths, misconceptions and mis-memory: Holocaust education in England'. In *Remembering the Holocaust in Educational Settings*, edited by Andy Pearce. London: Routledge.

Foster, S.J. and Crawford, K.A. eds. 2006. *What Shall We Tell the Children? International perspectives on school history textbooks.* Greenwich, CT: Information Age Publishing.

Foster, S.J., Pettigrew, A., Pearce, A., Hale, R., Burgess, A., Salmons, P. and Lenga, R.-A. 2016. *What Do Students Know and Understand about the Holocaust? Evidence from English Secondary Schools*. London: UCL Institute of Education.

Foster, S.J. and Yeager, E. 1999. '"You've got to put together the pieces": English 12-year-olds encounter and learn from historical evidence', *Journal of Curriculum and Supervision* 14 (4): 286–318.

Foster, S. and Yeager, E. 2001. 'Historical empathy in theory and practice: Some final thoughts'. In *Historical Empathy and Perspective Taking in the Social Studies*, edited by O.L. Davis, Elizabeth A. Yeager and Stuart J. Foster, 167–81. Oxford: Rowman and Littlefield.

Gibb, N. 2017. 'Importance of core knowledge sees return of textbooks: School Standards Minister speaks at a panel discussion at the Policy Exchange (Thursday 30 November 2017)'. Online. https://www.gov.uk/government/speeches/nick-gibb-importance-of-core-knowledge-sees-return-of-textbooks.

Granatstein, J.L. 1998. *Who Killed Canadian History?* Toronto: Harper Collins.

Gray, M. 2014a. 'Preconceptions of the Holocaust among thirteen and fourteen year olds in English schools'. Ph.D. diss., Institute of Education, University of London.

Gray, M. 2014b. '*The Boy in the Striped Pyjamas*: A blessing or curse for Holocaust education?' *Holocaust Studies: A Journal of Culture and History* 20 (3): 109–36.

Hirsch. E.D., Jr. 1983. 'Cultural Literacy', *The American Scholar* 52 (2): 159–69.

Hirsch, E.D., Jr. 1987. *Cultural Literacy: What every American needs to know*. Boston: Houghton Mifflin.

Hirsch, E.D., Jr. 2016. *Why Knowledge Matters: Rescuing our children from failed educational theories*. Cambridge, MA: Harvard Education Press.

Husbands, C., Kitson, A. and Seward, S. 2011. *Teaching and Learning History 11–18: Understanding the past*. Maidenhead: Open University Press.

Kershaw, I. 2000. *The Nazi Dictatorship: Problems and perspectives of interpretation*. London: Hodder.

Kershaw, I. 2008. *Hitler, the Germans and the Final Solution*. New Haven, CT: Yale University Press.

Kinloch, N. 1998. 'Learning about the Holocaust: Moral or historical question?' *Teaching History* 93: 44–6.

Lawson, T. 2017. 'Britain's promise to forget: Some historiographical reflections on *What Do Students Know and Understand about the Holocaust?*'*Holocaust Studies: A Journal of Culture and History* 23 (3): 345–63.

Lee, P.J. 1999. 'Putting principles into practice: Understanding history'. In *HowPeople Learn: Brain, mind, experience, and school*, edited by J.D. Bransford, A. Brown and R. Cocking. Washington, DC: National Research Council.

Lee, P. 2005. 'Historical Literacy', *International Journal of Historical Learning, Teaching and Research* 5 (1): 27–40.

Lee, P. and Ashby, R. 2000. 'Progression in historical understanding among students ages 7–14'. In *Knowing, Teaching, and Learning History: National and international perspectives*, edited by P.N. Stearns, P. Seixas and S. Wineburg, 199–222. New York: New York University Press.

Marrus, M. 1987. *The Holocaust in History*. Hanover, NH: University Press of New England.

Nash, G.B., Crabtree, C. and Dunn, R.E. 1997. *History on Trial: Culture wars and the teaching of the past*. New York: Knopf.

Peal, R. 2014. *Progressively Worse: The burden of bad ideas in British schools*. London: Civitas.

Pearce, A. 2014. *Holocaust Consciousness in Contemporary Britain*. New York: Routledge.

Pearce, A. 2017. 'The Holocaust in the national curriculum after 25 years', *Holocaust Studies: A Journal of Culture and History* 23 (3): 231–63.

Pettigrew, A. 2017. 'Why teach or learn about the Holocaust? Teaching aims and student knowledge in English secondary schools', *Holocaust Studies: A Journal of Culture and History* 23 (3): 263–88.

Pettigrew, A., Foster, S., Howson, J., Salmons, P., Lenga, R.-A. and Andrews, K. 2009. *Teaching about the Holocaust in English Secondary Schools: An empirical study of national trends, perspectives and practice*. London: Institute of Education.

Phillips, R. 1998. *History Teaching, Nationhood, and the State: A study in educational politics*. London: Cassell.

Russell, L. 2006. *Teaching the Holocaust in School History: Teachers or preachers?* London: Continuum.

Salmons, P. 2003. 'Teaching or preaching? The Holocaust and intercultural education in the UK', *Intercultural Education* 14 (2): 139–49.

Seixas, P. ed. 2004. *Theorizing Historical Consciousness*. Toronto: University of Toronto Press.

Shemilt, D. 1987. 'Adolescent ideas about evidence and methodology in history'. In *The History Curriculum for Teachers*, edited by Christopher Portal, 39–61. London: Falmer Press.

Short, G. 1994. 'Teaching about the Holocaust: A consideration of ethical and pedagogic issues', *Educational Studies* 20 (1): 53–67.

Slater, J. 1989. *The Politics of History Teaching: A humanity dehumanized?* London: Institute of Education, University of London.

Spencer, H. 1860. 'What knowledge is of most worth?' In H. Spencer, *Education: Intellectual, moral, and physical*, 21–96. New York: D. Appleton and Company.

Stone, D. 2010. *Histories of the Holocaust*. Oxford: Oxford University Press.

Symcox, L. and Wilschut, A. eds. 2009. *National History Standards: The problem of the canon and the future of teaching history: International Review of History Education*, Volume 5. Charlotte, NC: Information Age Publishing.

Taylor, T. 2004. 'Disputed territory: The politics of historical consciousness in Australia'. In *Theorizing Historical Consciousness*, edited by Peter Seixas, 217–39. Toronto: University of Toronto Press.

VanSledright, B.A. 2004. 'What does it mean to think historically . . . and how do you teach it?' *Social Education* 68 (3): 230–3.

VanSledright, B.A. 2011. *The Challenge of Re-thinking History Education: On practices, theories and policy*. New York: Routledge.

Wineburg, S.S. 2001. *Historical Thinking and Other Unnatural Acts: Charting the future of teaching the past*. Philadelphia: Temple University Press.

Young, M. and Muller, J. 2013. 'On the powers of powerful knowledge', *Review of Education* 1 (3): 229–50.

Young, M. and Muller, J. 2016. *Curriculum and the Specialization of Knowledge: Studies in the sociology of education*. London: Routledge.

3
Learning the lessons of the Holocaust: A critical exploration

Arthur Chapman

Introduction

> Every generation has to confront the Holocaust: how did it happen, who made it happen, who allowed it to happen and who will make sure it does not happen again? Recent events in Paris and the tyranny and barbarity we continue to witness in Iraq and Syria are telling testimony of this need. It is vital that people from all walks of life learn about and understand the Holocaust, for the sake of the people who died and as a way of honouring those who survived, as well as to learn the contemporary lessons from this, the darkest hour of human history.
>
> (The Cabinet Office 2015, 6)

The Holocaust has come to have a prominent place in much international educational discourse during the last generation, since the collapse of the Berlin Wall and the USSR that unfroze the memory of the Shoah in much of Europe (Judt 2007, 3) and, in particular, in the years since the Stockholm Declaration of 2000 (International Holocaust Remembrance Alliance n.d.) and the mandating of 'Holocaust Memorial Day', developments associated with the embedding of the Holocaust in an increasingly globalised Human Rights discourse (Marrus 2016, 148–51). Often, it is the 'lessons' of the Holocaust that feature most prominently in Holocaust education language and practice. In England, the Holocaust became one of the small number of specific topics mandated by name in the National Curriculum when it was first introduced in 1991, and the theme of 'lessons' has played an influential role since, in packs of educational materials provided for schools to support them in teaching this topic (Spiro Institute and Holocaust Educational Trust 1997), through programmes of educational visits funded by English and other UK governments focused on drawing 'lessons' from Auschwitz (Foreign and Commonwealth Office 2012; Jewish News Reporter, 2018; Holocaust Educational Trust, n.d.; Hargrave 2018), in the Prime Minister's Holocaust Commission Report *Britain's Promise to Remember* (2015), and in Holocaust Memorial Day commemorations, presentations and assemblies (e.g. Bedford Borough Council 2019).

The idea that we might learn lessons from history has a long pedigree – reaching back to the Ciceronian personification of history as a 'teacher of life' (*historia magistra vitae*) who can help us understand the present and inform action to change the future (Assis 2014, 24–5) and 'mirror for princes' literature in the Renaissance (Paul 2015, 125) – and is very widespread in contemporary culture:

- Newspapers frequently offer 'lessons' from history, or complain that they have not been learned (e.g. Sandbrook 2009; First Dog on the Moon 2016; Smith 2018)
- Popular histories are frequently structured around lists of 'lessons' (e.g. Snyder 2017; Harari 2018)
- Politicians frequently invoke 'lessons of history' when calling for action or seeking to justify action (e.g. Gove 2010; May 2018; Major 2018)
- The analogical use of the past to describe and help characterise present problems and concerns is widespread – as in the frequent use of analogies between contemporary contexts and the appeasement of Hitler in the 1930s (Tosh 2008, 64–7) and the use of the Holocaust as a paradigm through which to think a range of contemporary concerns, ranging from gun control to animal exploitation (e.g. Marrus 2016, 137–9; Karlsen, n.d.).

The discourse in which 'lessons' are embedded is complex, indicating that we are dealing with a multi-faceted phenomenon. Typically – as in our epigraph, above, from *Britain's Promise to Remember* (The Cabinet Office 2015, 6) – this discourse mixes:

- Memory (' . . . for the sake of the people who died and as a way of honouring those who survived . . .')
- History (' . . . how did it happen . . .?')

- 'Para-historical' enquiry (Megill 2002), mixing historical and moral questions (' . . . who made it happen, who allowed it to happen?')
- Calls for practical reflection and action (' . . . who will make sure it does not happen again?')
- A determination to link the past and the immediate present ('events in Paris . . . the tyranny and barbarity we continue to witness in Iraq and Syria').

'Lessons' themselves, as we will see below, can take many forms, ranging from meditations on the nature of the human condition, at one end of the spectrum, to the articulation of maxims and guides to action, at the other. Despite their ubiquity, 'lessons' are frequently perceived as problematic by historians and history educators, as we will see below. Two recent works by prominent Holocaust historians (Marrus 2016; Cesarani 2016) indicate, perhaps, increasing frustration, in some areas of the historical academy at least, at the ease with which 'lessons' and conclusions are drawn from the stories about the Holocaust in our present.

David Cesarani's last book, *Final Solution: The Fate of the Jews 1933–1949* (2016), begins with a critique of the ways in which the Holocaust is constructed in public discourse and in education, things that Cesarani was well-positioned to comment on as an historian and public intellectual who had, for example, written a history of the Holocaust for the Holocaust Educational Trust (Cesarani 1998). 'The Holocaust has never been so ubiquitous', Cesarani argued. However, there was 'a yawning gulf between popular understanding of this history and current scholarship on the subject' (Cesarani 2016, xxv). As he went on to note:

> This is hardly surprising given that most people acquire their knowledge of the Nazi past and the fate of the Jews through novels, films or earnest but ill-informed lessons at school, which frequently rely on novels for young adults or their filmic versions. Misconceptions are reinforced by the edited and instrumentalized versions purveyed by campaigning bodies and the constellation of organizations devoted to education and commemoration. Although these efforts are made in good faith, they are subordinate to extraneous agendas, be it the desire to cultivate an inclusive national identity or the laudable determination to combat anti-Semitism, racism, homophobia and other forms of political, religious or ethnic intolerance. Some lazily draw on an outdated body of research, while others utilize state-of-the-art research but downplay inconvenient aspects of the newer findings.
>
> (Cesarani 2016, xxv)

In other words, Cesarani contended, first, that the Holocaust culturally constructed in much contemporary education and popular culture bore little resemblance to the historical Holocaust, reconstructed in contemporary scholarship, and that this unhistorical Holocaust was pedagogised in educational contexts in highly instrumental ways – the 'lessons' drawn from this past were, increasingly, inferences from inaccuracy and, therefore, flawed from the start.

In this 'standardised version' the Holocaust is presented as the 'outcome of racist and anti-Semitic policies' unfolding from 1933 and leading, from 1939 onwards, through deportation to annihilation in 'death camps in Poland', and ending with the collapse of the German Reich in 1945 (Cesarani 2016, xxix–xxx). Cesarani argues that this teleological narrative, inaccurate in a number of ways, ignores the impact of a range of drivers of policy – such as 'the German way of war', unexpected victories and later defeats (Cesarani 2016, xxxii–xxxvii) – and imposes a spurious retrospective inevitability on contingent events, which are understood as the bureaucratic and technocratic unfolding of ideologically driven policy formulated early in the Nazi period.

Like Cesarani, Michael Marrus's *Lessons of the Holocaust* (2016) is concerned about historical accuracy and about the instrumentalisation of the past. Whilst acknowledging that 'a degree of trivialization' is inevitable when complex historical scholarship is refunctioned educationally and re-inscribed into 'any widely accepted discourse', Marrus argues against predominant pedagogic and popular cultural framings of this history in terms of 'formulaic lessons' (Marrus 2015) that, he argues, stereotype and misconstrue both the past and the future. Furthermore, Marrus contends, a lessons-based approach fails to appreciate the nature and the limits of historical sense-making in the present (Marrus 2016). Marrus's *Lessons of the Holocaust* argues, above all, that '[a]s acknowledgement of the significance of the Holocaust has increased globally, an unfortunate accompaniment has been a loss of respect for detailed knowledge of what actually happened' and that the 'principal lesson of the Holocaust is, therefore, beware of lessons' (Marrus 2016, 160).

This chapter, which takes a theoretical rather than an empirical focus, will explore the forms that 'lessons' of the Holocaust can take, as well as some of the criticisms that have been made, particularly by historians and history educators, of a lessons-based approach, before attempting an appraisal of the affordances and constraints of 'lessons of the Holocaust' discourse as educational practice.

'Learning about' and 'learning from' the Holocaust

Learning '*about* the Holocaust' denotes a kind of education – formally or informally delivered – through which one comes to knowledge and understanding of the past realities to which the term 'Holocaust' refers (e.g. knowledge and understanding of the extermination camp at Treblinka) and also, perhaps, knowledge of the ways in which those past realities are – and have been – understood (for example, knowledge and understanding of The Treblinka Memorial). There is much room for debate and discussion of what children and adults should come to learn *about* the Holocaust (e.g. What is it most important to know?) and much debate and discussion about how these things should be taught and learned, in general and at different stages of education (e.g. When should learning begin? What aspects should be learned first and how should they be taught?).

When one moves from 'learning *about*' to 'learning *from*' or learning the lessons '*of*' the Holocaust, things become more complex. Learning '*from* X' denotes that one draws conclusions from the study of 'X' for some other topic that one learns about, and learning the lessons '*of* X' personifies it, such that it teaches one something of a wider applicability. These are both *secondary* kinds of learning – *meta*-learning – in which one learns about the *significance* of what one has learned *about* the Holocaust *for* things *beyond* the Holocaust itself. As they both share this common feature, I will treat '*of*' and '*from*' interchangeably in what follows. One cannot learn '*from*' or '*of*' if one has not already learned '*about*', and this learning '*from*' or '*of*' involves a transfer of knowledge and understanding from one topic (the Holocaust) to another (for example, how to act in the present and future). This is potentially a highly complex area of learning: there are many ways in which one topic might have significance for another topic; significance and signification are multifaceted; transfer depends upon structural or other types of connection between the topics, and such links can be both hard to make and open to debate. These two types of learning are schematised in Figure 3.1.

Things are more complex still, however, since both the objects that we can 'learn *about*' and 'learn *from*' can be approached through a number of distinct optics or ways of seeing. We can distinguish distinct intellectual optics – or disciplines – that approach the objects of human experience, and that experience itself, in differing and distinctive ways – for example, 'Visual Arts' and 'History' (Dawes Duraisingh and Boix Mansilla 2007). Disciplines constitute their objects of study in different ways and we can speak of distinct epistemologies linked to different disciplines.

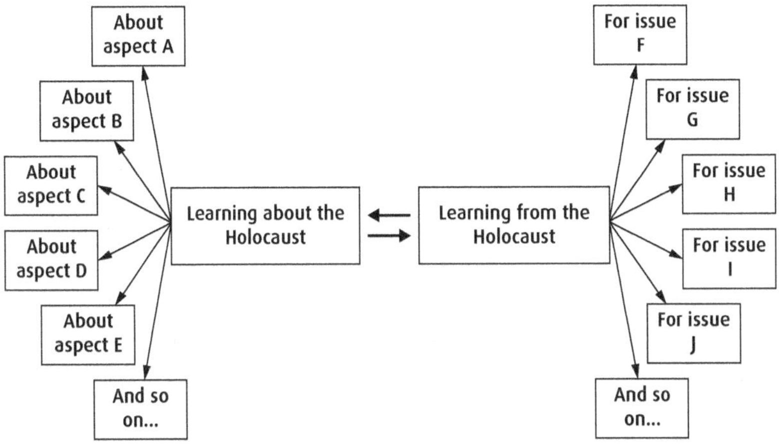

Fig 3.1 Learning about and learning from the Holocaust (drawn by author).

Learning '*about*' and '*from*' the Holocaust are likely, then, to mean rather different things depending on the discipline through which the learning is taking place.

In addition to distinguishing, in general, between different disciplinary optics that can be used to understand areas and types of experience, we can distinguish more specifically between differing approaches to the public past. Just as disciplines shape learning, so the approaches to the past that are adopted will have consequences, also, for how that past is understood. As Megill has argued, the principal task of the historian is to 'attempt to say what actually happened in the past, let the chips fall where they may' (Megill 2002, 123); nevertheless, 'historians have the task not only of describing and explaining the past but also of trying to show how the past makes sense for "us" now' (Megill 2002, 105–6). Making sense of the public past inevitably takes us beyond the empirical and explanatory modes of historical scholarship and into questions of identity (including the identity of 'us'). This is likely to be particularly true of attempts to make sense of the past in institutions such as schools where the strictly 'analytic' stance towards the past central to the discipline of history often sits parallel to learning focused on cultivating what Barton and Levstik call 'moral' and 'identification' stances (Barton and Levstik 2004, 7). Even in the context of the discipline of history, Megill argues, dealing with topics such as the Holocaust 'involves some attempt to confront the ethical breach that atrocity makes in our world' (Megill 2002, 106), and what is true of the academy is likely to be even truer of schools where all teaching is multi-stranded and involves pastoral as well as academic functions, to one degree or another.

Lessons from the Holocaust

Broadly speaking, it seems to me, one can divide the 'lessons' that students are urged to learn from the Holocaust into three broad types:

- *Deontological* lessons, of a categorical and unconditional kind, about how to act or think or feel; that is to say, lessons indicating what it simply is, *in* and *of itself*, moral to do or to be
- *Consequentialist* lessons, of a conditional or prudential kind, about how to act or think or feel; that is to say, lessons indicating what one should do or how one should be, *if* one wishes to secure a particular outcome
- *Ontological* lessons about the nature of human and or social or political reality – for example, lessons about 'human nature' and what human beings are like in some fundamental sense, or, to give another example, lessons about the fundamental nature of politics, ideology and so on.[1]

Deontological lessons are exemplified by the following comment made by a pupil:

> All people are equal and . . . no one should be treated like [the Jews were].
>
> (Short 2005, 372)

The following, from an article outlining seven 'universal' lessons of the Holocaust published in the *Jerusalem Post*, is equally deontological in nature:

> The first lesson is the importance of *zachor*, of remembrance. For as we remember the six million Jewish victims of the Shoah – defamed, demonized and dehumanized, as prologue or justification for genocide – we have to understand that the mass murder of six million Jews, and millions of non-Jews, is not a matter of abstract statistics. For unto each person there is a name, an identity; each person is a universe. As our sages tell us, 'Whoever saves a single life, it is as if he or she has saved an entire universe.' Conversely, whoever has killed a person, it is as if he has killed an entire universe. Thus, the abiding imperative: We are each, wherever we are, the guarantors of each other's destiny.
>
> (Cotler 2014)

Cotler's argument here is about remembrance as a *duty* and about the *imperative* duties that individuals owe each other as members of a collective 'we', and the register of the text is rich with religious connotation and quotation.

Consequentialist lessons are exemplified by the following pupil comment:

> We have to work together with other religions. We have to get to know their side of things and if we get together, things like [the Holocaust] won't happen.
>
> (Short 2005, 273)

Primo Levi's argument, made in his 1979 'Afterword' to *If This Is A Man*, and a number of other places, that '[i]n every part of the world, wherever you begin by denying the fundamental liberties of mankind, and equality among people, you move toward the concentration camp system, and it is a road on which it is difficult to halt' (Levi 1987, 390–1), also embodies a consequentialist imperative and 'if . . . then . . . ' reasoning: *if* you will the denial of liberties and human equality, Levi argues, *then* you have begun a process that may lead to Auschwitz.

Ontological lessons are exemplified by this comment by a History teacher:

> [I]t is not something which is one country or one particular set of circumstances . . . actually maybe it is something deeper about the human condition. It's something that actually exists within all of us.
>
> (Pettigrew *et al.* 2009, 81)

Equally, the following – elaborating the sixth of eight 'general theses' developed to explain why 'ethnic cleansing' occurs (Mann 2005, 2) – takes an ontological approach, albeit of a more prosaic kind generalising about the nature of socio-political processes and exemplifying 'lessons' about *the nature* of ethnic cleansing derived from comparative sociological analysis of the Holocaust, other cases of genocide and case studies of ethnic cleansing:

> 6. *Murderous cleansing is rarely the initial intent of perpetrators.* It is rare to find evil geniuses plotting mass murder from the very beginning. Not even Hitler did so. Murderous cleansing typically emerges as a kind of Plan C, developed only after ... responses to a perceived ethnic threat fail.
>
> (Mann 2005, 7)

All three types of 'lesson' can be differentiated further in various ways: in terms of the degrees of specificity or generality with which they are offered, in terms of the content of the claims that are made and in terms of the disciplinary frame through which the 'lessons' are stated. It is worth noting – in general – that there are likely to be relationships between different modes of apprehending the world (e.g. subject disciplines) and different lesson types: universal deontological 'lessons', for example, are more likely to be found in disciplines such as theology or moral philosophy, that explore universal principles, than they are to be found in disciplines like history, that explore contextualised particulars.

Debates on the validity of a lessons-based approach to the Holocaust

A range of criticisms have been made about a lessons-based approach to Holocaust education. We can distinguish between objections to lessons *per se* and objections to lessons of particular kinds. Objections of the first type are often made by historians and history educators, as we shall see below, and are exemplified by the following claims, that:

- the Holocaust is not a suitable topic from which to learn lessons for the present and the future
- a 'lessons'-based approach presupposes degrees of knowledge that we simply cannot have of both past and future
- lessons distort history by imposing a moralising presentist agenda on our approach to the past
- a focus on lessons can simplify and distort through anachronism and monocausal explanation.

A related criticism – and one that is made by an advocate of particular types of 'lesson' – is the following:

- That lessons are typically vacuous – too vague to be of value in achieving their aims.

These objections will be reviewed in turn prior to attempting an overall evaluation.

Lessons rest on a category error and inference from the extreme to the normal

Peter Novick has expressed doubts about learning lessons from the Holocaust 'because of its extremity' (Novick 1999, 13). The objections are of two types.

First, Novick objects on 'pedagogic grounds', contending, although Novick does not use precisely these terms, that drawing lessons involves a kind of category error: an inference from (a) extreme experiences and/or actions in extreme circumstances to (b) action and/or experience in normal circumstances: '[l]essons for dealing with the sort of issues that confront us in ordinary life, public or private, are not likely to be found in this most extraordinary of events' (Novick 1999, 13). Novick argues that we should focus on 'the behaviour of normal Americans in normal times', if we want to learn 'important lessons about how easily we become victimizers' (Novick 1999, 13).

Second, Novick objects to 'lessons' on 'pragmatic grounds' (Novick 1999, 14), arguing that, far from sensitising 'us to oppression and atrocity', the extremity of the Holocaust can set our moral bar too high and thus result in 'trivializing crimes of lesser magnitude' (Novick 1999, 14). This, Novick contends, happened during the Bosnian war in the early 1990s, when efforts to deploy a 'Holocaust framework' (Novick 1999, 253) to interpret events failed, and when doubts were expressed about whether ethnic cleansing actions were truly genocidal, thus meriting international intervention, or merely atrocious (Novick 1999, 14).

Lessons presuppose knowledge that we cannot have

Whereas Novick's doubts about lessons rest on the extremity of the events of the Holocaust, Marrus's scepticism about 'lessons' arises from epistemic doubts about the viability of the types of knowledge of both past and future that he argues are presupposed in lessons-based approaches (Marrus 2015 and 2016).

Lessons arise, Marrus argues, when we ruminate 'on the conclusions that historians draw from their study of the past' (Marrus 2016, 32). Marrus objects to attempting to infer the universal from the subjective and the particular: 'history is subject to interpretation, and the effort to derive universally accepted lessons from it [is] a hazardous enterprise' (Marrus 2016, 32). Interpretations, he goes on to argue, are highly

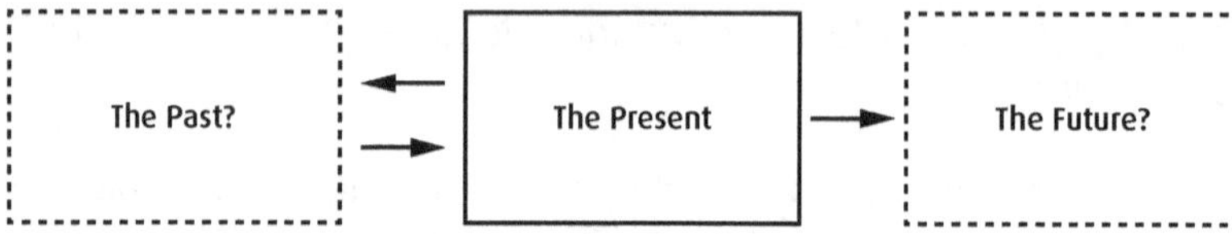

Fig 3.2 Barriers to 'Lessons' – uncertain knowledge of both past and future (drawn by author, based on Marrus 2016, 29–51)

variable and shaped by a range of considerations linked to the subjectivity of the historian enquiring into the past. Marrus argues that to draw lessons is to take significant intellectual risks, by making claims about things that it is very hard to know with any certainty – the past and the future (Figure 3.2).

Of the future, Marrus argues that 'without having a good idea about how things are likely to turn out, one is hardly in a position to recommend one thing or another' (Marrus 2016, 50), and he points to failed futures-past in order to underline the folly of projecting the past into the future, such as the Maginot Line (35–6), constructed on the basis of erroneous predictions about the nature of future wars grounded in the assumption that the future would resemble the past.

Marrus further argues that lessons-based approaches are premised on the erroneous assumption 'that the past is a given, and that the real problem is understanding the future' (Marrus 2016, 39), an assumption that Marrus criticises by discussing how interpretations of the outbreak of World War I have changed since the 1960s: 'history is subject constantly to interpretation, that the focus of history constantly shifts, depending upon what questions people choose to address' (Marrus 2016, 48).

Finally, Marrus advances a more fundamental objection to 'lessons' – one that would apply even if an historian were to succeed in creating a perdurable interpretation and successfully predicting the future. It is not only our interpretations of the past and the future that are subject to change, but human action and human contexts of action themselves, such that what may have held true in the past may no longer apply in the future:

> World views change. Cultures operate differently. Leaders face new challenges. What moved some at one time might not work in another. . . . Drawing lessons . . . on the basis of what people did . . . becomes a very complicated process indeed, not to mention an extremely hazardous one.
>
> (Marrus 2016, 42)

Lessons moralise history in inappropriate ways

Writing in 1998 and 2001, Nicholas Kinloch developed a critique of what he described as a 'dangerously non-historical set of assumptions' (Kinloch 1998, 44) underlying the use of Holocaust history to explore moral and other lessons of the past (Kinloch 1998, 45). Kinloch argued that history teachers should 'help their students become better historians' (Kinloch 2001, 13) and 'start and end with what happened and why' without burdening their history lessons with 'any attempt at "making the world a better place"'. Kinloch objected to using analogies with Nazism – a paradigm of an extreme case – to learn lessons about Britain, a dramatically different context:

> Of course there is much racism in British society. The extermination of ethnic minorities is not yet, however, government policy. Nor do most of us believe that it is likely to become so. Racism will not be eradicated by drawing false comparisons with Nazi Germany.
>
> (Kinloch 1998, 45)

In addition to challenging the appropriateness of using the Holocaust to learn about contemporary anti-racism, Kinloch objected to the efficacy of trying to use history in these ways:

> . . . students, in the real world beyond their classrooms, will continue to make their own moral and social judgements, probably not really much affected by their well-meaning History teachers.
>
> (Kinloch 1998, 46)

Kinloch also objected, in principle, to using history to teach morality:

> There may be good reason to teach children that killing other human beings is generally undesirable. Whether the history class is really the place for such lessons, however, remains debatable.
>
> (Kinloch 2001, 13)

Paul Salmons challenges Kinloch's arguments, as we shall see below. However, like Kinloch, he expresses reservations about what he regards as the simplifying, unhistorical and moralising approach to the past that is often embodied in 'lessons':

> Comfortable 'explanations' that people made the wrong moral choices may lead to resolutions that we will act more morally than

> our forebears. We can then experience the catharsis of saying 'Never again', and congratulate ourselves on our strong moral values. . . . Our attempt to galvanise our students to stand against injustice today then comes at the cost of denigrating people in the past, whose behaviour we have not explained.
>
> (Salmons 2001, 35)

Furthermore, Salmons also argues that simplifying approaches have self-defeating aspects: in the attempt to ensure that children learn the right lessons, young people are presented with conclusions to consume rather than challenged to enquire into the complexity of the past; and that we thus leave 'young people open to manipulation and coercion from those who use the past to push their own social, political or other agendas' (Salmons 2010, 58).

Finally, Salmons argues that a simplistic 'lessons-focused' approach trivialises the Holocaust in important ways:

> The Holocaust is frequently invoked in the classroom to teach universal lessons about the dangers of man's inhumanity to man, the evils of racism and the need for a more tolerant society. The sentiments are noble and important, but do we really need the Holocaust to demonstrate their value? Racism is wrong not because of the gas chambers of Treblinka, but – intellectually – for its weak and faulty view of human beings, and – morally – for the widespread injustice and suffering it causes in the contemporary world on a daily basis.
>
> (Salmons 2010, 58)

Lessons can simplify and distort past realities through anachronism and monocausal explanation

Both Salmons and Marrus agree in arguing that a focus on contemporary lessons distorts the history of the Holocaust, refunctioning it for contemporary ends in ways that obscure more than they illuminate. Salmons contends – as did Cesarani in objecting to an inaccurate 'standardised version' of Holocaust history – that a 'lessons'-based approach can inhibit our understanding of the Holocaust itself:

> While it is clearly the case that without the Nazis' racist ideology and radical antisemitism the Holocaust could not have happened,

> still to reduce the Holocaust to a lesson in anti-racism is an oversimplification which . . . does not reveal the complexities of historical process to the student. It leads to the assumption that there was a straight path from racist ideology to the extinction of a people. It overlooks the possibility that there was a 'twisted road to Auschwitz'.
>
> (Salmons 2010, 59)

Marrus makes his case against neat, pre-packaged Holocaust-history by critiquing a number of 'lessons' frequently invoked in contemporary Holocaust discourse (Marrus 2016, 155–6), including the 'lessons' that:

- It began with words.
- All that it takes for the triumph of evil is that good men do nothing.
- One person can make a difference.

Marrus's objection to these lessons, as to the other examples that he discusses, is that they impose anachronistic assumptions on the past and – as often as not – present simplistic and irrelevant explanations for past action or draw facile and inaccurate conclusions from individual past actions about past action-contexts in general.

In respect of the proposition 'it began with words', which Marrus shows has been used to validate deprivations of liberty encroaching on free speech in France and elsewhere, he argues that the 'lesson' confuses cause with consequence (many Germans became antisemitic because they became Nazi and *not* the other way around). It also elevates one of many causes to particular importance with 'no grounds' for doing so, and thus 'distorts the history we claim to be trying to understand' (Marrus 2016, 154–5).

In respect of the 'lesson' 'all that it takes for the triumph of evil is that good men do nothing' Marrus shows, again, that this is a distortion of history – many good men did much more than nothing, often at great personal cost, and still the Holocaust happened – and argues that it 'presents a childishly simple view of how genocide functions' (Marrus 2016, 156).

Finally, objecting to the lesson that '[o]ne person can make a difference' Marrus argues that many performed brave actions in defiance of the policies of the Nazis but with no effect whatever on the overall direction of policy. Like Salmons, Marrus finds implicit derogation of past actors in the implied moral judgements these lessons make and concludes that, overall, the approach recommended by this 'lesson' 'obscures the historical reality of wartime genocide and falsifies the situation that bystanders actually faced' (Marrus 2016, 157).

Lessons can be vacuous – too vague to be of value

In a number of papers, between 2003 and 2015, Geoffrey Short has made a qualified argument for the importance of lessons and for an antiracist approach to learning about the Holocaust, in direct and critical response to many of the authors discussed in this paper (such as Kinloch and Salmons) and others who have prioritised an historical approach to lessons. Short contends that antiracist Holocaust education should not simply be a matter for historians and that others – notably Citizenship teachers – are particularly well-placed to contribute to teaching antiracist lessons from these events (Short 2005, 379). Short's case for lessons is qualified because, like the other authors we have discussed, he finds many of the lessons that are advocated by Holocaust educators to be 'trite' – a judgment that Short passes (Short 2003, 278), for example, on the passage below:

> The Holocaust reminds us that hatred of others who are different from ourselves and whom we place beyond the pale of humanity can lead only to group violence and atrocity. It tells us that any society, however culturally, scientifically and technologically advanced, can become totally criminal once it loses the ability and the will to distinguish between right and wrong.
>
> (Spiro Institute/Holocaust Educational Trust 1997, 22; cited in Short 2003, 278)

He argues that there is poor provision for explicit learning of detailed practical lessons in education in England and that it is not surprising, therefore, to find – as he did, for example, in empirical studies of Holocaust Memorial Day in 2004 – deficiencies in aspects of children's learning about concrete action to prevent racism. As Short put it, summing up his findings:

> [M]ost often the 'lesson' they had in mind amounted to no more than a plea for greater tolerance. Nearly a third of the group was adamant that all individuals are of equal worth and that we should act towards one another accordingly. They either stated or implied that differences in ethnic or religious identity could never justify

discrimination. . . . Only a dozen students articulated a clear-cut lesson in the sense of proposing action of some kind intended to avert genocide.

(Short 2005, 373–4)

As has been said, Short's key focus, where lessons are concerned, is on antiracist education and on measures understood to be essential to the prevention of escalating racism and persecution. He argues that the key focus of antiracist education about the Holocaust should be *not* on the genocide of European Jews during the Second World War but, rather, on the processes through which the Nazi party secured dictatorship in the 1930s and on 'the way in which a relatively normal society was transformed into a highly abnormal one infused with a lethal racist ideology (Short 2005, 369). As Short put it in a 2003 paper:

> [T]he lessons provided by the Holocaust depend to some extent on how it is defined. If it is seen as referring only to the mass killing of Jews that occurred between 1941 and 1945 then the scope for profitable engagement is limited, though far from lacking. If, however, teachers operate on a broader canvas and focus on the background to the Holocaust, the lessons resonate more loudly, for they have a firmer purchase on contemporary society where racist groups operate both within and beyond the bounds of legitimate politics.
>
> (Short 2003, 285)

If students engage in reflection and study of this period, Short argues, they are likely to come to 'treat any manifestation of racism with concern', to appreciate 'the danger of ignoring an embryonic racist movement' (Short 2003, 285). A study 'of events antecedent to the Holocaust' will alert 'students to the main risk inherent in unrestricted free speech, namely, the possibility of racist demagogues garnering mass support for their dangerous and simplistic solutions to complex problems' (Short 2003, 285).[2]

The kinds of lesson that Short advocates (Short 2005) include, for example:

- Appreciation of the nature and significance of stereotyping and scapegoating
- Appreciation of the importance of legislation to outlaw incitement to religious or racial hatred

- Appreciation of the importance of banning of overtly racist organisations
- Awareness of the international dimension to the genocide and the need for bodies such as the UN to assume a more proactive and interventionist role.

In more recent work, Short has repeated many of these themes, under the categories 'Lessons Relating to the Nature of Racism' (including 'that Nazism, in respect of its racial policies is an unmitigated evil'), (Short 2015, 456) and 'Lessons Unrelated to the Nature of Racism' (including 'the realisation that ordinary people are not necessarily reduced to the role of impotent bystanders in the face of evil') (Short 2015, 459).

Discussion: Affordances and constraints of a lessons-based approach to Holocaust education

Many of the arguments outlined above have received critical comment and response in the literature. Kinloch's argument for a sharp boundary between history and moral reflection, for example, was criticised rapidly on publication, in the letters pages (e.g. Meagher 1999) and subsequent articles (Illingworth 2000; Salmons 2001) in the journal in which it was published. Counter-arguments included the claim that many of the historical questions that scholars pursue are also moral questions (e.g. 'How could "ordinary men" become brutal murderers?'), the claim that 'learning the history of the Holocaust and drawing moral lessons are not mutually exclusive' (Salmons 2001, 35) and the claim that, in practice, in learning the history of the Holocaust 'pupils will', inevitably and naturally, 'be disturbed into reflection of a deep and personal kind' (e.g. Meagher 1999, 3).

Rather than engaging with each argument in turn, I propose to consider the wider question, implicit in almost all of them, about the value and the limitation of a specifically historical approach to reflection on the implications of the Holocaust for subsequent generations.

There are some significant tensions in Marrus's arguments for the limitations of an historical approach. Marrus's argument for the impossibility of 'lessons' grounded in the fragility of our knowledge of past and future seems, for example, to sit uneasily with his wider endeavour to evaluate the adequacy of particular 'lessons' by testing their consistency with what we know about the events of the Holocaust. There is also, perhaps, a presumption, in setting high criteria of unchangeability for lessons linking past and future, of an a-historical standard of judgement. It is, indeed, commonplace, in the philosophy of history and in historiography, that both the past and the future can change – and that we can speak of both 'futures past' and 'past pasts' (Koselleck 2004; Danto 2007). The radical instability of our knowledge of the past by no means follows from this, however: although our accounts of the past can change dramatically over time, for much of the story for much of the time, many of the changes are marginal rather than central and incremental rather than dramatic. And even if the future does turn out to be radically different from what we currently expect, it does not follow that one should not infer conclusions for present or future action from the past *as it is known to us now*. If location in time – historicity – is a fundamental condition of human action, then knowledgeable human action can only ever mean action informed by the *best* of *our* knowledge *now*.

It is true, however, that we should be very circumspect in reasoning consequentially about future action on the basis of what we know about the Holocaust, and not simply because our knowledge is – as it always must be – subject to revision and change. As disabling here is the fact that the Holocaust – like all unfolding narratives – was bounded by and specific to the times and places in which it happened. This is not to say, however, that we have to read it in that way. As Todorov argues, we can read histories 'literally', as referring, solely and exclusively, to the states of affairs, actors and events that they describe and narrate, and we can also read histories 'paradigmatically', treating what is narrated 'as one instance among others of a more general category, in which case it can be used as a model by which to understand new situations and new perpetrators' (Todorov 1994, 258). This is, of course, what happens when the Holocaust is understood as a genocide – an instance of a wider category. However, understanding a general category entails comparison and consideration of cases that fall within it, a conclusion that suggests that any inferences that may arise and enable future cases to be understood cannot be 'lessons of the Holocaust' alone. 'Consequential' learning about the dynamics of social and political processes – of the kind that enables Michael Mann to differentiate 'types of violence and cleansing in intergroup relations' and to model the conditions under which genocides have arisen to date (Mann 2005, 12) – requires *both* the kinds of attention to the specific histories and details of those histories that Cesarani points to when critiquing the teleological 'standard version' of Holocaust history (Cesarani 2016, xxix) *and* a comparative historical sociological approach that goes beyond the boundaries of narrative history.

There are certainly likely to be dangers arising, however, from generalising prematurely about future possibilities from a limited range of data, and this seems likely to arise if we begin, overly confidently, to focus on the kinds of action that we 'know' are necessary to pre-empt the rise of murderous racisms. Although it may be true, as Short argues, that banning overtly racist organisations is likely to make a positive contribution to preventing the spread of racial hatred (Short 2015), there is no guarantee that it will do so, and it is conceivable that focusing on actions that previous experience indicates will be important may lead to a failure to see novel and specific aspects of the processes that confront us in the present. As Tosh has argued:

> The . . . benefits of analogy . . . depend not on a presumed convergence between past and present, but on the demonstration of difference alongside similarity. . . . Our readiness to see repetition between past and present must always be qualified by a presumption of difference . . . analogies which serve to refine understanding of the present are a genuine asset to critical debate.
>
> (Tosh 2008, 77)

Whilst it is crucial to have empirical controls placing limits on the kinds of inference one seeks to draw from the past – of the kind that allow Marrus to point to the hollowness of what purport to be universal 'lessons' of an ontological kind, such as 'One person can make a difference' (Marrus 2016, 156) – it is important, also, to acknowledge the limitations of purely historical approaches to the Holocaust. Whilst detailed historical study can help to give students some sense of the enormities of the Holocaust and to experience the ontological shock that follows from realising the atrocities that human groups are capable of inflicting on each other, historians do not have the tools to answer the compelling ontological and ethical questions that often arise:

> Arno Mayer's question, 'Why did the heavens not darken?,' . . . asks not about causation but about ultimate justification. Mayer's question is ontological in character. It is the question as to how the universe itself could justify such an event. . . . But it is not itself a historical question. The historian *qua* historian is powerless to answer it.
>
> (Megill 2002, 105)

In other words, many of the 'Why?' questions that often arise as students study the Holocaust are beyond the scope of the discipline of history to answer. Even though historical perspectives are essential to understanding what the Holocaust was – because 'learning about' must precede 'learning from' or 'lessons of' – there is a further limitation to the role played by historical understanding in this and other aspects of making sense of the world. As Mark Day, Herman Paul and others have argued (Day 2008; Paul 2015), to be human is to live multiple forms of relationship to the past – for example, material, aesthetic, political, epistemic and moral relationships (Paul 2015) and, as Gottlieb and Wineburg have shown, in a study of readings of historical and non-historical documents by a range of readers including religious and secular historians, not only can individuals approach the past through differing frameworks of assumptions, but the same individuals can also engage in simultaneous or serial 'epistemic switching' between different ways of knowing, when the task they are engaged in has salience for different aspects of their personal and professional identities (Gottlieb and Wineburg 2012, 114).

Coda: 'Understand in order to judge'

I will end this chapter with some reflections on Primo Levi's thinking about the broader significance of the Holocaust. I end in this way because Levi was a Holocaust survivor – an inmate in Auschwitz III/Monowitz-Buna for 11 months prior to liberation in January 1945 – and one who reflected at length on the wider meaning of the events he had experienced between 1945 and his death in 1987. Levi's works are instructive in a number of senses and not least in that they attend to many of the considerations that we have discussed whilst also refusing many of the binaries that tend to structure debate on 'lessons' (Levi 2015, I:xxx–xxxiii).

Primo Levi wrote about Auschwitz for many reasons – to achieve 'interior liberation' (Levi 1987, 15) to 'shout from the rooftops' (Levi 1988, 138), 'to furnish documentation for a quiet study of the human mind' (Levi 1987, 15), 'to understand . . . in order to judge' (Levi 1987, 143) – and always with a sense of moral urgency and purpose. Because 'it happened . . . it can happen again' and 'it can happen everywhere' (Levi 1988, 167), Levi argued, and he found parallels in the actions of the *conquistadores*, in the Argentina of the generals and in the Cambodia of *Khmer Rouge* (Levi 1988, 9–10; 66–7). What had happened, then, was minatory and a warning – there were 'lessons' to be learned in the present from the Holocaust.

However, in *The Drowned and The Saved* Levi argued that the road from racism and intolerance to Auschwitz was a complex one: although 'denying the fundamental liberties of mankind, and equality among people' (Levi 1987, 391) was a necessary condition for Auschwitz, it was not sufficient to bring it about. 'The German slaughter' arose, he argued, from 'the doctrine of contempt', was enabled by 'a desire for servitude and smallness of soul' among its perpetrators, and was possible only because of

> the concurrence of a number of factors (the state of war; German technological and organisational perfectionism; Hitler's will and charisma; the lack in Germany of solid democratic roots), not very numerous, all of them indispensable but insufficient if taken singly.
>
> (Levi 1988, 66)

The specificity of the concentration camp universe arose from its historical context, its location in its time and place. The behaviour of Jews who did not emigrate in the 1930s and who complied with Nazi orders during the Holocaust, right up to the doors of the gas chambers in many cases, and the behaviour of prisoners who did not fight back or try to escape, had to be contextualised to be understood, and Levi contextualised using historicist tools (Beiser 2011). Levi protested against 'a stereotyped and anachronistic conception of history' (Levi 1988, 132) and argued that:

> One must beware of hindsight and stereotypes. More generally one must beware of the error of judging distant epochs and places with the yardstick that prevails in the here and now: an error all the more difficult to avoid as the distance in space and time increases.
>
> (1988, 134–5)

Jews did not emigrate, in ways that people in Levi's audiences often thought they should have done, he argued, because to leave the 'fatherland' meant something fundamentally different to people in the 1930s than it does for 'citizens eternally on the move' in 'countries and times of intense mobility' (Levi 1988, 132–3); German Jews did not emigrate, or see what with 'hindsight' seems so obvious, he argued, because 'like their "Aryan" quasi-compatriots they loved law and order and . . . were organically incapable of conceiving of a terrorism directed by the state' (Levi 1988, 134).

Levi's arguments in *The Drowned and The Saved* imply that the effort to understand Auschwitz, by those who were not there and for whom these events are 'distant, blurred, historical' (Levi 1988, 128), entails at least two forms of engagement, both of which challenge simplifications, binaries and stereotypes: first, the effort to grasp the context from which Auschwitz arose, and, second, an effort at empathy or rational understanding, that aims to 'perceive the experience of others' (Levi 1988, 128) in terms of the situated knowledge, assumptions and forms of thinking operative in their time and their context and not in ours. Understanding, then, entailed the contestation of stereotypes and presentism and a focus on context and specificity. Stereotypical binary thinking was at the base of the rhetorics of hatred that helped to drive the Holocaust as a historical process, but they alone were insufficient to explain it since they were mediated in specific cultural contexts of belief and expectation. To understand what had happened one had also to contest the operation of precisely the same tendency to simplify and reduce complexity in the present.

For Levi, then, a focus on judgement, 'lessons' and moral reflection was essential when responding to the enormity of the Holocaust, and contextualised historical thinking was essential to success in these tasks. Thinking about lessons involved a combination of historical and ethical thinking and a form of thinking that attended closely to specificity rather than one that traded in absolutes and universals.

Notes

1. Deontology, consequentialism and ontology are all explained systematically in open access articles in the online *Stanford Encyclopedia of Philosophy* (Alexander and Moore 2016; Sinnott-Armstrong 2015; Epstein 2018). The contrast between deontological and consequentialist imperatives is a common contrast in moral and political philosophy, used, for example, to differentiate Kantian and Utilitarian positions.
2. The proposition that it is most profitable not to study the Holocaust itself but, rather, to focus on discrimination in the pre-war period, is one that is certainly likely to be questioned by historians – not least because it appears to embody the kind of teleology that Cesarani argued against and the assumption that the road to Auschwitz was much straighter and predetermined than scholarship allows us to conclude it was.

References

Alexander, L. and Moore, M. 2016. 'Deontological Ethics'. In *The Stanford Encyclopedia of Philosophy*, edited by Edward N. Zalta, Winter 2016. Metaphysics Research Lab, Stanford University. https://plato.stanford.edu/archives/win2016/entries/ethics-deontological/.

Assis, A. 2014. *What Is History For? Johann Gustav Droysen and the functions of historiography*. New York and Oxford: Berghahn Books.

Barton, K.C. and Levstik, L. 2004. *Teaching History for the Common Good*. Mahwah, NJ: Lawrence Erlbaum Associates.

Bedford Borough Council. 2019. 'Holocaust Memorial Day Commemoration: Bedford Borough Council'. https://www.bedford.gov.uk/news/Latest-News/2019-01-17-holocaust-memorial-day-commemoration/.

Beiser, F.C. 2011. *The German Historicist Tradition*. Oxford: Oxford University Press.

Cesarani, D. 1998. *Britain and the Holocaust*. London: The Holocaust Educational Trust.

Cesarani, D. 2016. *Final Solution: The fate of the Jews 1933–1949*. London: Macmillan.

Cotler, I. 2014. 'Universal Lessons of the Holocaust', *Jerusalem Post*, 23 January. Online. https://www.jpost.com/Opinion/Op-Ed-Contributors/Universal-lessons-of-the-Holocaust-339230.

Danto, A.C. 2007. *Narration and Knowledge*. New York: Columbia University Press.

Dawes Duraisingh, L. and Boix Mansilla, V. 2007. 'Interdisciplinary forays within the history classroom: How the visual arts can enhance (or hinder) historical understanding', *Teaching History* 129: 22–30.

Day, M. 2008. 'Our relations with the past', *Philosophia* 36 (4): 417–27.

Epstein, B. 2018. 'Social Ontology'. In *The Stanford Encyclopedia of Philosophy*, edited by Edward N. Zalta, Summer 2018. Metaphysics Research Lab, Stanford University. https://plato.stanford.edu/archives/sum2018/entries/social-ontology/.

First Dog on the Moon. 2016. 'Will Malcolm Turnbull learn the lessons of history? [First Dog on the Moon Cartoon]'. *The Guardian*, 2016, sec. Opinion. https://www.theguardian.com/commentisfree/2016/jun/29/will-malcolm-turnbull-learn-the-lessons-of-history.

Foreign and Commonwealth Office. 2012. 'UK Country Report on Holocaust Education'. Online. https://www.gov.uk/government/publications/uk-country-report-on-holocaust-education.

Gottlieb, E. and Wineburg, S. 2012. 'Between "Veritas" and "Communitas": Epistemic Switching in the Reading of Academic and Sacred History', *Journal of the Learning Sciences* 21 (1): 84–129. Online. https://doi.org/10.1080/10508406.2011.582376.

Gove, Michael. 2010. 'All pupils will learn our island story: Speech to the Conservative Party Conference, 5th October 2010.' Online. https://conservative-speeches.sayit.mysociety.org/speech/601441.

Harari, Y. 2018. *21 Lessons for the 21st Century*. London: Jonathan Cape.

Hargrave, R. 2018. 'Government to Set up £1.7m Fund for Holocaust Education Charities', *Third Sector*. Online. https://www.thirdsector.co.uk/article/1497298.

Holocaust Educational Trust. n.d. 'Lessons from Auschwitz Project to be reintroduced in Northern Ireland'. Online. https://www.het.org.uk/news-and-events/609-lessons-from-auschwitz-project-to-be-reintroduced-in-northern-ireland.

Illingworth, S. 2000. 'Hearts, minds and souls: Exploring values through history', *Teaching History* 100: 20–4.

International Holocaust Remembrance Alliance. n.d. 'Stockholm Declaration: A commitment shared by 32 member countries'. Online. https://www.holocaustremembrance.com/stockholm-declaration (accessed 15 February 2020).

Jewish News Reporter. 2018. 'Government funds Auschwitz trips for university students,' *Jewish News*. Online. https://jewishnews.timesofisrael.com/government-creates-144000-fund-to-tackle-anti-semitism-on-campus-students/.

Judt, T. 2007. *Postwar: A history of Europe since 1945*. London: Pimlico.

Karlsen, S. n.d. 'Is it offensive to compare the Holocaust with the meat industry?' *Ethical Vegan* (blog). n.d. http://ethicalvegan.net/read/animal-holocaust.

Kinloch, N. 1998. 'Learning about the Holocaust: Moral or historical question?', *Teaching History* 93: 44–6.

Kinloch, N. 2001. 'Parallel catastrophes? Uniqueness, redemption and the Shoah', *Teaching History* 104: 8–14.

Koselleck, R. 2004. *Futures Past: On the semantics of historical time*. Trans. Tribe, K. New York: Columbia University Press.

Levi, P. 1987. *If This Is a Man and The Truce*. Trans. Woolf, S. London: Abacus.

Levi, P. 1988. *The Drowned and The Saved*. Trans. Rosenthal, R. London: Abacus.

Levi, P. 2015. *The Complete Works of Primo Levi*. Ed. Goldstein, A. Vol. I. London: Penguin.

Major, J. 2018. 'John Major's astonishing Brexit attack on Theresa May in full', *The Mirror*. Online. https://www.mirror.co.uk/news/politics/john-majors-astonishing-brexit-speech-12103931.

Mann, M. 2005. *The Dark Side of Democracy: Explaining ethnic cleansing*. Cambridge: Cambridge University Press.

Marrus, M.R. 2015. 'Many lessons still to be learned from the horrors at Auschwitz', *The Globe and Mail*. Online. https://www.theglobeandmail.com/opinion/many-lessons-still-to-be-learned-from-the-horrors-at-auschwitz/article22646774/.

Marrus, M.R. 2016. *Lessons of the Holocaust*. Toronto: University of Toronto Press.

May, T. 2018. 'Theresa May's speech on military strikes against Syria – full text', *The Guardian*. Online. https://www.theguardian.com/world/2018/apr/14/theresa-may-speech-military-strikes-syria-full-text.

Meagher, M. 1999. 'Holocaust: A moral and historical question (Letters Pages)', *Teaching History* 94: 3.

Megill, A. 2002. 'Two para-historical approaches to atrocity', *History and Theory* 41 (4): 104–23.

Novick, P. 1999. *The Holocaust and Collective Memory*. London: Bloomsbury.

Paul, H. 2015. *Key Issues in Historical Theory*. Abingdon: Routledge.

Pettigrew, A., Foster, S., Howson, J., Salmons, P., Lenga, R.-A. and Andrews, K. 2009. *Teaching about the Holocaust in English Secondary Schools: An empirical study of national trends, perspectives and practice*. London: Institute of Education.

Salmons, P. 2001. 'Moral dilemmas: History teaching and the Holocaust', *Teaching History* 104: 34–40.

Salmons, P. 2010. 'Universal meaning or historical understanding? The Holocaust in history and history in the curriculum', *Teaching History* 141: 57–63.

Sandbrook, D. 2009. 'Darling blind to the lessons of history', *Daily Mail*. Online. https://www.dailymail.co.uk/debate/article-1235202/Blind-lessons-history.html.

Short, G. 2003. 'Lessons of the Holocaust: A response to the critics', *Educational Review* 55 (3): 277–87. https://doi.org/10.1080/0013191032000118938.

Short, G. 2005. 'Learning from genocide? A study in the failure of Holocaust education', *Intercultural Education* 16 (4): 367–80. https://doi.org/10.1080/14675980500303845.

Short, G. 2015. 'Failing to learn from the Holocaust'. In *As the Witnesses Fall Silent: 21st century Holocaust education in curriculum, policy and practice*, edited by Zehavit Gross and E. Doyle Stevick, 455–68. London: Springer.

Sinnott-Armstrong, W. 2015. 'Consequentialism'. In *The Stanford Encyclopedia of Philosophy,* edited by Edward N. Zalta, Winter 2015. Metaphysics Research Lab, Stanford University. Online. https://plato.stanford.edu/archives/win2015/entries/consequentialism/.

Smith, G. 2018. 'We should never forget the lessons from history', *Morning Star*. Online. https://morningstaronline.co.uk/article/we-should-never-forget-lessons-history.

Snyder, T. 2017. *On Tyranny: Twenty lessons from the twentieth century*. New York: Tim Duggan Books.

Spiro Institute, and Holocaust Educational Trust. 1997. *Lessons of the Holocaust*. London: Spiro Institute / Holocaust Educational Trust.

The Cabinet Office. 2015. 'Britain's promise to remember: The Prime Minister's Holocaust Commission Report'. London: The Cabinet Office. Online. https://www.gov.uk/government/publications/prime-ministers-holocaust-commission-report.

Todorov, Tzvetan. 1994. *Facing the Extreme: Moral life in the concentration camps*. Trans. Denner, A. and Pollack, A. London: Phoenix.

Tosh, J. 2008. *Why History Matters*. Houndmills: Palgrave Macmillan.

4

'They were just following orders': Relationships between Milgram's obedience experiments and conceptions of Holocaust perpetration

Rebecca Hale

Introduction

In 1963, Stanley Milgram published his first experiment on obedience, using a procedure where participants believed they were administering harmful electric shocks to another participant under the orders of an authority figure. In formulating this research, Milgram made explicit links to the Holocaust from the outset:

> Obedience, as a determinant of behavior, is of particular relevance to our time. It has been reliably established that from 1933–45 millions of innocent persons were systematically slaughtered on command. Gas chambers were built, death camps were guarded, daily quotas of corpses were produced with the same efficiency as the manufacture of appliances. These inhumane policies may have originated in the mind of a single person, but they could only be carried out on a massive scale if a very large number of persons obeyed orders.
>
> (Milgram 1963, 371)

Milgram's research is amongst the most famous and significant ever conducted in social psychology. While the distinctive methodology and unsettling results have undoubtedly contributed to this reputation, the research had particular purchase on people's consciousness because it ran concurrently with Adolf Eichmann's trial (Benjamin and Simpson 2009, 14–15; Jetten and Mols 2014, 587). Indeed, in later publications about the obedience experiments, Milgram did identify links with Eichmann's trial and in particular to Hannah Arendt's analysis. In Milgram (1967, 4), he stated 'after witnessing hundreds of ordinary persons submit to the authority in our own experiments, I must conclude that Arendt's conception of the *banality of evil* comes closer to the truth than one might dare to imagine'. Over the last 50 years, the experiments have been a staple of psychology courses and have permeated popular culture (Perry 2013, 7), meaning millions of people worldwide have encountered this work and the posited link to the Holocaust.

However, the experiments have triggered accusations of unethical treatment of participants and raised numerous methodological concerns. These and other aspersions have led to debate about the validity of the research for explaining the actions of perpetrators during the Holocaust. Yet evidence suggests that students are unlikely to be exposed to a detailed critique of the experiments (Griggs and Whitehead 2015, 317–18). Additionally, while social psychology textbooks often present information about the Holocaust to give some context to the research, the historical detail is usually at a cursory level (Miller 2004, 228).

This is problematic because presenting students with superficial information about the Holocaust could engender or reinforce ubiquitous misconceptions about the reasons for perpetrators' actions during the Holocaust. For example, a common misconception about the Holocaust is that soldiers had to obey orders to kill Jewish people; otherwise they would have been shot themselves (Foster *et al.* 2016, 163). However, no evidence has been found to indicate that refusing to obey an order to kill unarmed civilians resulted in members of the police or military (or their families) being killed (Browning 1992, 170). Hayes (2017, 141) noted that where soldiers experienced any compunction about killing, rather than being viewed negatively, this was seen as an opportunity for them to engage in self-pity and retaliate at the group responsible for their discomfort. Historical evidence demonstrates that Nazi campaigns to cultivate widespread antisemitism, convey the Jewish threat, and dehumanise the Jews were successful in creating a climate where 'ordinary Germans could and did become willing executors of Nazi persecution and even in many cases willing executioners' (Hayes 2017, 142).

The historical record is testament to the caution needed when linking Milgram's research with the Holocaust. Psychological literature highlighting issues with the experiments and the nuance required in interpreting the results also raises questions about the efficacy of 'obedience to authority' as an adequate explanation for the actions of Holocaust perpetrators. This chapter will examine the relationship between knowledge of Milgram's studies and interpretations of the Holocaust among psychology A-level students in England. Given the prominence of Milgram in psychology curricula, both in England and worldwide, exploring this relationship is something which warrants close investigation.

Milgram's obedience experiments

Milgram ran 24 experimental conditions manipulating variables such as the proximity of the participants to one another (see Perry 2013, 351–7). However, psychology A-level students tend to be most familiar with his first published condition (see Milgram 1963), also referred to as the 'baseline experiment' (Jetten and Mols 2014, 589) because it is often the condition cited in exam specifications and outlined in textbooks.

The baseline experiment was framed as being about the effects of punishment on memory. Naïve participants were assigned the role of 'teacher' and had to administer electric shocks to another participant ('the learner') every time they gave an inaccurate answer on a learning task. The learner was actually an associate of the experimenter. The shock generator was clearly marked with voltage levels in increments of 15 volts ranging from 15 to 450 volts and supplemented with labels such as 'strong shock' at 135–180 volts, 'extreme intensity shock' at 315–360 volts and ominously 'XXX' at 435–450 volts. Unbeknownst to the naïve participant, the shocks were actually fake.

Throughout the experiment, the learner was in a different room to the participant. At 300 volts the learner pounded on the wall and stopped giving answers; this happened again at 315 volts, and then afterwards there was no further sound. The participant had to continue asking the questions and the learner's silence was taken as an incorrect answer which required a shock as punishment. If the participant indicated they wanted to stop while working through the voltage levels, the experimenter prompted them to continue using four prods: 'please continue', 'the experiment requires that you continue', 'it is absolutely essential that you continue', and 'you have no other choice you must continue'. The point of disobedience was indicated when the participant absolutely refused to continue with the experiment.

Forty men took part in the baseline experiment, with none of them stopping prior to administering 300 volts. Five of the men refused to obey beyond 300 volts. The rest continued, with nine of them administering shocks between 315 and 375 volts, and 26 of them (65 per cent) going to the maximum voltage of 450 volts.

To account for participants' obedience to authority, Milgram (1974, 133) argued for the role of the agentic state. This occurs in situations where a person no longer sees themselves as responsible for their actions, and instead views themselves as the instrument for carrying out another person's requests. Milgram did not see this as a thin alibi for an individual's actions, but instead as a fundamental change in their thinking (Milgram 1967, 6). The findings of his research have been used as evidence of obedience to authority from ordinary and unwilling people, and as such have been argued to provide an explanation for the actions of Nazis during the Holocaust (Mastroianni 2002, 159).

This raises key considerations about the extent to which psychology students subscribe to this interpretation of Milgram's findings and fit it with their existing knowledge and understanding of the Holocaust. In England, most students will learn about the Holocaust by the age of 14 years as part of the Key Stage 3 National Curriculum for history. Therefore, A-level psychology students will usually have learned about the Holocaust when in lower school (although, since there is no stipulation for the topics taught or the number of lessons required, students' experiences of learning about the Holocaust will vary).

A national study conducted by Foster *et al.* (2016, 152–63) found that secondary school students held a number of embedded misconceptions about the Holocaust. This included notions about the perpetrators being 'quite normal' people who followed the orders of authority figures due to fear and intimidation. Evidence suggests knowledge acquisition is never a passive process and students will seek to make personal sense of new information they encounter, and this will draw on existing frames of reference (Foster *et al.* 2016, 38–9). Thus, it is possible that if psychology students hold similar pre-existing notions about the nature of perpetrators, this will limit their ability to reflect on and problematise the different interpretations of Milgram's studies.

At a most basic level, there are numerous obvious differences between Milgram's experiments and the events of the Holocaust (see Fenigstein 2015), and it is likely the majority of psychology students could easily identify them. A laboratory experiment where variables were manipulated and controlled, which took place at a prestigious university, and involved participants who were engaged in the experiment for a short amount of time, is incomparable with the complex and tragic realities of the Holocaust. Indeed, Milgram acknowledged the differences between his participants and Nazi perpetrators, but dismissed these 'surface' differences, drawing attention instead to the similarities he perceived in the core psychological processes operating in both situations (Fenigstein 2015, 586). However, academics (for example, Fenigstein 2015; Haslam *et al.* 2015; Jetten and Mols 2014; Perry 2013) have cautioned against this argument, because the fundamentals of his experiments (including all the variations), raise problems in using obedience as an explanation for the Holocaust.

Concerns about Milgram's conclusions and the ethical issues his research raised were identified at the outset. Baumrind (1964, 422–3) was especially critical, pointing out there were no parallels between Milgram's research and the Holocaust, and the experiment was so far removed from real-life experience that the deception and distress participants were exposed to could not be justified. Recent analysis of the data held in the Milgram archives at Yale University has revealed further concerns. This includes participants who, after refusing to obey the fourth prod (when the experiment should have been terminated), were subjected to repeated commands to continue. For several participants the number of prods went into double figures and in the only condition to use female participants, one woman was ordered to continue 26 times. For these participants it probably appeared the only way to exit the experiment was to administer all the shocks (Perry 2013, 134). Not only is this scenario highly unethical, but arguably points to a study which provides insight into processes related to harassment rather than obedience.

Partial replication of Milgram's studies using more ethical procedures (see Burger 2009, 5–8) have provided evidence to suggest that while the first three prods in Milgram's studies do trigger participants to continue to varying degrees, the fourth prod actually triggers disobedience (Burger *et al.* 2011, 464). This has contributed to some researchers (e.g. Burger *et al.* 2011, 464; Haslam *et al.* 2015, 62) questioning the obedience explanation because it is only the fourth prod that gives a concrete command ('you have no other choice, you must go on'). Consequently, it could be argued that participants continued to 450 volts for reasons other than blindly obeying authority. Haslam *et al.* (2015, 60) assert that participants' behaviour can be better understood by engaged followership. That is, the participants knew the consequences of their actions and administered the shocks because they identified with the scientific goals of the experiment and believed they were contributing to a moral, worthy and progressive cause.

Milgram ran 24 experimental conditions from 1961 to 1962, with obedience levels (going to 450 volts) varying from 2 per cent to 100 per cent (Perry 2013, 351–7). For example, in the touch condition, after 150 volts, the experimenter instructed the teacher (the naïve participant) to hold the learner's hand on a metal plate to receive the shocks. In this condition, 30 per cent of participants went to 450 volts. In the group pressure to disobey condition, there were three teachers (two were associates of the experimenter and one was a real participant). By 210 volts both associates refused to continue with the experiment, leaving the participant to continue to administer shocks while the associates watched. In this condition, 10 per cent of participants went to 450 volts.

For many academics, the experimental variations provide evidence that the majority of participants actually *disobeyed* the authority figure. As Jetten and Mols (2014, 588) suggest, by becoming cognisant with the variations and how participants reacted, Milgram's findings present a far more complex picture of how people respond to authority figures. Indeed, the simplistic blind obedience explanation that his baseline study has typically been reduced to becomes very problematic, and consequently the argument for its relevance to the Holocaust becomes similarly contentious. This view is further reinforced because participants administered the shocks under extreme stress, assisted the learner by emphasising the correct answer, gave lower shocks when they were able to, and repeatedly tried to exit the situation (Jetten and Mols 2014, 591–2). However, Nazi perpetrators largely expressed no such reluctance to harm or kill, and where they did abstain it was because of physical disgust rather than moral opposition (Fenigstein 2015, 591).

The brevity of the above summary evidently does not outline the full catalogue of concerns that have emerged in relation to Milgram's research. However, it does point towards the difficulty of using Milgram's findings as evidence of people's willingness to obey authority, and in turn the complexity of drawing on the research to explain the actions of perpetrators during the Holocaust. Of course, it would be remiss to completely disregard Milgram's experiments, and some psychologists and historians have argued that his research does provide insight into the processes behind the actions of perpetrators. For instance, Browning (1992, 175–6) cites Milgram's experimental variation where participants were more likely to administer higher shocks when in the presence of other participants (actually associates of the experimenter) who proposed an escalation of shocks, demonstrating the role of conformity. Also, congruent with Milgram's findings, Browning noted that when the officers were in close proximity to the victims they were less likely to obey orders. Whereas, when the killing process was divided between the men and transferred to the death camps, orders were more willingly carried out because the men felt less responsible for their actions.

Milgram's studies have also been used to inform historical thinking about the role of orders which gradually increased in brutality and perpetrators' preoccupation with diligently focusing on procedures to perform their assigned tasks (Overy 2014, 521–4). Additionally, recent scholarship has argued the design and refinement of Milgram's experiments to create conditions for optimum obedience resonate with the 'trial and error' approach utilised by Nazi officers to make the procedures for the mass shooting of Jewish people more efficient and palatable for the *Einsatzgruppen* (Russell 2017, 282–7).

Exploring students' understandings of Milgram and the Holocaust

Clearly, there are important considerations for what is taught about Milgram's experiments, the nature and accuracy of information presented about the Holocaust, and the extent to which students are able to scrutinise the link between Milgram's research and the Holocaust. These issues were explored by conducting focus groups with psychology A-level students in England. While this data was collected from students participating in a specific course and within a particular national context, the findings are relevant to introductory psychology courses across the world.

Forty-eight schools were notified about the focus groups, and five agreed to participate. One school was based in the East of England, one in the South East, one in London, one in the West Midlands and one in Yorkshire and Humber. Although the schools were diverse in terms of their location, academic performance and composition of different ethnic groups, sampling was not done systematically because schools and students were volunteers, thus introducing bias to the sample.

In total, 9 focus groups were conducted with 47 students. All students had learned about Milgram's obedience research as part of their A-level psychology course. Eight students were in year 12 and the remainder were in year 13. There was an almost even split of boys and girls (23 and 24 respectively) and students were aged 16 to 18 years.

Students were given a consent form and information sheet which explained the research, including how their data would be used and stored. Students could withdraw from the research at any time. Parental consent was not required because students were aged over 16 years (although opt-in parental consent was used in one school where this was requested). Focus groups comprising four to eight students, and within each group students attended the same school. A small number of questions were used to guide the discussion, but the conversation was mainly led by the students. The discussions took place at the schools and each lasted for approximately 30 minutes. All discussions were audio recorded (with each student's permission).

To start the discussion, students were asked to summarise what they could remember about Milgram's research and the Holocaust. All students were able to cite key pieces of information from Milgram's 1963 baseline experiment. The following points were also frequently made: the research was 'only' a laboratory experiment and not 'real life' like the Holocaust; only 40 participants took part; the study occurred at a prestigious university so participants would have been sceptical about the reality of being asked to harm the learner; and the participants were not really killing people. Just one student knew the fourth prod was the only concrete command and the least effective in triggering obedience. Some of the students also mentioned there were experimental variations, but did not provide much detail about what these involved.

In terms of their knowledge of the Holocaust, students tended to give the same pattern of responses found in research by Foster *et al.* (2016, 41–4) when students were asked to describe in one or two sentences what the Holocaust was. That is to say, foremost in the psychology students' responses were the victims, the perpetrator(s) and an action. For example:

> Six million Jewish people were murdered by Hitler basically. (Zaid, Focus Group 2)
>
> The Germans took over and took all the Jews to concentration camps and they had like gas chambers and things like that. (Hassan, Focus Group 7)

The psychology students always identified Jewish people as the principal victims and Hitler as the key perpetrator, with some references made to the Nazis and/or individuals like Himmler. Reference was also made (though to a lesser extent) to the Second World War, other victim groups, Germany, genocide, the Aryan race, ghettos, Auschwitz and Anne Frank. The aim of this research was not to examine in detail what the psychology students knew and understood about the Holocaust. Instead, this element of the focus group sought to establish that the students were familiar with the word 'Holocaust' and the history it describes. Moreover, students were only asked to briefly summarise what they knew about the Holocaust and it is probable that with greater opportunity to elaborate, other historical details would have emerged. Despite this, it is still noteworthy that the form of their descriptions shared similarities with the descriptions provided by students in the research by Foster *et al.* (2016, 44).

After briefly finding out what students knew about the Holocaust and Milgram's research (as two separate entities), the focus of the discussion was the relationship between the two entities. The salient themes from these discussions are presented in the next section. The researcher asked the students if they were aware of Milgram linking his study with the Holocaust. They were all aware of this. The researcher then read the excerpt from Milgram (1963, 371) presented at the start of this chapter (excluding the sentence 'These inhumane policies may have originated in the mind of a single person, but they could only be carried out on a massive scale if a very large number of persons obeyed orders', so not to influence students' opinions about who they thought might be ultimately responsible given Milgram's reference to a 'single person').

After hearing this excerpt, the students discussed whether or not they thought Milgram's studies were related to the Holocaust. Where appropriate students were asked to elaborate on their comments. The students were also invited to refer to any other relevant theories or studies. They were asked what they thought would have happened to the military or police if they refused an order to kill a Jewish person. Once they had discussed their answers, the researcher told them that on 13 July 1942, in Józefów, Poland, the men of Reserve Police Battalion 101 received orders to kill all the Jews in the village. Their commander, Major Wilhelm Trapp, made an offer that if any of the older men did not feel up to this task they could step out and await another duty. A small minority did this; the rest of the men carried out their orders (Browning 1992, 57). This example was selected because it features in some textbooks to encourage reflection on Milgram's conclusions, although none of the students in this research had previously heard about this incident. The researcher then asked students to discuss what they thought about the actions of this Battalion in relation to Milgram's research. Finally, students were invited to make any additional comments about Milgram's research and/or the Holocaust that they felt were relevant.

The discussions were transcribed verbatim by the researcher. Drawing on guidance from Braun and Clarke (2006), the transcripts were analysed by carefully reading the text and identifying initial codes that reflected the content in each sentence and/or short segment. Codes included ‘surface limitation of Milgram’s research’, ‘perpetrators were shot’, ‘distressed participants’, ‘antisemitism’, ‘perpetrators as ordinary people’, ‘role of situation’, and ‘Hitler-centricity’. The codes were then reviewed to explore relationships between them and to identify potential themes across students’ accounts. The themes were refined by reviewing the codes and data extracts they encompassed, and then exploring the validity of the themes across the data set. From this process, three overarching themes were identified: the role of fear, the role of propaganda in Nazi Germany and the nature of the ‘ordinary’ soldier.

The role of fear

Across the focus groups there was consensus that the perpetrators participated in the mass murder of Jewish people because they feared that if they did not obey orders they and/or their families would be killed.

> Didn’t they get shot? (Beatrice, Focus Group 4)
>
> With the people in the Holocaust if they didn’t carry out what they’d been told to do in the camps, their families would get killed and things like that. (Dominic, Focus Group 1)
>
> In the Holocaust, during that time, if you didn’t obey they would kill you. (Esmee, Focus Group 8)

Students were aware that Milgram’s participants exhibited distress during the experiment and showed resistance to inflicting harm on the learner. Tellingly, they saw this as indicative of the responses of perpetrators during the Holocaust, arguing that perpetrators did not want to kill Jewish people, but did so under duress and fear of the consequences if they disobeyed.

> Not many people wanted to kill innocent people but because they were told to do something especially by someone in higher command like Hitler then they had no choice. But the same thing as in Milgram. . . . There was many observations to show that the teacher didn’t want to do it, there were even moments when they said that they had seizures . . . but they did it anyway because they were told by someone higher in command, which was the experimenter. So they know it was wrong, they had to do it because it was against their own morals, it was against their own will basically. So,

> it shows a relationship between the Holocaust and the experiment. (Max, Focus Group 5)
>
> As a soldier in a concentration camp watching people die every day and then like if you didn't carry out what you were meant to do, you'd be the same, so it's like watching your own future. . . . It wasn't like anything to do with the fact that they believed in it, it was just they were scared . . . the results [of Milgram's study] showed that lots of people showed signs of distress but it didn't mean that they stopped anyway. So, all these soldiers could have like personal turmoil and like in their heads be really against it but do it anyway because they've got higher figures above them that will force them to do so. (Hazel, Focus Group 6)

When students were presented with information about Major Trapp's offer to opt out of killing Jewish people in Józefów, most suggested the men did not take this opportunity because they were conforming to the majority decision of the battalion. The students explained the men would have been concerned about fitting in with the group and worried about what others might think about them if they did not participate in the killing process.

> Maybe those soldiers, that's not them yeah, they're just . . . 'I want to fit in with everyone else, I don't want to be the one who's against everyone else', so maybe a sense of belonging could have made some people who are good people kill other people. (Manisha, Focus Group 3)
>
> Like they want to fit in so they're going to do it anyway, so they are fighting for their lives themselves really. (Beatrice, Focus Group 4)

Most students expressed views alluding to the 'choice' to opt out of killing as not actually being a choice, as succinctly expressed by Varsha:

> They still felt that they didn't really have a choice even if they were given a choice. (Varsha, Focus Group 6)

Instead, the students suspected opportunities to withdraw from killing were a ruse; a ruse which the men would have been keenly aware of. Therefore, the students thought the fear of later reprisals contributed to the majority of the battalion electing to proceed with murdering the Jewish population of Józefów.

> It could be the fear of what the other duty is, because they're not specifying what the other duty is. They might be lying and they might just kill them. (Max, Focus Group 5)
>
> Maybe they could have feared that if they had like not agreed to do it that the other officers could come like later on, like the night after or something and then something bad could have happened. (Saskia, Focus Group 9)

It should be noted that across all focus groups, the students made repeated references to events in Germany and the actions and experiences of German officers, soldiers and people, without any mention of other countries. Thus, despite engaging in discussions about the incident in Józefów (which the researcher informed them was in occupied Poland), the students' interpretations were positioned within the framework of what they thought happened in Germany and the actions and responses of German perpetrators.

The role of propaganda in Nazi Germany

While the initial response to the actions of Reserve Police Battalion 101 across all focus groups was that conformity and fear could account for what happened, this explanation seemed to sit uncomfortably with some students, triggering reflection about the validity of the obedience to authority explanation.

> If they're told 'oh you don't actually have to kill people, you don't have to do this, that's fine, you can back out', and then they didn't, then obviously they have some sort of attachment to it still, and it's not about obedience then, it's about how far they agree with it. (Nessa, Focus Group 6)

It was at this point when a minority of students began to grapple with alternative explanations related to anti-Jewish propaganda and the evolution of Nazi discriminatory policies towards Jewish people.

> By 1942, they might just be desensitised to it over years of it . . . I mean Hitler has been giving these rallying speeches about Jewish

> people being demons or whatever and causing all the problems for Germany, so they might truly believe that they're doing the right thing, and might not consider them to be human anymore because they've just seen them as these horrible problems that they need to get rid of, and that's the nationalist and the right way of doing it, solving things. So, I don't know if it's conformity still. I think at that point, you're changing your moral basis. I think it's a lot deeper than conformity is what I'm trying to say. (Elliot, Focus Group 2)
>
> I think that the result of Nazi propaganda and eugenics and that sort of thing, saying that Jews were responsible for all of the failures and the collapse of Germany, I think that's all built up that a lot of German people sort of accepted that Jews were wrong or that they should hate Jews, so I think that that, and then there were a load of laws that came in that sort of dehumanised them and took away their citizenship, so it became easier to sort of attack them. So, I think that's probably quite a big part of it as well. (Dylan, Focus Group 3)

Data was not collected on students' academic background (such as whether or not they were studying history at A-level), so the factors that informed their history-based explanations remain unclear. However, it should be noted this type of commentary was relatively infrequent in the discussions or, when mentioned, not comprehensively fleshed out. Indeed, there were numerous instances where misconceptions and inadequate knowledge hindered students in their attempts to evaluate the extent to which Milgram's studies were related to what happened during the Holocaust. For example, Matilda (below) explained the soldiers' actions with reference to factors sometimes related to authority figures (such as age and status), rather than the role of ideological indoctrination:

> [The German soldiers] were young because a lot of them didn't actually choose to be part of the army, they just got taken because they'd reached a certain age. So they could have felt like, like as younger people with older people in higher up positions and giving the orders, they might have felt like they should obey because of their status in the whole hierarchy of people. (Matilda, Focus Group 9)

Overall a paradox emerged where students could identify there were problems with linking Milgram's studies to the Holocaust, yet without sound historical knowledge to draw upon, they struggled to articulate what these problems were. Consequently, they returned to their original position that fear and pressure to obey were important factors in explaining Holocaust perpetration, and any limitations in linking Milgram's research to this behaviour were thought to arise from the surface differences between the studies and the Holocaust.

> I think [Milgram's study] does help explain the Holocaust to an extent . . . it kind of let us know how they might have been thinking at that point, which can help us understand that ok, maybe they were under pressure, maybe they couldn't resist pressure at that point, so they just went with it. But it still doesn't explain, you know like how you said they had a choice to not kill them but they did. So I guess it doesn't explain that part. (Florence, Focus Group 8)
>
> I don't think there is a link really. Because, obviously you've got issues with the sample sizes and that you can't really generalise. I think they're such different things. Like this was a major event in life, like you were possibly fighting for your life and this was sort of a small scale experiment. (Beatrice, Focus Group 4)

The nature of the 'ordinary' soldier

As part of the students' accounts of fear and conformity, there was reference to the 'normal', 'ordinary' (and sometimes 'good') character of the perpetrators that belied outward appearances. For example, as previously outlined, Hazel suggested the soldiers had 'personal turmoil' and Manisha thought that conformity made 'people who are good' become murderers. Accordingly, students thought the perpetrators were not inherently bad, but instead were put in an impossible situation where they had no other choice but to follow the orders of their superiors. The behaviour of 'regular people' who took part in Milgram's study seemed to reinforce this view:

> I think it does relate to be honest quite well because [Milgram] was trying to show like the, sort of how being submissive to authority can be really important. So, people who went into Milgram's study were just regular people, they weren't like, well considered like dispositionally, you know, they weren't seeking to harm people. So, I think it's trying to show up, sort of Hitler's people working under him, where those situational factors were really at play, more than probably just the fact that they were bad people I think. (Glen, Focus Group 1)

Throughout the discussions, Hitler was frequently identified as the most superior authority figure, and on occasion psychology students lapsed into narrating their stories with reference to 'he', 'him' and 'his'. This was also seen in the research by Foster *et al.* (2016, 146), especially with younger students aged under 14 years. On the surface, this sort of short circuiting gave the impression of the psychology students having a narrow view of culpability. However, as the discussion developed, a notion of there being a hierarchy of responsibility emerged, sometimes stated and at other times inferred. Students tended to believe that being forced to kill against one's will was the ubiquitous experience of the lower-ranking soldiers, an experience which made them different to the Nazis, and to some extent exonerated their actions:

> I think like lower level officials, they can sort of get away with it, I think, but with like, it doesn't provide a reason for it, but with the lower people who were just following orders, I do, to an extent, understand why they did that. (Carl, Focus Group 3)
>
> I think it's more of a fear thing to be honest. I have faith that they were more human than that. I'm not sympathising with Nazis, I'm sympathising with the German soldiers who were forced to do things, some of the things they did. (Elliot, Focus Group 2)

It is interesting to contrast Elliot's comment above with another presented earlier in this chapter where he argued for the role of defamatory propaganda against the Jewish people and widespread antisemitism. Conflict in his thinking is discernible: on the one hand he argued for those being responsible as 'changing their moral basis', but on the other hand alluded to German soldiers being forced to kill against their will. This inconsistency suggests that while he can draw on historical evidence to better understand Holocaust perpetration, he can counter this by drawing on his 'faith' in humans to not innately want to act in this way.

This sort of dissonance is something for educators to be aware of. Indeed, learning about the Holocaust and the actions of the perpetrators is a challenging task which raises many difficult questions about behaviour and what it means to be 'human'; considerations which are particularly apposite for psychology students. As shown in Foster *et al.*'s research (2016, 163), not only did the majority of secondary school students believe the police and military were shot if they refused to obey an order to kill Jewish people, two-thirds of students were confident this was the case. This suggests an embedded belief about the reasons for the actions of the perpetrators, reasons that point towards the situation determining the action, rather than the disposition or attitudes of the perpetrators. For the psychology students in this study, it is possible that Milgram's experiments provided some extenuation for the actions of 'regular' or 'ordinary' German soldiers which was less disturbing than reflecting on the capability of normal people, indeed whole societies, to act in this way due to dispositional factors as well as situational factors.

Considerations and implications

Across the focus groups, students thought Milgram's obedience experiments were related to the Holocaust. In particular, the experiments indicated that perpetrators participated in the mass murder of Jewish people because they were following the orders of an authority figure (typically narrated as Hitler, and to a lesser extent the Nazis). This was not seen as thoughtless obedience; instead, students erroneously believed the perpetrators acted out of fear that they would be killed if they disobeyed. When presented with an historical example of perpetrators not taking the opportunity to opt out of killing, the majority of the psychology students were unable to draw on robust or confident historical knowledge to understand why most of the men in Reserve Police Battalion 101 acted as they did. Consequently, the students maintained their view that the men acted out of fear.

There was some suggestion that Nazi ideology played a role as a motivational force, and where students had some knowledge and understanding of the Holocaust to draw upon, they were able to move beyond purely psychological theories and challenge the interpretations of Milgram's studies in relation to the Holocaust. However, this was a minority perspective across the focus groups. Students instead tended to believe the majority of perpetrators were essentially normal people who had been put in a 'life or death' situation and had no choice but to kill Jewish people. Occasionally, students articulated a distinction between senior Nazi officials (who were the reprehensible ones) and the low-ranking German soldiers (who were ultimately decent people but acted out of fear). Arguably, one of the most salient issues to emerge from the focus groups was that Milgram's experiments appeared to provide some mitigation for the actions of 'regular' or 'ordinary' German soldiers. This line of thinking perhaps afforded a protection mechanism for students in which believing these soldiers acted out of fear for their lives was easier and safer to comprehend than believing soldiers actively supported the genocide of Jewish people and willingly participated in mass murder.

It is unclear whether the psychology students' notions were in place before learning about Milgram's experiments. Research by Foster *et al.* (2016, 152) indicates students nationally thought the perpetrators were 'quite normal'. Additionally, 66.5 per cent of students thought the military/police would be shot if they refused to obey an order, and two-thirds of that group were confident in their answer. This suggests a significant and embedded misconception. Thus, it is plausible that learning about the obedience studies reinforces a pre-existing and erroneous belief. Milgram (1963, 376) cited the extreme stress that his participants exhibited during the experiments, and academics have drawn upon this to suggest the obedience studies cannot be generalised to the Holocaust. That is, the distress shown by the participants is completely at odds with the depraved and unabating murderous acts that the Holocaust perpetrators carried out (Fenigstein 2015, 592–3; Haslam *et al.* 2015, 78). In contrast, the psychology students viewed the participants' distress as evidence of the perpetrators being normal people who were not inherently bad, and instead committed these atrocities out of fear.

While the conclusions of the psychology students were contrary to what many historians and psychologists have argued (for example, Baumrind 1964; Haslam *et al.* 2015; Hayes 2017; Jetten and Mols 2014), they were reasonable conclusions for students to draw given the information available to them. Milgram's research has been influential in discourse about the validity of situational and dispositional explanations for obedience. Numerous situational factors have been identified in Milgram's studies including the incremental nature of the task and the opportunity to shift responsibility to another (Burger 2014, 491). The role of personality traits and personal values was not dismissed by Milgram, but the power of the situation was considered a potent factor in the obedience process (Milgram 1967, 7; Benjamin and Simpson 2009, 16; Burger 2014, 489). Therefore, students' convictions that it was the situation and not perpetrators' characters that dictated their actions are consistent with this discourse.

Milgram came from a positivist background seeking to be an unbiased and value-neutral experimenter. Therefore, despite collating extensive and complex qualitative information, he focused on statistics in the form of voltage levels and percentages as his primary data (Perry 2013, 247–8). It is this primary data, condensed (and used selectively) in textbooks, which is accessible to students and can give the illusion of more straightforward obedience processes than was actually the case. This has been exacerbated by binary conclusions that present the participants as either obeying or disobeying, and in doing so overlooking the numerous and complex reactions they exhibited (Hoffman *et al.* 2015, 677).

As a small-scale exploratory study, this research evidently has limitations and cannot provide evidence of the impact of psychology teaching on students' knowledge and understanding of the Holocaust. This is because the data were collected at one point in time, and so causation pathways cannot be established. Moreover, detailed information about what students had learned about Milgram's research and the Holocaust was not collected. However, the study can be used as a starting point to conduct further research examining the patterns that emerged.

The views of these psychology students should not be used to criticise them or their teachers. The general belief that perpetrators acted out of fear, and were at risk of being shot if they refused an order to kill a Jewish person, is a prevalent misconception in public discourse (Foster *et al.* 2016, 163). Furthermore, limited curriculum time for history teachers when teaching about the Holocaust, and for psychology teachers when teaching about Milgram's research, present a challenge to thoroughly examining issues related to Holocaust perpetration.

Still, these focus groups highlight significant issues, not only for teaching practice, but given the reputation of Milgram's research, also for public discourse. In the case of the latter, Milgram's experiments (and/or replications of them) have permeated popular culture including cartoons, game shows and films across the world (Perry 2013, 7). In light of this, and the worldwide popularity of psychology courses, it is entirely feasible that the conjectures about the motivations and actions of Holocaust perpetrators formulated by the students in this research are indicative of those held by the majority of people who are familiar with Milgram's experiments. This is problematic because surmising that mass murder and genocide occurred because the protagonists feared for their lives is a severe distortion of what happened. It provides a means to exonerate the perpetrators and overlooks the complex interplay of factors that both historians and psychologists have argued contributed to the Holocaust occurring. This includes relentless propaganda justifying the harming of Jews and redefining morality so that inflicting pain on the Jewish 'enemy' was seen as moral progress (Hayes 2017, 140–1). Subscribing to Milgram's studies also precludes understanding about broader levels of collaboration across Europe and the role of individuals and communities who were complicit in the persecution and murder of Jews. Indeed, a prevalent goal of learning about the Holocaust is to 'learn the lessons of the past', yet thinking that perpetrators obeyed out of fear for their lives leads to erroneous 'lessons' being learned (Foster *et al.* 2016, 163).

In terms of considerations for teaching practice, across the focus groups students were able to identify a number of complications with Milgram's studies, but in general did not appear familiar with recent salient criticisms. For instance, only one student made reference to the fourth prod being the only command, and where students mentioned experimental variations this was done briefly. As Jetten and Mols (2014, 588) point out, engaging with the different experimental variations shows there is no simple explanation to account for the many different ways that participants responded. Consequently, it is important for teachers to highlight the existence of the variations and help students to reflect on what this means for the ubiquitous interpretations of Milgram's research, as well as looking at other issues which question the role of obedience, like the fourth prod triggering disobedience in participants.

Some students suggested the will to make a contribution to scientific research might account for why participants administered the shocks. A few also mentioned that participants reported being glad to have taken part, though the students did not discuss this further. Recent scholarship has looked at the role of engaged followership and has highlighted the importance of reflecting on why Milgram's participants felt happy about administering what they believed to be lethal shocks to a helpless stranger (Haslam *et al.* 2015, 76–9). It is thought the answer lies in Milgram's efforts to reassure participants about the value of the study for science and humanity. But as Haslam *et al.* (2015, 80) argue 'we need to ask whether this is the kind of service with which we want people to be quite so happy'. Undoubtedly, this is something psychology teachers should discuss with their students, not least as participants' willingness to absolve themselves through justifications to helping science has particular import when talking about the Holocaust.

Milgram's research tends to lead students into wrongly concluding obedience is ubiquitous and easy to activate (Jetten and Mols 2014, 590). Thus, it is perhaps not surprising that the psychology students in this study who believed participants followed the orders of the authority figure (the experimenter) could be generalised to their believing that the military and police followed the orders of the authority figure (principally narrated as Hitler). Students must therefore have sound knowledge of the different agents and agencies across Europe who were involved in the mass murder of Jewish people, including individuals and communities who were complicit in what was happening. This will better equip students to challenge the generalisation of Milgram's experiments to the Holocaust. Teaching can also include reflection on the motivations of the perpetrators. For example, discussing the events that took place in Józefów in July 1942 led some of the psychology students to consider explanations other than obedience and/or conformity. Arguably, it was this kind of historical knowledge that was missing from most of the psychology students' interpretations of Milgram's findings and in turn contributed to their impression that Holocaust perpetrators (similarly to Milgram's participants) acted as they did under the duress of an authority figure. Their discussions highlight the importance of students considering the historical context alongside psychological explanations.

It is unlikely psychology teachers will have in-depth knowledge of the historiography of the Holocaust, and it is not the intention of this chapter to argue they should. Certainly, the aim of studying Milgram's research as part of a psychology course will not be to conduct a detailed historical study, but instead to learn about a prominent study within the field of social psychology, to reflect on and critique the methodology, and to discuss the importance of ethical issues when conducting research. Even so, given the enduring links between Milgram's research and the Holocaust, psychology teachers should become acquainted with some key pieces of information about the Holocaust – especially information related to responsibility, and the different agents and agencies involved.

The British Psychological Society defines psychology as: 'The scientific study of the mind and how it dictates and influences our behaviour, from communication and memory to thought and emotion. It's about understanding what makes people tick and how this understanding can help us address many of the problems and issues in society today' (British Psychological Society 2019). As such, psychology students are especially well placed to scrutinise the actions of Holocaust perpetrators, grapple with matters of responsibility, and critically reflect on the relevance and significance of this for contemporary society. This is essential when learning about Milgram's research and its connection to the Holocaust, especially as this series of experiments continue to be a staple of most introductory psychology courses. Having sound historical knowledge will enable students to more meaningfully and accurately critique the relationship between Milgram's experiments and the Holocaust, and in doing so develop the analytical skills required to problematise, unpack and interpret human behaviour recorded in past events and observed in present-day situations.

Acknowledgements

Sincere thanks are due to the students who took part in this study and to the teachers who facilitated research visits to their schools.

References

Baumrind, D. 1964. 'Some thoughts on ethics of research: After reading Milgram's "Behavioral Study of Obedience"', *American Psychologist* 19 (6): 421–3.

Benjamin, L.T. and Simpson, J. 2009. 'The power of the situation: The impact of Milgram's obedience studies on personality and social psychology', *American Psychologist* 64 (1): 12–19.

Braun, V. and Clarke, V. 2006. 'Using thematic analysis in psychology', *Qualitative Research in Psychology* 3 (2): 77–101.

British Psychological Society. 2019. 'What is Psychology?' Online. https://www.bps.org.uk/public/what-is-psychology (accessed 15 February 2020).

Browning, C.R. 1992. *Ordinary Men: Reserve Police Battalion 101 and the Final Solution in Poland.* New York: Harper Collins.

Burger, J.M. 2009. 'Replicating Milgram: Would people still obey today?' *American Psychologist* 64 (1): 1–11.

Burger, J.M. 2014. 'Situational features in Milgram's experiment that kept his participants shocking', *Journal of Social Issues* 70 (3): 489–500.

Burger, J.M., Girgis, Z.M. and Manning, C. 2011. 'In their own words: Explaining obedience to authority through an examination of participants' comments', *Social Psychology and Personality Science* 2 (5): 460–6.

Fenigstein, A. 2015. 'Milgram's shock experiments and the Nazi perpetrators: A contrarian perspective on the role of obedience pressures during the Holocaust', *Theory and Psychology* 25 (5): 581–98.

Foster, S.J., Pettigrew, A., Pearce, A., Hale, R., Burgess, A., Salmons, P. and Lenga, R.-A. 2016. *What Do Students Know and Understand about the Holocaust? Evidence from English secondary schools*. London: UCL Institute of Education.

Griggs, R.A. and Whitehead III, G.I. 2015 'Coverage of Milgram's obedience experiments in social psychology textbooks: Where have all the criticisms gone?' *Teaching of Psychology* 42 (4): 315–22.

Haslam, S.A., Reicher, S.D., Millard, K. and McDonald, R. 2015. '"Happy to have been of service": The Yale archive as a window into the engaged followership of participants in Milgram's "obedience" experiments', *British Journal of Social Psychology* 54 (1): 55–83.

Hayes, P. 2017. *Why? Explaining the Holocaust*. New York: Norton.

Hoffman, E., Myerberg, N.R. and Morawski, J.G. 2015. 'Acting otherwise: Resistance, agency, and subjectivities in Milgram's studies of obedience', *Theory and Psychology* 25 (5): 670–89.

Jetten, J. and Mols, F. 2014. '50:50 hindsight: Appreciating anew the contributions of Milgram's experiments', *Journal of Social Issues* 70 (3): 587–602.

Mastroianni, G.R. 2002. 'Milgram and the Holocaust: A re-examination', *Journal of Theoretical and Philosophical Psychology* 22 (2): 158–73.

Milgram, S. 1963. 'Behavioral study of obedience', *The Journal of Abnormal and Social Psychology* 67: 371–8.

Milgram, S. 1967. 'The compulsion to do evil', *Patterns of Justice* 1: 3–7.

Milgram, S. 1974. *Obedience to Authority: An experimental view*. New York: Harper and Row.

Miller, A.G. 2004. 'What can the Milgram obedience experiments tell us about the Holocaust? Generalising from the social psychology laboratory'. In *The Social Psychology of Good and Evil*, edited by Arthur G. Miller, 193–239. New York: Guilford Press.

Overy, R. 2014. '"Ordinary men," extraordinary circumstances: Historians, social psychology, and the Holocaust', *Journal of Social Issues* 70: 515–30.

Perry, G. 2013. *Behind the Shock Machine: The untold story of the notorious Milgram psychology experiments*. Melbourne: Scribe Publications.

Russell, N. 2017. 'An important Milgram-Holocaust linkage: Formal rationality', *Canadian Journal of Sociology* 42 (3): 261–92.

5

Look before you leap: Teaching about the Holocaust in primary schools

Eleni Karayianni

Introduction

In England, there is currently no requirement to teach about the Holocaust in the primary school. Despite this, evidence exists to suggest primary schools are including the Holocaust in their curriculum. As the UCL student study (Foster *et al.* 2016) reported, 28.5 per cent of almost 8,000 student participants said they first encountered the Holocaust in primary school. The survey responses of this study, along with desk-based research focused on online information of Holocaust Education organisations' programmes and resources,[1] and primary schools' curriculum plans, indicate that these encounters are taking many forms. For example, some schools choose to mark Holocaust Memorial Day with assemblies and survivor testimonies, others read the book or watch the film *The Boy in the Striped Pyjamas*, or encounter *Anne Frank's Diary*, and some primary school pupils learn about *Kindertransport* as part of a study of the Second World War. The growing body of academic and practitioner literature, as well as the increasing availability of resources, guides, teacher training and museum education programmes specifically aimed at primary school children, indicate the emergence of an educational trend or, perhaps, a drive from certain invested parties to increase the Holocaust's presence in the primary curriculum.

Whether a trend or drive, this development raises a number of critical issues. The most important is the stark absence of research upon which to make informed decisions about the appropriateness of the subject for primary aged pupils. This includes consideration of the content that such teaching could include, the objectives it could pursue and the potential impact on pupils' cognitive, emotional, or moral development. Indeed, much advocacy for such teaching from academics, educators, and Holocaust education institutions is largely based on assumptions and perceptions of benefits for pupils' attitudes and values rather than on robust empirical evidence. This chapter argues that advocating for, or implementing teaching about, such an important and difficult topic as the Holocaust should go hand in hand with careful consideration of the rationale for such an inclusion, and empirical explorations of the ways context, content and pedagogies can impact pupils. Overall, this chapter argues for a more thoughtful approach to the teaching of the Holocaust in the primary school. It aims to add to the limited existing body of literature on primary school pupils' encounters with the Holocaust and to challenge common assumptions made about the benefits of Holocaust education for the development of positive attitudes and values in young people.

The analysis is based on a sub-sample of the existing database produced for the UCL student study described in detail elsewhere in this collection (Foster *et al.* 2016). Analysis of this database focused on a specific section of the study and explored whether or not learning about the Holocaust in the primary school is related to students' attitudes towards immigrants and their attitudes towards neighbourhood diversity. As such, the analysis problematises the assumptions commonly made about the value of Holocaust education in countering prejudice, discrimination and racism and calls for more empirical research on the objectives, delivery and outcomes of Holocaust inclusion in the primary curriculum.

The findings of this analysis and the questions it raises have important implications not only for primary and secondary school teachers, but also for academics, policy makers and Holocaust education organisations nationally and internationally. A recent investigation carried out by UNESCO and the Georg Eckert Institute indicated that the Holocaust is currently included in the curricula of more than half of the 135 countries investigated across all continents (Carrier *et al.* 2015). Thus, the present analysis contributes to discussions about when, how and why to teach about the Holocaust which are of international significance and interest.

Holocaust education in the primary school

In England, the Holocaust is currently a compulsory subject for Key Stage 3 History and is usually taught to Year 9 students (13–14-year-olds) (Pettigrew *et al.* 2009). Teachers at primary level are not required to teach the subject, and as Hale (2018, 222) stated:

> There remain too few empirical studies in the field, contributing to a myriad of unknowns including: the extent that the Holocaust is part of primary school curriculum; how the topic is approached; the knowledge on non-history specialist primary teachers delivering the subject; the impact that learning about the Holocaust has on children (including their emotional, attitudinal and cognitive responses); and consequently, if and/or how it should be taught to children of this age.

This latter issue of whether or not the Holocaust is an age-appropriate subject to teach at primary school level is one that has been fiercely contested. Those who are against the teaching of the Holocaust in primary schools have cited a number of different arguments. Heyl (in Mittnik 2018) claims that early exposure to the topic would overwhelm children both cognitively and emotionally with the danger of traumatising them. Totten (1999) has argued that the history is too horrific for lower primary aged pupils and so complex that any attempt to teach it at this level will result in simplifications that distort the history beyond recognition.[2] Short (2003), while claiming that some of Totten's criticisms were misdirected, nevertheless argued that fatigue, reactance and primary pupils' lack of understanding of Jewish identity and culture strengthen the case for not including the Holocaust in the primary curriculum. According to Short (2003), fatigue may result from too much exposure to the topic when students, who having learned about the Holocaust in primary school, encounter it again in secondary school (and perhaps not just in history lessons but in other subjects too). Furthermore, Short (2003) uses Brehm's psychological notion of 'reactance' to describe the feeling of manipulation that pupils may experience because of pressure to recognise the importance of the Holocaust and to learn its lessons.

On the other hand, those advocating the inclusion of Holocaust education in primary schools argue that pupils in the upper primary level are 'intellectually and emotionally ready to explore complex and challenging histories' (Holocaust Educational Trust 2016, 3) and can manage the difficult content of the Holocaust (Supple 1998). Others have claimed that the primary school is a good place to do some foundation work as it offers vast cross-curricular, multi-disciplinary opportunities, and more continuity as primary teachers have the flexibility to respond to pupils' responses instantly or follow up their lessons the next day (Maitles and Cowan 1999). Yet others have cited pupils' familiarity with the subject – through the media and society – as reason to deal with the subject in the safe and controlled environment of the school (Richler-Friedman 2018; see also Mittnik 2018).

Of crucial importance for the discussion in this chapter is that the appropriateness of the topic has been linked by advocates for its inclusion in the primary curriculum with what they see as the positive outcomes of such an encounter. They claim that studying this subject is not only appropriate but also essential and worthwhile because it can help develop pupils' understanding of racism, injustice, prejudice, stereotyping and discrimination, and can develop the positive values of empathy, tolerance and respect for others (Collin 2000; Cowan 2018; Cowan and Maitles 2007; Jennings 2010; Maitles and Cowan 1999; Sepinwall 1999; Szejnmann *et al.* 2018).

The civic and moral development of young people has been a large part of the justification for Holocaust education not only at primary but also the secondary level. Beyond historical knowledge, as Clements (2007) claims, moral and social education objectives such as countering racism and encouraging active citizenship have provided the rationale for the inclusion of the Holocaust in the National Curriculum since its inception. Furthermore, the aim of establishing the Holocaust Memorial Day in 2001 was clearly explained by the Home Office as an opportunity for a national focus on education which will promote 'a democratic and tolerant society, free of the evils of prejudice and racism' (Home Office 1999). These civic aims do not simply express politicians' and policy makers' hopes and aspirations for Holocaust education. Empirical evidence suggests that they are also central to the aims and practices of many teachers. For example, the IOE teacher study revealed that secondary teachers mainly prioritise civic-based objectives over subject-specific ones (Pettigrew *et al.* 2009). Specifically, a total of 71 per cent of survey respondents in a sample of 2,108 secondary teachers said they taught about the Holocaust 'to develop an understanding of the roots and ramifications of prejudice, racism and stereotyping in any society' and 55.9 per cent said they aimed for their students 'to learn the lessons of the

Holocaust and to ensure that a similar human atrocity never happens again' (Pettigrew *et al.* 2009, 76).

Whether or not the teaching of the Holocaust has been successful in contributing to students' citizenship and values, education at the secondary level is a matter still to be determined as very few empirical studies have examined the issue (see for example Brown and Davies 1998; Carrington and Short 1997; Clements 2007). Research in Holocaust education in primary schools is even scarcer. A comprehensive literature review of studies published in the English language revealed only a handful of empirical studies examining what teachers at this level teach or what pupils learn. In the United States, Schweber's (2008) research into one third grade classroom (children aged 8–9) led her to conclude that pupils at that age should not be learning about the Holocaust because they either fail to understand it, or because they do understand but are horrified by it. Jennings's (2010) study into a fifth grade classroom (children aged 10–11), on the other hand, concluded that Holocaust education has exciting possibilities for critical citizenship if teachers make a long-term engagement and build a layered curriculum. In Scotland, Maitles and Cowan (1999) interviewed eight primary school teachers about their inclusion of the Holocaust in their lessons and examined the methods and content used. Later, Cowan and Maitles (2002) explored the practices of primary schools in one local authority and concluded that after the establishment of Holocaust Memorial Day, the presence and quality of Holocaust education in primary schools had increased with evidence of positive effects on pupils (see also Cowan and Maitles 2010). The same researchers conducted a small-scale longitudinal study into the immediate and lasting effects of Holocaust education on primary pupils. They concluded that learning about the Holocaust in the primary school has positive effects on pupils' values and attitudes (Cowan and Maitles 2005; Cowan and Maitles 2007; Maitles 2008). In England, the work of Short and Carrington (Short 1991; Short 2003; Short and Carrington 1995) is notable but it does not focus on the Holocaust directly; rather their research has examined primary pupils' understanding of Jewish culture and identity and concluded that teachers need to first address possible stereotypes or misconceptions pupils have about the Jews if Holocaust education is to be meaningful and have the desired outcomes in the future.

The studies described here offer interesting and important findings but are not sufficient to create a rich empirical framework in which meaningful considerations of *if* and *what* is appropriate can take place. Indeed, it is starkly apparent that current practices in schools (and among Holocaust education institutions) and their impact on pupils are under-researched and typically based more on assumptions rather than empirical evidence. Educators and institutions have claimed that the subject is or is not appropriate for primary school pupils in intellectual or emotional terms, but there are to date very limited – in number and methodology – studies that examine and assess the actual impact of studying the Holocaust on primary pupils. Furthermore, it seems that much advocacy and practice has been based on the assumption that including the Holocaust in the primary school can help achieve civic and moral goals, but again empirical evidence has not been forthcoming. The chapter now moves to further problematise these assumptions by examining a sub-sample of the database of the UCL student study. In doing so, it aims to open up discussions about the purpose, place and function of Holocaust education in the primary school and to make suggestions for future directions.

Researching students' civic attitudes

The analysis presented here is based on the data collected by the UCL student study on knowledge and understanding about the Holocaust. For the purposes of this analysis, I used a small sub-sample of this study: the Year 7 students (aged 11–12) who completed the survey. Specific cases were further selected from this sub-sample and were divided into two groups: Group A consisted of those Year 7 students who said they had studied the Holocaust in primary school but not yet in secondary school (n = 243; 131 girls, 112 boys), and Group B consisted of those who said they had never studied the Holocaust in any school environment (n = 410; 233 girls, 177 boys). I compared the two groups' answers to the *Attitudes Towards Equal Rights for Immigrants* scale (Schulz *et al.* 2010) along with their answers to the *Attitudes Towards Neighbourhood Diversity* scale (Schulz *et al.* 2011). The two scales were taken from the 2009 International Civic and Citizenship Education Study (ICCS),[3] which is the largest international study on civic and citizenship education ever conducted.[4]

The discussion of the findings into students' attitudes is supplemented by examples of students' answers to knowledge questions as such a connection is deemed useful. It should be emphasised that because this is not a longitudinal study, and as the survey did not ask for details about students' learning experiences, we cannot determine cause and effect relationships. However, it was believed that comparing the two groups could provide some insight into the presence or absence of potential links between studying the Holocaust in primary school and students' attitudes or values.

Attitudes towards equal rights for immigrants

In the UCL student study, the *Attitudes Towards Equal Rights for Immigrants* scale was introduced to participants with the following information: 'People sometimes move from one country to another, and are often known as "immigrants"'. Students were then presented with a list of statements about immigrants and asked to indicate their level of agreement or disagreement with each item, using a four-point Likert scale in which 1 = 'strongly disagree' and 4 = 'strongly agree'.

Figure 5.1 shows the proportion of Year 7 students giving each response on the items of this scale. The responses of those who learned

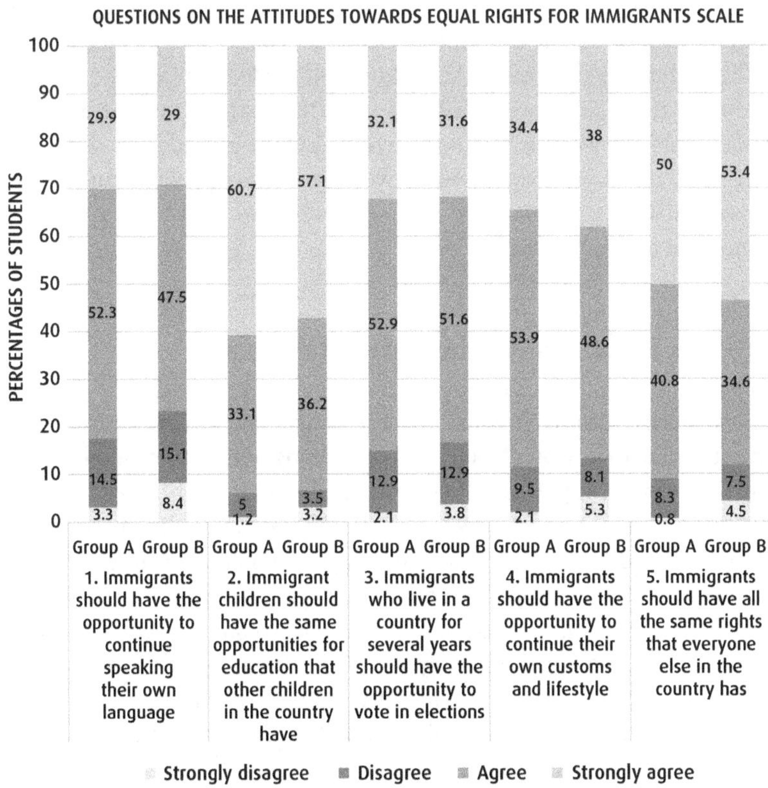

Fig 5.1 Responses of the two groups to the *Attitudes towards Equal Rights for Immigrants* scale (percentage of students by group) (graph by author based on data in Schulz *et al.* 2010, 275).

about the Holocaust in primary school (Group A) are compared with those who have never learned about the Holocaust in school (Group B). Overall, the majority of students in both groups either agreed or strongly agreed with the statements, suggesting positive attitudes towards rights for immigrants. Importantly, the results indicated remarkably similar attitudes towards immigrants between those students who had studied the Holocaust in the primary school and those who had never studied the Holocaust in any school setting.

Each question was scored from 1 to 4, where 1 indicated strong disagreement and 4 indicated strong agreement. Thus, mean total scores on this scale could range from 5 to 20, with higher scores showing more accepting attitudes towards equal rights for immigrants. For those who learned about the Holocaust in primary school, the mean score was 16.37 (with standard deviation = 2.66) and for those who had never learned about the Holocaust in a school environment, the mean score was 16.17 (with standard deviation = 3.06). The means were compared using an unrelated t-test to determine whether there is a statistically significant difference between the two groups' attitudes. The result indicated no significant difference between the attitudes of students in the two groups ($t = .83$, $DF = 624$, two tailed $p = .41$). In simple terms, the analysis of students' answers in this scale indicated that attitudes towards immigrants' rights were the same between students who had studied the Holocaust in the primary school and students who had never learned about it in a school setting.

Attitudes towards neighbourhood diversity

The *Attitudes Towards Neighbourhood Diversity* scale was introduced with the question 'How would you feel about having neighbours belonging to the following groups?' and then presented students with a list of nine different groups of people ('people of a different nationality than yours'; 'people of a different religion than yours'; 'people of a different skin colour than yours'; 'people of a different social class than yours'; 'homosexuals (gay men and/or lesbians)'; 'people who come from another part of the country'; 'people with physical disabilities'; 'people with mental health problems'; and 'people with HIV/AIDS'). The question asked students to state whether they 'wouldn't mind' or they 'would dislike' having each of these groups as their neighbours.

Total scores on this scale were calculated by how many groups the students would not like to live next to. Scores could range from 0 to 8, with higher scores showing more groups that students did not want to live next to, so higher intolerance to neighbourhood diversity. For those that learned about the Holocaust in primary school, the mean score was 0.92 (standard deviation = 1.21) and for those who had never learned about the Holocaust in a school environment, their mean score was 1.32 (standard deviation = 1.5). An unrelated t-test performed on the data showed a statistically significant difference between the two groups: ($t = -3.45$, $DF = 603$, two tailed $p < .01$). However, we should remember that we are comparing means with very little real difference between them (0.92 and 1.32 where it is possible for these values to have ranged from 0 to 8). So, to explore the effect size, Cohen's *d* was calculated and showed a small effect ($d = 0.29$), meaning that the difference between the two groups is minor, even if it's statistically significant. In other words, while there was a difference between the two groups, it was very small, and consequently we should be cautious about overstating this difference. In general, there was a very high level of acceptance of neighbourhood diversity in both groups.

The results indicate that students seem to leave the primary school and enter secondary school with very positive attitudes towards immigrants as well as towards people of difference or minority groups. The data could be used to claim that primary school teachers appear to be doing a good job in teaching students about racism, human rights, diversity, tolerance and respect whether they teach about the Holocaust or not. Or the data could be an indication of positive values additionally learned outside school, from students' family and social environment. Of course, we should also exercise caution as students can be very aware of what answer is acceptable during surveys like this one and thus the percentages may be artificially high due to students' understanding of what answers are more socially desirable. While that may be true to some extent, we have no reason to doubt that there are negligible differences in attitudes towards others between the two groups. In fact, other studies have had similar results. For example, Maitles *et al.* (2006) compared secondary students who had learned about the Holocaust in primary school with peers who hadn't. While there was some evidence that might suggest differences in voting attitudes and perceived knowledge, they found negligible differences between the two groups to the questions 'I think that it is OK for children to make racist comments about Jews/Blacks/Chinese/Asians/Gypsy Travellers/ refugees' and 'I think there are too many Jews/Blacks/Chinese/Asians/ refugees in Scotland' as both groups strongly disagreed with all these statements.

The findings from the analysis of these attitudinal scales clearly pose questions regarding the purpose of Holocaust education in the primary school. The data do not seem to justify assumptions regarding the benefits of studying the Holocaust for the promotion of civic and moral objectives as the study of the Holocaust in primary school does not seem to have added value on these students' attitudes and values. In fact, the findings presented here stand in contrast to a study conducted by Cowan and Maitles (2002; 2005; 2007) who have claimed positive effects on primary pupils after studying the Holocaust (see also Maitles 2008; Maitles *et al.* 2006). Above all, it points to the need for more research on this issue and the need for quantitative and qualitative research to clearly define and capture the moral or attitudinal effect of Holocaust education on primary pupils.

Knowledge about the Holocaust

The possibility of developing positive attitudes towards others or informing young people's moral development through the study of the Holocaust cannot be considered without due attention to the history of the Holocaust. In other words, without historical knowledge *about* the Holocaust – of what the Holocaust was and, most importantly, why it happened – we cannot acquire lessons *from* the Holocaust; we cannot reach ethical judgements and cannot draw moral or attitudinal lessons of contemporary significance. To illustrate and substantiate this point, the discussion now turns attention to evidence of students' historical understanding from the same UCL student study.

First, when these Year 7 students were asked during the survey to indicate whether they knew the meaning of 'antisemitism', only 16 per cent of those who had studied the Holocaust in primary school recognised the term. Compared to 7.3 per cent of those who knew the term without ever studying the Holocaust in school, this is not an impressive result.[5] Of course, not knowing the term does not necessarily mean that students don't know its meaning. However, it is not unreasonable to expect that the term should be explicitly mentioned when studying the Holocaust. A possible explanation of this finding is that the Holocaust is taught in primary schools as part of broader lessons about racism in general rather than antisemitism in particular. The studies of Dawidowicz (1992) and Short (2005) on how the Holocaust was taught in secondary schools support this argument. They provided evidence that the specificity of antisemitism was often lost because the Holocaust was taught only in terms of racism and prejudice. Certainly, when students in the UCL student study were asked about 'racism', 90.7 per cent of those who had studied the Holocaust recognised the term compared to 74.4 per cent of those who never studied the Holocaust. But, an essential question remains: if students learned about the Holocaust without reference to antisemitism, how are they to begin to understand why it happened? As Dawidowicz (1992) argues: 'the trouble with this kind of universalization is that it . . . ignores the particular religious and historical roots that nurture specific prejudices' (Dawidowicz 1992, 74). And so, if antisemitism is not explicitly addressed in the classroom, are students to understand that Jews were persecuted just because they were different? As Short remarked:

> If that were the case, one has to ask why others who were in some sense 'different' such as the red-haired, the seriously overweight and the sporting elite did not have to endure the same fate. The reality, of course, is that the Jews were singled out because they were held responsible for Germany losing the war; they were seen as exercising a malign influence over the economy and were suspected of harbouring communist sympathies. That said, their persecution cannot be explained adequately without also taking account of the less immediate but nonetheless potent influence of the long tradition in Germany (and elsewhere in Europe) of Christian anti-Semitism.
>
> (Short 2003, 121)

Alongside Short, the argument that I intend to make here is that lessons which present the Holocaust as a generalised paradigm of the evils of racism or prejudice and the virtues of respect for others do very little to promote real understanding of the actual processes of stereotyping and scapegoating.

Furthermore, if students don't understand antisemitism and why the Jews were persecuted, what stops them from blaming the victims? Certainly, during interviews with secondary students, Foster *et al.* (2016) found a tendency on behalf of some students of all ages to answer the question 'why the Jews?' by providing distorted understandings and misconceptions about who the Jewish people were. For example, students referred to Jews as having better jobs, better education and more money than ordinary Germans. In addition, Short (1991; 2015) has argued that children's natural inclination to believe in a just world can lead them to think that if Jews suffered they must have done something to deserve it. This raises an important pedagogical concern as students are unlikely to respond appropriately when learning about the Holocaust if they don't come to see the Jewish people as innocent people, undeserving of their fate (Short 1991; Short 2015).

During the survey, students indicated a lack of understanding of who the Jewish people were on a number of occasions. For example, when asked about the size of the Jewish population in pre-war Germany, only 7 per cent of those Year 7s who had studied the Holocaust in primary school gave the correct answer (that 'less than 1%' were Jewish) in a multiple choice question. Just over a third of these students (34.7 per cent) thought that Jewish people accounted for 'approximately 15%' of the German population in 1933 and 39.3 per cent estimated the proportion of Jewish population at 'more than 30%'. Students' responses to this question raise concerns about what they have learned and how that knowledge may relate to the formation of attitudes. For, how are students expected to draw lessons about the dangers of stereotyping, prejudice and discrimination, if they don't come to recognise the myths and negative stereotypes about Jews that 'are woven into the very fabric of western culture' (Short 1991, 29) and they don't come to see the persecuted Jews as a small minority in German society? Furthermore, if Nazi propaganda claiming that Jews were a dominant group in Germany is not addressed when teaching about the Holocaust, how are students to even begin to understand their social duties and responsibilities towards others and especially towards the weaker members of their society?

A further research finding warrants careful consideration here. When during the survey those Year 7 students who had learned about the Holocaust in the primary school were asked who they thought was responsible for the genocide, out of 235 open-text responses received, the most common answer by a vast majority was 'Adolf Hitler'. A total of 143 students assigned responsibility to Hitler alone. A small number of students followed this by explaining that 'he was a bad man', 'he was a really terrible man', and 'he hated Jews'. An additional 45 students blamed Hitler along with the Nazis or the Nazi party and 19 students blamed the Nazi party without reference to Hitler. Only 21 students extended responsibility beyond Hitler and/or the Nazis. A dozen added the Germans as responsible along with Hitler and an additional eight students said the Germans were responsible without reference to Hitler. One student held 'the SS, Hitler, Heinrich, Himmler, the Nazis and all the soldiers who obeyed these orders' responsible. One additional student said that Hitler was to blame 'along with people who agreed with him' and, remarkably, only one student out of 235 who had studied the Holocaust in the primary school and replied to this question, explicitly extended responsibility beyond

Germany by holding accountable 'Adolf Hitler and his soldiers and all the other participating countries in Europe'.

Thus, the research revealed a significant Hitler-centrism (see Stuart Foster's chapter in this volume). This is not a surprising finding as students commonly see Hitler as the 'evil', 'mad' individual who caused the Holocaust to happen (Carrington and Short 1997; Foster *et al.* 2016; Mathis 2018; Mittnik 2016, 2018). However, it is a finding that raises questions about the purpose of teaching the Holocaust at the primary level. If students see the Holocaust as the result of one isolated 'bad man', how are they expected to understand that suppressing and discriminating against minority groups is embedded within society at large? How are they to comprehend notions of prejudice and discrimination, culpability and complicity, and how are they to take social action or learn to stand up to injustice if they don't understand how to recognise it?

One could counteract these arguments by saying that we simply cannot expect primary school pupils to acquire such historical knowledge and understanding about Europe-wide collaboration and complicity but that they are still capable of taking away civic or moral lessons. However, what this discussion has emphasised is that, without sound historical knowledge, pupils may not be able to truly achieve any kind of citizenship, personal, social, or values-based educational objectives. They may not be able to move beyond superficial slogans about respect and equal rights (or perhaps beyond merely ticking the socially desirable answer on a survey) to true, deep understandings of social phenomena. Thus, they may not truly learn the 'lessons' of the Holocaust. Fundamentally, if we really think pupils are not ready to understand the history of the Holocaust, why then teach about it at this age?

Implications for future directions

The purpose of this chapter is not to proclaim the work of primary school teachers as ineffective in cognitive, attitudinal or moral terms. We certainly know nothing about the way the students in the sample were taught about the Holocaust, with what resources or pedagogical approaches and in pursuit of what objectives. However, the data presented here suggest no – or very little – difference in attitudes related to immigrants and neighbourhood diversity between those who had and those who hadn't learned about the Holocaust in the primary school. Students' answers to knowledge questions further suggest that they hold misconceptions and inaccuracies that could actively inhibit the development of the envisaged attitudes and values. These findings, therefore, raise important questions about the purpose and value of including the Holocaust in the primary curriculum.

They suggest that an encounter with the Holocaust in the primary school will not automatically inform or improve pupils' attitudes towards others. If pupils learn about the persecution of Jewish people during the Second World War, about *Kindertransport* or about Anne Frank, they will not automatically become more sympathetic towards immigrants or people different than themselves. Short (2005) – conducting research with secondary school students after they had participated in Holocaust Memorial Day activities – concluded that they failed to learn a number of important lessons from the Holocaust. This prompted him to state that students cannot be relied on to work lessons out for themselves but that such learning requires explicit focus. If this is the case for secondary school students, it can only be at least equally the case for younger pupils. What the present analysis does then is challenge those who argue that civic and moral development is the reason for including the Holocaust in the primary school curriculum or who assume that all encounters with the subject will benefit pupils in matters of contemporary significance.

Thus, this analysis points to the need to reconceptualise what we think Holocaust education can offer primary school pupils. In simple terms, it is crucial to step back and consider why we may want to include the Holocaust in the primary curriculum. Why the Holocaust specifically? Indeed, it is possible that the important civic and moral aims of anti-racist education, prejudice reduction, empathy, tolerance, and respect for others can be pursued by other means, other topics and subjects. As Heyl (in Mathis 2018) has argued, objectives such as tolerance and open-mindedness do not require discussion of the Holocaust. This is not by any means to deny the significance of the Holocaust as a subject and its potential for students' ethical and civic development. Rather it is to question the potential for in-depth study and meaning making of such a complex subject by primary aged pupils. The data certainly indicate that teachers who do not teach about the Holocaust are effective at developing positive attitudes in their pupils anyway. And perhaps teachers in both cases are only one of the many influential factors in pupils' learning which seem to be having positive effects on their values and attitudes. So why the Holocaust? What do we think the Holocaust has to offer to our young people that would justify its inclusion in the primary curriculum when it is already a part of the secondary curriculum? It is of course beyond the scope of this chapter to attempt to answer this question. But it is very important to ask it.

As Mathis (2018) claims, the question of *if* the topic should be taught at primary school needs to be answered first before we start thinking about how to teach it. When practitioners, academics and researchers have articulated their own response to this question, then we may be closer to a more clearly conceptualised purpose for Holocaust education in primary schools. In doing so, we need to take into account concerns such as those expressed by Short (2003) about the legitimacy of certain lessons (regarding tolerance and respect for others) and the ways in which such lessons fundamentally misrepresent the genocide and can create misunderstandings about it. The issue of creating misconceptions and misunderstandings in pursuit of civic aims or in the process of simplifying or generalising the content is a particularly salient one that deserves careful consideration. The concerns about trivialisation (didactic reduction as, for example, when dealing with the topic without referring to mass murder), instrumentalisation and exploitation (using the topic to teach general ethical principles) (Heyl in Mittnik, 2018; Heyl in Mathis, 2018) of the Holocaust need to be addressed.

After contemplation on purpose and objectives, serious attention needs to be given to how the intended educational objectives can be realised and assessed, with what content, what approach and what resources. As Hale clearly stated: 'for educators and academics who advocate the introduction of this topic to primary school curricula, thoughtful and critical consideration is needed to determine what should or could be expected from children of this age' (Hale 2018, 235). To this end, educators need to draw perspectives from a myriad of related fields and bodies of knowledge.

The entire process of designing and implementing Holocaust programmes needs to be grounded in research so that anticipated and desired outcomes are tested, methods revised and practice improved. In this sense, we need not only better informed, richer theoretical discussions on what the purpose of the Holocaust in the primary school could be, we also need to ground these discussions in rich empirical research. As has been illustrated here, analyses such as the one presented in this chapter and in the work of Cowan and Maitles (Cowan and Maitles, 2002; 2005; 2007; Maitles, 2008; Maitles *et al.* 2006) that examine the impact on attitudes in quantitative terms without first looking at what specific content pupils have been taught, why, how and for how long, are of little use in progressing our understanding of how the topic impacts pupils in attitudinal, emotional or cognitive ways.

An urgent need exists for empirical studies exploring what current practice actually looks like in England's primary classrooms to determine how common it is for primary schools to teach the Holocaust, what the teaching includes, why teachers choose to teach it and what they are aiming to achieve. We need qualitative research that looks at the educational processes more closely and assesses both teacher interventions and pupil outcomes. If we want to determine the impact on civic and moral development, we also need research studies that can establish links between Holocaust education and attitudes or values. Then, and if we decide that part of our purpose for including the Holocaust is to inform civic and moral development, we need to explore not only what kind of educational interventions are more effective, but also what kind of quantitative and qualitative research methods can more accurately measure pupils' attitudes, worldviews and values.

Conclusion

The place of the Holocaust in the primary school is an issue that has increasingly attracted the interest of Holocaust education institutions and academics in recent years. Despite this interest, we currently know too little about whether and to what degree primary school teachers include it in their curricula, for what purpose and with what content and approach they teach it. The analysis presented in this chapter aimed to problematise the purpose of including the Holocaust in the primary curriculum and to highlight a number of potential problems when dealing with its content. In an *Attitudes Towards Equal Rights for Immigrants* scale, it has illustrated no significant difference between those Year 7 students who had learned about the Holocaust in primary school and those who had never learned about it in a school setting. With regards to questions about attitudes towards neighbourhood diversity, it has illustrated very small differences in attitudes towards others between the two groups. The findings relating to students' knowledge about the Holocaust further indicated that advocated lessons relating to civic and moral development are not straightforward and that generalising or simplifying the history of the Holocaust potentially does very little towards achieving such goals. The chapter concludes by calling for more research to inform our understanding of current practice and provide assessment on its impact on pupils. Undoubtedly more empirical evidence is needed to inform theoretical discussions on the purpose and value of Holocaust education in the primary school.

Acknowledgments

I would like to thank my colleague, Dr Rebecca Hale, for her valuable assistance in carrying out the statistical analysis of the data presented in this chapter.

Notes

1. Such as the National Holocaust Centre and Museum, the Holocaust Memorial Day Trust, the Holocaust Educational Trust, and the Jewish Museum.
2. Totten was replying to Sepinwall (1999) and objecting to the teaching of the Holocaust below the age of 10.
3. The *Attitudes Towards Neighbourhood Diversity* scale was used with the Latin American sample, not the European sample (Schulz *et al.* 2011).
4. The ICCS was carried out by an independent, international cooperative of national research agencies; the International Association for the Evaluation of Educational Achievement (IEA).
5. A similar lack of knowledge of what 'antisemitism' means was found by Maitles *et al.* (2006).

References

All online material last accessed 24 July 2019 unless indicated otherwise.

Brown, M. and Davies, I. 1998. 'The Holocaust and education for citizenship: The teaching of history, religion and human rights in England', *Educational Review* 50 (1): 75–83.

Carrier, P., Fuchs, E. and Messinger, T. 2015. *The International Status of Education about the Holocaust: A global mapping of textbooks and curricula*. Paris: UNESCO and Georg Eckert Institute for International Textbook Research.

Carrington, B. and Short, G. 1997. 'Holocaust education, anti-racism and citizenship', *Educational Review* 49 (3): 271–82.

Clements, J.L. 2007. 'Difficult Knowledge: Possibilities of learning in Holocaust education'. Ph.D. diss., Institute of Education, University of London.

Collin, S. 2000. *Teaching about the Holocaust in Primary Schools*. Farmington Institute, Harris Manchester College, Oxford. Online. http://www.farmington.ac.uk/index.php/tt77-teaching-about-the-holocaust-in-primary-schools/

Cowan, P. 2018. 'There's no "J" in (the) Holocaust: Perceptions and practice of Holocaust education'. In *Holocaust Education in Primary Schools in the Twenty-First Century: Current practices, potentials and ways forward*, edited by C.C.W. Szejnmann, Paula Cowan and James Griffiths. London: Palgrave Macmillan.

Cowan, P. and Maitles, H. 2002. 'Developing positive values: A case study of Holocaust Memorial Day in primary schools of one local authority in Scotland', *Educational Review* 54 (3): 219–29.

Cowan, P. and Maitles, H. 2005. 'Values and attitudes – positive and negative: A study of the impact of teaching the Holocaust on citizenship among Scottish 11–12 year olds', *Scottish Educational Review* 37: 104–15.

Cowan, P. and Maitles, H. 2007. 'Does addressing prejudice and discrimination through Holocaust education produce better citizens?' *Educational Review* 59 (2): 115–30.

Cowan, P. and Maitles, H. 2010. 'Policy and practice of Holocaust education in Scotland', *Prospects* 40: 257–72.

Dawidowicz, L. 1992. 'How they teach the Holocaust'. In *What Is the Use of Jewish History?* edited by Lucy Dawidowicz. New York: Schocken Books.

Foster, S.J., Pettigrew, A., Pearce, A., Hale, R., Burgess, A., Salmons, P. and Lenga, R.-A. 2016. *What Do Students Know and Understand about the Holocaust? Evidence from English secondary schools*. London: UCL Institute of Education.

Hale, R. 2018. 'Reflections on what year 7 students know and understand about the Holocaust: An argument for empirical research in English primary schools'. In *Holocaust Education in Primary Schools in the Twenty-First Century: Current practices, potentials and ways forward*, edited by C.C.W. Szejnmann, Paula Cowan and James Griffiths. London: Palgrave Macmillan.

Holocaust Educational Trust (HET). 2016. *A Guide for Primary School Teachers*. London: HET. Online. https://www.het.org.uk/primary (accessed 15 February 2020).

Home Office. 1999. *Government Proposal for a Holocaust Remembrance Day*. London: Home Office. Online. http://webarchive.nationalarchives.gov.uk/20021220165530/http://www.homeoffice.gov.uk:80/reu/holrem.htm (accessed 15 February 2020).

Jennings, L.B. 2010. 'Challenges and possibilities of Holocaust education and critical citizenship: An ethnographic study of a fifth-grade bilingual class revisited', *Prospects* 40: 35–56.

Maitles, H. 2008. '"Why are we learning this?": Does studying the Holocaust encourage better citizenship values?' *Genocide Studies and Prevention: An International Journal* 3 (3): 341–52.

Maitles, H. and Cowan, P. 1999. 'Teaching the Holocaust in primary schools in Scotland: Modes, methodology, content', *Educational Review* 51 (3): 263–71.

Maitles, H., Cowan, P. and Butler, E. 2006. 'Never Again! Does Holocaust education have an effect on pupils' citizenship values and attitudes?' Scottish Executive Social Research. Online. https://www2.gov.scot/resource/doc/147037/0038530.pdf (accessed 15 February 2020).

Mathis, C. 2018. '". . . They locked them up in houses and let gas in": Swiss primary school pupils' conceptions of the Holocaust'. In *Holocaust Education in Primary Schools in the Twenty-First Century: Current practices, potentials and ways forward*, edited by C.C.W. Szejnmann, Paula Cowan and James Griffiths. London: Palgrave Macmillan.

Mittnik, P. 2016. 'Holocaust studies in Austrian elementary and secondary schools', *Global Education Review* 3 (3): 138–52.

Mittnik, P. 2018. 'Holocaust education in Austrian primary schools: A plea for teaching the history of National Socialism to 9- and 10-year-olds'. In *Holocaust Education in Primary Schools in the Twenty-First Century: Current practices, potentials and ways forward*, edited by C.C.W. Szejnmann, Paula Cowan and James Griffiths. London: Palgrave Macmillan.

Pettigrew, A., Foster, S., Howson, J., Salmons, P., Lenga, R.-A. and Andrews, K. 2009. *Teaching about the Holocaust in English Secondary Schools: An empirical study of national trends, perspectives and practice*. London: Institute of Education.

Richler-Friedman, Y. 2018. 'Teaching about trauma without traumatizing: Yad Vashem's spiral pedagogical approach in light of developmental psychology'. In *Holocaust Education in Primary Schools in the Twenty-First Century: Current practices, potentials and ways forward*, edited by C.C.W. Szejnmann, Paula Cowan and James Griffiths. London: Palgrave Macmillan.

Schulz, W., Ainley, J., Fraillon, J., Kerr, D. and Losito, B. 2010. *ICCS 2009 International Report: Civic knowledge, attitudes and engagement among lower secondary school students in thirty-eight countries*. Amsterdam: International Association for the Evaluation of Educational Achievement. Online. https://research.acer.edu.au/civics/6/ (accessed 24 March 2020).

Schulz, W., Ainley, J., Friedman, T. and Lietz, P. 2011. ICCS 2009 Latin American Report: Civic knowledge and attitudes among lower secondary students in six Latin American countries. Amsterdam: International Association for the Evaluation of Educational Achievement. Online. https://heefa.net/files/ICCS_2009_Latin_American_Report.pdf (accessed 15 February 2020).

Schweber, S. 2008. '"What Happened to Their Pets?": Third Graders Encounter the Holocaust', *Teachers College Record* 110 (10): 2073–115.

Sepinwall, H. 1999. 'Incorporating Holocaust education into K-4 curriculum and teaching in the United States', *Social Studies and the Young Learner* 10: 5–8.

Short, G. 1991. 'Teaching the Holocaust: Some reflections on a problematic area', *British Journal of Religious Education* 14 (1): 28–34.

Short, G. 2003. 'Holocaust education in the primary school: Some reflections on an emergent debate', *London Review of Education* 1 (2): 119–29.

Short, G. 2005. 'Learning from genocide? A study in the failure of Holocaust education', *Intercultural Education* 16 (4): 367–80.

Short, G. 2015. 'Failing to learn from the Holocaust'. In *As the Witnesses Fall Silent: 21st century Holocaust education in curriculum, policy and practice*, edited by Zehavit Gross and Doyle E. Stevick. Switzerland: Springer International Publishing.

Short, G. and Carrington, B. 1995. 'Antisemitism and the primary school: Children's perceptions of Jewish culture and identity', *Research in Education* 54: 14–24.

Supple, C. 1998. *From Prejudice to Genocide: Learning about the Holocaust*. Stoke-on-Trent: Trentham Books.

Szejnmann, C.C.W., Cowan, P. and Griffiths, J. (eds) 2018. *Holocaust Education in Primary Schools in the Twenty-First Century: Current practices, potentials and ways forward*. London: Palgrave Macmillan.

Totten, S. 1999. 'Should there be Holocaust education for K-4 students? The answer is no', *Social Studies and the Young Learner* 12: 36–9.

6

British Responses to the Holocaust: Student and teacher perspectives on the development of a new classroom resource

Tom Haward

Introduction

Within Britain, the government-led narrative of the country's relationship with the Holocaust treads a sometimes uneasy line between triumphalist eulogy, on the one hand, and acknowledgement Britain 'could have done more' (Prime Minister's Holocaust Commission Report 2015, 24), on the other. Nowhere is this better exemplified than in *Britain's Promise to Remember: The Prime Minister's Holocaust Commission Report*, which contains in its executive summary the following statement:

> Ensuring that the memory and the lessons of the Holocaust are never forgotten lies at the heart of Britain's values as a nation. In commemorating the Holocaust, Britain remembers the way it proudly stood up to Hitler and provided a home to tens of thousands of survivors and refugees, including almost 10,000 children who came on the *Kindertransports*. In debating the more challenging elements of Britain's history – such as the refusal to accept more refugees or the questions over whether more could have been done to disrupt the Final Solution – Britain reflects on its responsibilities in the world today. In educating young people about the Holocaust, Britain reaffirms its commitment to stand up against prejudice and hatred in all its forms.
>
> (Prime Minister's Holocaust Commission Report 2015, 9)

This passage holds a number of assumptions, frames thinking about Britain's role in particular ways, and is notable for what it doesn't say as much as for what it does. It seems a highly political and politicised statement – as is evidenced by the association of Holocaust memory and 'Britain's values as a nation', the conflation between standing up to Hitler and the acceptance of 'tens of thousands of survivors and refugees', and the admission there are 'challenging elements' but lack of clarity about what as a nation should be done differently.

It is within this context, and in response to it, that the teaching resource *British Responses to the Holocaust* was conceived and developed. Designed to open dialogue and encourage rethinking of dominant political and cultural narratives, this resource starts from the premise that Britain's role in and relationship with the Holocaust is understood as a complex and problematic history. This is not a specifically British phenomenon: all countries have problematic pasts, and how such pasts are represented, encountered, and considered in educational spaces is a key element of how students' knowledge and understanding of their historical culture are formed.

This chapter discusses the evolution of *British Responses to the Holocaust* and analyses its potential to effect changes in what both teachers and students know and understand about this history. It will be argued that encouraging students to consider Britain's relationship with the Holocaust is an inherently political act, one where the historical record can provide a counterpoint to the current dominant accounts. The resource exemplifies how primary archival sources can be used to offer counter-narratives, and foster more nuanced, complex, and altogether challenging understandings of connections between Britain and the Holocaust. The resource also has implications for teaching this history in the context of the teaching of 'British values', a requirement for English schools since 2014, allowing students the opportunity to reflect on the identification of Britain as a 'tolerant' country.

British responses to the Holocaust: Then and now

Key questions around what the Allies knew about the Holocaust, when they knew it, what options were available to them, and what actions they ultimately chose are critical to being able to understand the government's capacity to respond to the unfolding genocide and the context in which this developed. Such questions need to be considered not just in the war years, but in the policy approaches forged before. From

1933 on, emigration was a central tenet of the Nazis' policy towards the Jews, to the extent that by 1939, Jewish emigration from the Reich 'had become a major European problem' (Wasserstein 1988, 7). For Britain, this problem was compounded by tensions in its Mandate for Palestine, which from 1936 saw Arab uprisings for independence and against open-ended Jewish immigration. In consequence, the government White Paper of May 1939 restricted Jewish immigration to just 10,000 over the next five years. The year before, from 6–15 July, the Evian Conference called by President Roosevelt to discuss the refugee crisis resulted in only the Dominican Republic and later Costa Rica offering to accept Jewish refugees. Britain, as with the other 30 delegates, offered no new initiatives.

As the war unfolded, the British government accrued intelligence of the mass murder of Jews to the extent that by the end of 1942 these crimes had become widespread public knowledge. Two sources of information in particular came to Britain in 1942 that were particularly significant. The Riegner Telegram of August was intelligence from an anti-Nazi German industrialist who had close connections with high-ranking Nazi officials. It outlined for the first time the planned extermination of the Jews, who would 'after deportation and concentration in the East, be at one blow exterminated' (Foreign Office 1942). The 'Karski Report' of November was an eyewitness report given to the Foreign Office describing the liquidation of the Warsaw ghetto, deportations and gassings at Belzec. Both of these were key elements in an accumulation of evidence of unfolding genocide in Europe that had accumulated over time. By December 1942 the government felt it could no longer ignore the knowledge that had suffused into the public realm, a time when 'from the beginning to the end, few facts of Nazi anti-Semitism were left unstated by the British press' (Sharf 1964, 193).

On 17 December 1942, Foreign Secretary Anthony Eden's Allied Declaration given in the House of Commons was a very public acknowledgement that the British and American governments possessed sufficient knowledge and understanding about the Nazi policy towards the Jews to recognise its criminality, its fundamental abhorrence, and the necessity for punitive measures to be taken against its perpetrators. Yet despite this, within government circles there appeared to be inertia in terms of drawing up and taking tangible steps which might provide relief, sustenance, or rescue to those targeted for murder. The Anglo-American refugee conference in Bermuda of April 1943, convened to discuss potential collaborative efforts between the British and Americans to rescue

Jews, is a case in point. London (2000, 216) has spoken of its 'inadequacy' in terms of outcomes, and Cesarani (2016, 621) has described it as 'a place where every concrete proposal [to rescue Jews] was shot down' by the respective delegations.

Accounting for these behaviours, Kushner (1994, 36) persuasively argues 'it is . . . essential to understand that the available information would be channelled through domestic ideological considerations that were . . . to hinder understanding of the Jewish plight'. Foreign policy considerations were principally centred upon a strategic commitment to winning the war, and the accompanying belief this was the most effective means of ending the genocide and bringing its perpetrators to justice. Government reluctance to help save Jews was also compounded by a latent antisemitism within British society, and the complicating foreign policy issue of the volatile political situation in the British mandate of Palestine, which became effective from 1923. Ultimately, much of the historical scholarship evolving especially from the late 1970s (Wasserstein 1988; London 2000; Gilbert 2001) has tended to conclude, as Wasserstein (1988, 345) does at the end of his study of British policy, that 'there is little to celebrate in this account of British policy towards the Jews of Europe between 1939 and 1945'.

Such interpretations of British policy contrast with those proffered in political circles over the last decade or so. These have recently coalesced into a narrative that has connected to the government's concern with promoting 'British values', and its identification of the education system as a transmitter for these. This is because in some quarters, such as for MP Ian Austin, Britain's role in the Second World War, and in particular its role in the Holocaust, are seen as a defining moment in the demonstration of British values. In turn this raises questions about the sorts of stories politicians want educators to tell about British responses to the Holocaust, and how they reflect notions of the 'British values' outlined by Lord Nash (Department for Education 2014). First set out in the government's Prevent Strategy of 2011, he identified five specifically British key values: democracy; the rule of law; individual liberty; mutual respect; and tolerance for those with different faiths and beliefs. In the context of schools, OFSTED Chief Inspector Amanda Spielman has promoted this in proclaiming that 'pupils should learn how we became the country we are today and how our values make us a beacon of liberalism, tolerance and fairness' (cited in Bulman 2017).

Ian Austin, in 'Britain's Promise to Remember', is one MP who signals an attempt to position Britain's relationship with the Holocaust not only in exceptional and universalist terms, but also in a way that cuts to the core of what he understands 'British values' to be:

> Whilst Britain could have done more, no one can deny that when other European countries were rounding up their Jews and putting them on trains to concentration camps, Britain provided a safe haven for tens of thousands of refugees. In 1941, with Europe overrun and America not yet in the war, just one country – Britain – soldiered on, against all odds, fighting not just for our freedom, but for the world's liberty too. I believe this period defines Britain and what it means to be British. It is Britain's unique response to the Holocaust and its unique role in the war that gives us the right to claim a particular attachment to the values of democracy, equality, freedom, fairness and tolerance.
>
> (Prime Minister's Holocaust Commission Report 2015, 24)

There are many aspects of this interpretation, though, that invite interrogation. 'No one can deny', for instance, makes a claim towards an assumed common understanding that is somehow beyond questioning. Also, the repetition of the idea that in some way Britain's response to the Holocaust was 'unique', especially in the ways in which it aligns Britain in particular to values such as 'equality' and 'tolerance', as well as the conflation of Britain's relationship to the war with Britain's relationship to the Holocaust, presents a narrative of Britain's role as being of special significance in standing up to German aggression, and by implication to the Holocaust. Yet this is problematic, as such a conflation disguises the differences between the two: whilst at one point in the war the British government, despite being supported by the Empire and its dominions, promoted a narrative of being isolated in fighting against Hitler, it did little to rescue Jews from the European genocide, preferring instead to pledge to punish the perpetrators at the end of the war. There is also an assertion of a monolithic, homogenised understanding of how Britain responded, belying a more nuanced reality that British people responded in ways that were both fluid and at times contradictory and conflicting.

The creation of the UK Holocaust Memorial Foundation (UKHMF) in 2015 provides a specific lens through which such discourses can be viewed. Founded to deliver the recommendations of the Prime Minister's Holocaust Commission, the UKHMF has oversight for the construction of a new memorial and learning centre. Revealingly, the memorial is intended to 'stand beside Parliament as a permanent statement of our

British values' (Prime Minister's Office, 2016). Yet some see such a juxtaposition as problematic. Tollerton (2017), for instance, sees the move as an attempt 'to empower a similarly reinvigorated view of Britain and its governance'. In the context of British values, he goes on to note how

> underlying the interface between 'British values' and public Holocaust memory is a fundamental point that, because of the side Britain fought on in World War II, remembrance of Nazi atrocities can appear to offer a moral clarity that ultimately bolsters national pride. Unlike other, messier aspects of British history (especially those concerned with colonialism and empire) a sacred site of Holocaust remembrance is ripe with potential to empower veneration of the state.
>
> (Tollerton 2017)

British Responses to the Holocaust in context: Pedagogy and practice

British Responses to the Holocaust is a teaching resource that attempts to navigate a sometimes uneasy pathway between calls for 'veneration of the state' and an historical record where veneration may be more difficult to justify. It takes as its point of departure knowledge and understandings that the 2016 UCL Centre research reveals students have about what Britain 'knew' and 'did' in response to the Holocaust (Foster *et al.* 2016).

The clearest overall indicator of these was provided by responses to the question 'What happened when the British government knew about the mass murder of the Jews?' contained within the national survey. This multiple choice question was accompanied by a selection of seven possible answers, and was responded to by 7,166 secondary students of all year groups. The answers selected by students provided a striking insight into their substantive knowledge of this topic. Across the age-range, the most popular response (34.4 per cent) was that Britain 'declared war on Germany'. Second to this was that Britain 'didn't know anything until the end of the war' (23.8 per cent). The most appropriate answer, from the seven options available, was that Britain pledged to 'punish the killers after the war'. However, this was chosen by only 6.7 per cent of all students. Of those who chose this option only 3.8 per cent were 'very confident' of their answer, with 68.7 per cent stating they were either not very confident or didn't know and just guessed.

Discussions in focus group interviews provided further insight. A number of students suggested Britain and the Allies did not know about the killings as they happened in remote locations and were kept secret, and that if they had known about it they would have acted sooner: 'if we did know we would have done something' (2016, 185) suggested one Year 12 student in a response that typified the views of many others. As the report highlighted, 'students typically had a limited and often erroneous understanding of Britain's role during the Holocaust' and 'did not have the necessary contextual information to accurately explain Britain's response to the Holocaust' (2016, 200).

These findings have various implications. Students do not seem to know or understand why Britain went to war, and they tend to either incorrectly attribute the role of saviour to Britain, or absolve it of responsibility. At root then, there is a disconnect between how students understand British responses to the Holocaust, and the actual historical record. Mediating this is the crucial role of teachers and their own levels of knowledge and understanding of this history. Misconceptions in the classroom are reflective of a complex range of contemporary popular cultural and political discourses – but this only further underlines the critical importance of educational interventions which can work towards challenging and complicating erroneous assumptions.

The findings from the 2016 national survey provide the primary context for the pedagogical approach of *British Responses to the Holocaust* which rests on a socially constructivist approach to teaching and learning and a focus on the use of original archival source material. Bauman (1989, vii–viii) encapsulates one of the key tenets of this resource when he describes how 'my image of the Holocaust was like a picture on the wall: neatly framed', which then over time changed to become 'a window, rather than a picture on the wall' in terms of exposing the complexity of the past and its construction. Bauman's metaphor mirrors the pedagogical approach taken here, which seeks to replace 'pictures' for 'windows' in the way that Jenkins (2003, 7) sees history as 'being about, but categorically different from, the past', where describing the past is fundamentally about illuminating the present. As Kaiser and Salmons (2016, 101) note, this is where an interrogation of the sources is intended 'to allow students' own meanings to emerge out of that encounter with the past, rather than using the past to teach predetermined lessons'.

A key part of this construction involves working with primary source documents from a range of different archives located in England that articulate different voices and realms of knowledge that existed in

Britain through the course of the Second World War, be it the Foreign Office (The National Archives), Churchill himself (The Churchill Archives), Jewish immigrant communities (The Wiener Library and the Ben Uri Gallery), or the British public (Mass Observation). The intention is that students will move from a notion of a homogenised, unified conception of Britain's reaction, towards gaining a more differentiated understanding of what British responses there were, how they changed and interacted, and what, if anything, they meant. To do this whilst the research focuses exclusively on the response of the British government, *British Responses* also tries to illustrate how this intersects with other segments of British society.

A central feature of *British Responses to the Holocaust* has been its focus on developing student knowledge and understanding by revealing important information at key moments. As events unfold chronologically, information through primary sources is layered, prompting students to confirm or re-evaluate previous thinking. However, there are potential dangers here that teachers need to be aware of, such as the need to divert students away from thinking that events the sources describe were in some way predestined. It is intended that the teacher needs to play a key role in developing students' conceptual understanding both of evidence and of change and continuity.

In the spirit of research-informed practice, *British Responses to the Holocaust* starts with the same question in the student survey. This is to unpack student's existing knowledge and understanding of British responses, and enable teachers to calibrate their support for students appropriately as the lesson progresses. In a blind vote students respond to the question by choosing one of seven options. At the end of voting the responses are collated into a combined 'class vote' to synthesise how they thought the government responded, which is then shown to them for comment.

With the survey question duly framed as an enquiry question, the notion of 'British responses' is problematised through a juxtaposition of two historical sources that seem paradoxical. One of these is the declaration from a British soldier involved in the liberation of Bergen-Belsen on 15 April 1945 that while Nazi atrocities had previously been 'whispers . . . *now I know* what we had been fighting for'. Set against this is another source: Eden's 'Allied Declaration' speech to the House of Commons in December 1942, with its statement that there were 'reliable reports . . . of Hitler's oft repeated intention to exterminate the Jewish people of Europe'. Students are invited to speculate on why realms of knowledge of the unfolding genocide might have seemed widespread in late 1942, yet paradoxically not prevalent amongst British soldiers in 1945.

In the main section of the lesson students examine a range of archival sources showcasing various British responses. Drawing from a range of different institutions such as the National Archives, the Wiener Library and Mass Observation, this material complicates the notion of a monolithic singular 'British' response by presenting a medley of different voices in different contexts from different quarters across British society. In small groups students are provided with envelopes containing large A3 cards with a source related to the enquiry question on it, as well as a smaller A5 envelope with some contextual information about the source.

Following the main activity, students end by reflecting on where their new knowledge has taken them. First, they return to the original survey question, with teachers encouraging students to consider Churchill's statement to the House of Commons of 8 December 1942, that 'when the hour of liberation strikes in Europe, as strike it will, it will also be the hour of retribution' (Churchill Archives 1942). Second, students reflect on the earlier juxtaposition of narratives from British soldiers after the liberation of Bergen-Belsen with Eden's 'Allied Declaration' to the House of Commons, contemplating how new knowledge may cast a different light on such an apparent paradox. Finally, teachers open up space for students to reflect on broader issues which have been animated by this investigation: the ways sources may be problematised; wider issues that the sources generate that might connect past with present; and further questions students may wish to ask about how narratives of British responses to the Holocaust are constructed.

Piloting and development

In the process of developing this resource, different aspects of it were trialled with a variety of teachers and students in different parts of the country. These consisted of a Year 9 class in a mixed secondary school in the South of England in July 2016 (A); a teacher residential at the Wiener Library in October 2017 (B); a teacher Continuing Professional Development (CPD) session in a school in the North of England in December 2017 (C); a Year 9 class in a mixed secondary school in South-East England in January 2017 (D); a teacher CPD session in a school in North-East England in March 2017 (E); and a Year 9 class from a mixed comprehensive school in the Midlands in May 2017 (F). It is acknowledged that this is a small-scale investigation: as a consequence, whilst more general conclusions may be elusive, there are initial, tentative directions in which the data points. In particular these coalesce around how students understand the present through the lens of the past, and how they understand constructions of self and national identity, informed as they are by contemporary notions of 'British values'.

Student responses

In student pilot studies, all groups were presented with the student survey question. In school F, initial responses took two positions: one holding that the government didn't know anything, and the other that the government did know about the unfolding genocide but faced pragmatic, logistical barriers to helping that rendered intervention futile. It is interesting that both these positions constructed a benign view of Britain's role. Jack, for instance, declared 'I said that I don't think the government knew anything because I assumed if they knew they'd have done something' (F: 50–1). The use of 'assumed' is revealing here, seeming to indicate a belief in inherent benevolence or government actions being underpinned by well-intentioned motives.

William agreed with Jack, and went further in providing some contextual factors to explain why the British government wouldn't have helped:

> Same with me. Because it was quite hard to get to, because obviously we're quite an isolated country; it was quite hard to get from France, because I was thinking of Dunkirk and D-Day and events like that. And it was hard to get to Germany if it wasn't by plane. So we couldn't really shut down the camps anywhere else, apart from liberating through France.
>
> (F: 52–5)

However, William also seemed to be saying something different to Jack in trying to justify why pragmatically, to his understanding, Britain couldn't have helped, rather than saying the British government had no knowledge of the genocide. The difference may be the result of wider contextual knowledge of the war, as references to Dunkirk and D-Day and 'liberating through France' suggest. It was apparent in the UCL Centre's 2016 research that often when students were able to integrate wider contextual knowledge to their understandings, their explanatory accounts tended to be more rigorous. It could be that the same sort of process was being repeated here. George reiterated this position, saying 'The government did know but they couldn't really control the actions that were going on' (F: 57). The only divergence from these two positions came from Olivia, who was the only student to acknowledge that the best answer was 'they wanted to focus all their efforts on, you know, fighting the war and so they wanted to deal with it afterwards' (F: 70–1).

Mark, in focus group A, gave voice to what most students described as a sense of confusion in trying to reconcile the knowledge he assumed the government had, and their subsequent apparent lack of action:

> I thought they must have known really because it was such a massive event. I thought they must have known but then if they'd known then they must have done something about it so it was a bit confusing as to why they didn't do that.
>
> (A: 96–8)

Especially revealing were responses students gave when asked to reflect on how their views had changed on how the British government responded having completed the lesson. In focus group F they unanimously declared, like Olivia, that 'they [the British government] definitely knew' (F: 82), showing that the original survey option that the British government 'didn't know anything until the end of the war' was inaccurate. When pressed on what was then done with this information however, the nuances in student accounts, sometimes subtle and sometimes more flagrant, seemed to suggest something more complex. Jack, for instance, exemplified the position some students held that there was a fluidity in the government's approach, where

> They planned to attack or punish the Nazis after the war, but at first they ignored it – only the government knew, as they wanted to protect the British citizens, well, I think, to keep the morale high. Because if morale dropped Hitler could have had an advantage on us.
>
> (F: 85–7)

Jack's qualification of Britain's expressed intention to punish the perpetrators after the war is noteworthy for its coexistence with an understanding of 'wilful ignorance'; a benign interpretation of the British government's intentions to strategically withhold information of the unfolding genocide to bolster morale. To defend this further, William went on to support Jack's position, offering the explanation:

> We just ignored it. We couldn't. . . . We didn't ignore it because we're selfish, we just ignored it because we couldn't do anything. . . . It's not that we wanted to agree with Hitler and him persecuting the Jews because we're not like that. We were allied with the people who were fighting the Nazis, so we couldn't have done anything about it.
>
> (F: 89–94)

Particularly intriguing is the way William constructs his defence of Britain's position. Three things seem salient: William's repeated use of the word 'we'; the refutation that Britain ignored the unfolding genocide 'because we're selfish'; and the further moral distancing from the perpetrators in the phrase 'we're not like that'. In terms of classroom practice this highlights the need for teachers to be aware of the language students use in making sense of this history: understanding how students construct their accounts of the past may also help address any myths and misconceptions they may hold.

Firstly, William's use of the first person plural 'we' seems to signal an association of the self with nation, in terms of the kind of 'imagined' ways that Anderson (2006) talks of. It also seems to indicate William's sense of moral positioning with the nation he identifies with that conflates the past with present. In doing so, educators need to be aware that students may also reference contemporary events when learning about the past, and that these may mediate their understandings of the past.

Taking the use of 'we' further, William then explains the British government's lack of action as an inability to pragmatically do anything, rather than 'because we're selfish'. It could be argued here that he is trying to construct a rationale for British responses that seems morally acceptable and comforting. The contention that 'we couldn't do anything' is problematic, though. Whilst acknowledging that there were contingent logistical complexities around rescuing Jews in wartime, both the Evian Conference of 1938 and the Bermuda Conference of 1943 offered clear opportunities to rescue at least some Jews. William's claim then lacks contextual knowledge and understanding that leads him to construct a reductive misconception of British responses.

Finally, William's idea that 'we're not like that' can be seen as a form of in-group identification that seeks to draw distinct lines between behaviours that are acceptable and those that are not. It could be argued, however, that it implicitly obscures more than it reveals: if the British response is not one of 'persecuting the Jews', then neither necessarily is it its implicit antithesis that all was done to explicitly rescue them. William's use of the term 'we' in identifying with British responses to the Holocaust also refers to assumptions of what it is to 'do' History in terms of how 'all History is a conversation between past and present' (Lawson 2010, 9). I argue that it goes further here in being less of a present-past dialogue and more of a conflation of identities; both between self-and-other, and now-and-then.

There are also resonances in how William's use of language reflects Billig's (1995, 29) notion of 'banal nationalism', where 'the creation of a national hegemony often involves a hegemony of language'. Here, Billig's contention that 'common-sense' assumptions that nationalism, and identification with the nation, are seen in some way as being 'natural' and embedded in everyday language as a response to political motivations seems compelling. So when William says 'we just ignored it' or 'we're not like that', teachers need to be aware that the use of such language is far from 'natural', and that the relationship between student and nation, in both the past and present, is complex. In particular, how students may tend to conflate or analogise issues around British responses and contemporary accounts of issues such as displacement, refugees and immigration need to be handled carefully to avoid slippage into all-encompassing, reductive understandings, whilst at the same time using opportunities in the classroom to explore contemporary settings of historical themes.

The moral positioning of students in relation to government action also emerges in more ambivalent constructions of British identity. This emerged in a focus group of Year 9 students in a school A where, in response to the Riegner Telegram, Helen suggested:

> There is no harm in saying what they did was bad I mean, cause we . . . I know we had hindsight but we worked out what the document meant with very few prompts within a lesson so I think that if there was some scrutiny over what the British government did it would have helped. So if you look at it from both sides, we are not saying oh the British government is great, oh it's amazing.
>
> (A: 113–17)

Helen's adoption of a more critical stance toward British policy suggests the substantive knowledge that can be derived from archival sources may become a tool to interrogate British responses, rather than just affirm them. Whilst she refers to a specific source, the opportunity to consider a range of sources which cumulatively provide alternative, and at times conflicting, narratives of British responses, creates opportunities to reflect and construct different narratives. It is in such spaces, and the way they relate past and present, that hold the capacity to disrupt more fixed, hegemonic narratives of British responses. However, realising these potential explorations requires teacher intervention. It cannot be presumed that a disruptive space will necessarily be understood and processed as such by students, who will then move forward towards refining and recalibrating their thinking. Indeed, without teacher interventions some students may even refute the new or alternative information as incorrect for how it challenges or does not conform to their understandings. This raises pedagogic issues for teachers: a need to gauge where student knowledge and understanding is at different points in the lesson, and identify and challenge the misconceptions they may hold. It also means that while students may have ownership of their own learning and the construction of knowledge, this yet needs to be mitigated by teachers to avoid a relativism where all constructions are seen as equally valid.

Another interesting aspect that emerged from student focus group responses was how the intersection between the British government and the British public was understood by them as they considered the historical sources. Leo, for instance, from school F, commented that:

> I think that the government would have done something if the majority of the people had believed them. Because they didn't, they didn't have full support which would have ended up with, like Kyle said, low morale, lower morale, which could have allowed Germany to take advantage of that.
>
> (F: 103–5)

George felt that 'the British public I think knew what was happening, but they couldn't do anything to control it because they had nothing to do with it' (F: 148–9).

Three key aspects of Leo's and George's comments appear significant: a tentativeness in the language used by both students; a seeming lack of clarity over how much the British public knew of what was happening; and a contemporary semblance of Wasserstein's (1988, 356) notion of both physical and psychological distance as having a 'disinhibiting effect'.

Leo's way of understanding government inertia was to explain it in terms of a sense of public disbelief in what they were being told. This reflected how some students attempted to resolve the paradox between Eden's Allied Declaration and the sorts of narratives that emerged from British soldiers liberating Bergen-Belsen in 1945, whose literal confrontation with the 'traumatic' (Reilly *et al.* 1997) conditions of the camp provided a visceral sense of an aspect of the Holocaust that up to then hadn't been encountered in such starkness. Some students felt that whilst Eden may have spelt out the Nazi intention to exterminate the Jews of Europe in 1942, it wasn't until the British eyewitness evidence from the liberation of Bergen-Belsen that disbelief turned to a more unsettling confrontation with the reality of such camps. George's comment that the British public were aware of what was happening yet were in a sense distanced from it seems to deny them an agency that other sources suggest: a public protest at the Royal Albert Hall on 29 October 1942, to express outrage at the atrocities, and Eleanor Rathbone's 'Rescue the Perishing' pamphlet call-to-action from June 1943, being two such examples.

Student responses, then, reveal a complex interaction between notions of identity and identification with the nation, ways of explaining British responses in light of historical archival records, and affective reactions. It is argued here that when teachers are conscious of and acknowledge such student constructions and responses, deeper understandings of this history are made more possible through an appreciation of the constructed nature in the present of narratives of the past.

Teacher responses

At times the potential cognitive disruption created by the sources produced affective responses that revealed a sense of discomfort amongst teachers. After reading the Riegner Telegram Karl, a Head of History, declared 'I'm a historian, I'm reading this, and I feel ashamed' (E). His response showed the affect it had on him of realising that the British government clearly had knowledge on 10 August 1942, of the plan for all Jews in countries controlled or occupied by Germany to 'be at one blow exterminated', as well as the identification he felt with the response of the British government, the shame felt on behalf of the actions of others in the past.

Amongst teacher groups in particular there seemed to be a sense of heaviness and internalisation towards the end of the session around what the sources seemed to imply. Some of these were observed by my colleague, Eleni Karayianni, in her field notes. Whilst observing a session with teachers in school B for instance, Karayianni described how

> One teacher commented that the specific focus on the British response, instead of everybody else's response, could suggest that the British were somehow to blame for the Holocaust. So, perhaps it would be useful to include a little bit about how other countries responded to the Holocaust.
>
> (C: 76–9)

Further, she noted that

> They also felt that the lesson ends quite negatively and it would be good to add something on 'Jewish life in Britain after the war' and to talk about stories of survivors who came in Britain after liberation ('the Boys' for example).
>
> (C: 82–4)

This urge to shift the focus from Britain both spatially and temporally could be seen to be a call to contextualise British responses alongside those of other countries, possibly to enable a better understanding of, or even to allow for a more informed judgement on, Britain's role. It could also be seen as an apparent desire to mitigate negative portrayals of the British government at the time in order to, in a sense, 'redress the balance'. Yet this is something some historians are wary of, a number of whom see explanations for the actions of the British government as being many and interlinked, rather than the more monocausal explanations teachers tended to articulate around the government's perceived lack of knowledge of the unfolding genocide. Gilbert (2001, 341), for instance, in speaking of the Allied response in a more general sense, describes how whilst the story of the negative Allied response to many of the Jewish appeals for help was one of a lack of comprehension in the face of the 'unbelievable', concludes the story is ultimately one of 'many failures'. Speaking specifically of the British response, Wasserstein (1988, 345) also suggests multiple reasons for British inaction, including the British government's 'imaginative failure to grasp the full meaning of the consequences of decisions', the 'low priority' accorded to Jews in the context of the war effort, and the spatial notion of how 'distance had a disinhibiting effect' (Wasserstein 1988: 356). In light of this, his ultimate assessment is damning: 'there is', he writes, 'little to celebrate in this account of British policy towards the Jews of Europe between 1939 and 1945' (1988, 345).

Although the sample was fairly small, some teacher responses tended to show a sense of needing to frame British responses in a more benign light, primarily in the interest of perceived 'balance'. It should also be remembered that students' knowledge and understanding will be impacted by how far teachers are able to identify and address issues within their own knowledge and understanding of such issues, which if left unaddressed will inevitably have a negative impact on their teaching. It is argued here that this also develops beyond ideas of knowledge and understanding, as teachers' comments at times also reflected broader paradigms of thought and belief, be they reflective of more benign or critical views of British responses.

Conclusions

Three implications of the development of *British Responses to the Holocaust* and data collected from fieldwork from it warrant particular remark: the dialectic between past and present that emerges from student accounts; the political, tied up as it is with notions of personal and national identity; and the current discourse of 'British values' and their pedagogical implications for teacher practice. None of these areas is discrete: all intersect and inform each other with the notion of affect, for instance, interplaying between all three.

Firstly, a number of student accounts reveal a sense of conflating past and present, especially in ways relating to moral positioning. The idea expressed, for example, that 'we're not like that' when comparing the British with Nazis suggests an atemporal stance that sees moral positions in terms of national identity, and as being binary and unwavering. It can also be seen in Mbembe's (2001, 14) notion of temporal 'entanglement' which acknowledges the difficulties in navigating 'the complex interaction of pasts, presents and imagined futures' (Mirzoeff 2009, 127).

Secondly, this also has political implications. In the more specific context of History education, this is encapsulated in Seixas's view (2000, 21) of how such 'entanglement' is ultimately a contested political terrain, where what is fought over is 'the power of the past to define who we are in the present, our relations with others, relations in civil society . . . and broad parameters for action in the future'. Taking a wider view, Connerton (1989, 2) sees this as an intrinsic aspect of a dialectic between past and present, where in attempting to construct a narrative of national identity, 'our experience of the present very much depends on our knowledge of the past'. Yet this knowledge has a political hue. When Rieff (2016, 23) asks, 'must we deform the past to preserve it?', student and teacher reactions to *British Responses to the Holocaust* suggest a tension between the uncovering of different narratives of British responses and notions of the way truth and the past can be manipulated for a range of ends. Brotherton's observation that 'we build a fortress of positive information around our beliefs, and we rarely step outside – or even peek out of the window' hints at an instance of 'positive test strategy' (cited in D'Ancona 2017) where we look for what we expect to find. So when we find what we don't expect, either a form of wilful amnesia descends, or feelings of discomfort and, as revealed in this study, of 'shame' emerge.

Thirdly, such feelings also become problematic when set in the context of 'British values'; of how such values as 'tolerance', 'individual liberty', and 'democracy' (Department for Education 2014) sit in British schools, especially as the teaching of them has become mandatory. Issues of tolerance, for instance, could be said to sit uncomfortably with evidence of British reluctance to aid Jewish immigration at the Bermuda Conference, ironically at the same time as the start of the Warsaw Ghetto Uprising on 9 April 1943. Questions therefore arise over the choices made, and who makes them, as to what is remembered of Britain's role. It raises questions of why, for instance, stories of the *Kindertransport* programme gain such cultural appeal and traction in Britain, at the expense of the failures of the Bermuda Conference. It raises questions of which stories we are wanting to remember, and which to forget. Lawson (2017) goes so far as to argue that the sorts of misconceptions students hold about the Holocaust, as highlighted in the 2016 student survey, are as a consequence of the dominant culture of Holocaust remembrance in the UK. If we prefer to tell comforting stories that vindicate the British role, then questions need to be asked about what the implications of this are. When Amanda Spielman, as Chief Inspector of OFSTED, the English schools' inspectorate system, declared that 'pupils should learn how we became the country we are today and how our values make us a beacon of liberalism, tolerance and fairness' (cited in Bulman 2017), how this can be reconciled in the classroom with feelings of 'shame' that were articulated in this research is moot.

The research data also points to four key findings for teacher pedagogy. Firstly, it is argued here that for students to understand ideas around British responses to the Holocaust as being constructed in the present, as being fluid and always under construction both in and beyond the classroom, constitutes a more sophisticated way of seeing the past than more static, hegemonic accounts. The aim is to move towards a more robust understanding of British responses that is complex and nuanced: for students to see that different accounts of Britain's role exist, whether at the time in the strategic justification of winning the war first and then punishing the perpetrators, especially in the triumphalism of 1945 and its immediate aftermath, or more contemporary historians who are left with a 'profoundly saddening impression' (Wasserstein 1988, 345) of Britain's actions. This is especially so when students are able to start to see how the past is constructed by different people at different times for different purposes.

Secondly, *British Responses to the Holocaust* is designed to open a landscape and dialogue that aims to rethink dominant political and cultural narratives about the role Britain played. In this it attempts to develop an appreciation of complexity, where many of the questions around British responses are contingent on issues of who knew what, when, and the options available to them for action in a constantly shifting context of war. In this sense, the idea that, as Foster *et al.* note, 'a study of the past can provide straightforward "lessons" for the present is problematic for a number of reasons' (Foster *et al.* 2016, 220) is of significance. This resource is rather designed to open a space for critical thinking founded on historical sources to offer alternative considerations of British responses rather than teaching predetermined lessons.

In rethinking dominant cultural narratives, London (2000, 273) directly refers to what she terms 'a number of myths: that refugee policy was more humane than it was; that Britain put no limits on aid to persecuted Jews; or even that Britain has never turned its back on genuine refugees'. A number of student and teacher comments seem ready to paint a more benign picture of British policy in these respects; be it looking at the stories of survivors who came to Britain or looking at how other Allied countries responded. Seixas (2000) opens up the idea that this past-present relationship has potentially interesting curricular implications when the question is asked 'Should pupils themselves directly study ways in which their own, present subjective contexts shape interpretation of the past?' (Counsell *et al.* 2016, 84). With so much written of the symbolic relationship between past and present, it seems hard not to avoid thinking about how their own positioning effects their interpretation of events.

Thirdly, language used in the classroom such as 'we're not like that' can be slippery and problematic, excluding as it includes, but yet which can potentially be used as a reflective tool to help students consider the construction of identity and its implications. Considerations of who the 'we' refers to open up issues of inclusion and exclusion. The case of Ludwig Neumann, which students read about in one of the historical sources, is instructive here. Ludwig was a German-Jewish industrialist who ultimately fled to Britain after his textile factory was requisitioned by the Nazis. Interned in a camp on the Isle of Man as an enemy alien, Ludwig later fought in the war for the British, operating anti-aircraft guns. His story raises issues of who are included and who excluded in constructions of national identity, and so who is meant by the 'we' that students identify with.

Fourthly, when the proclaimed record of Britain as a 'beacon of liberalism, tolerance and fairness' is greeted with feelings of shame, this has implications for the classroom and beyond in how responses such as this can be acknowledged. As this research shows, this sense of friction and unease with discomforting national narratives has affective implications for both teachers and students: they may be embraced, evoking feelings of shame or guilt, or rebuked through more benign interpretations of British responses. Confronted with conflicted and 'difficult' histories, both students and teachers show themselves often caught in a cognitive gap in the way historical sources indicate narratives other than those they feel comfortable and familiar with. Psychologically, this seems to have the potential to limit the ability of students and teachers to absorb the true implications of what they are confronted with. This at times plays out in their affective responses, expressed in terms of emotions such as shame, guilt and confusion. How such responses are accounted for in the classroom is prescient in the current time as Britain engages with contemporary issues of displacement, refugees and immigration.

References

Anderson, B. 2006. *Imagined Communities: Reflections on the origin and spread of nationalism*. Rev. ed. London: Verso.

Bauman, Z. 1989. *Modernity and the Holocaust*. Cambridge: Polity Press.

Billig, M. 1995. *Banal Nationalism*. London: Sage.

Bulman, M. 2017. 'Schools must teach British values, says head of OFSTED', *The Independent*, 23 September. Online. https://www.independent.co.uk/news/uk/home-news/schools-teach-british-values-ofsted-amanda-spielman-a7962706.html

Cesarani, D. 2016. *Final Solution: The fate of the Jews 1933–49*. London: Macmillan.

Churchill Archives Centre. 1942. *Churchill's speaking notes for the House of Commons, 18th September–10th December, 1942.*CHAR 9/156A. Churchill College, Cambridge.

Connerton, P. 1989. *How Societies Remember*. Cambridge: Cambridge University Press.

Counsell, C., Burn, K. and Chapman, A. (eds) 2016. *Masterclass in History Education: Transforming teaching and learning*. London: Bloomsbury.

Department for Education. 2014. *Guidance on promoting British valuesin schools published*. Published 27th November, 2014. Online. https://www.gov.uk/government/news/guidance-on-promoting-british-values-in-schools-published

D'Ancona, M. 2017. *Post-Truth: The new war on truth and how to fight back*. London: Ebury Press.
Eden, A. 1942. *The Joint Declaration by Members of the United Nations Against Extermination of the Jews*. Hansard. HC Dec.17 Vol 385 cc2082-7.
Foreign Office. 1942. *From Berne to Foreign Office (aka the Riegner Telegram)* 11 August 1942, The National Archives: FO 371–30917.
Foster, S.J., Pettigrew, A., Pearce, A., Hale, R., Burgess, A., Salmons, P. and Lenga, R.-A. 2016. *What Do Students Know and Understand about the Holocaust? Evidence from English secondary schools*. London: UCL Institute of Education.
Gilbert, M. 2001. *Auschwitz and the Allies*. London: Pimlico.
Jenkins, K. 2003. *Re-Thinking History*. London: Routledge Classics.
Kaiser, W. and Salmons, P. 2016. 'Encountering the Holocaust through primary documents'. In *Essentials of Holocaust Education: Fundamental issues and approaches*, edited by Samuel Totten and Stephen Feinberg. New York: Routledge.
Karpf, A. 2002. 'We've Been Here Before'. *The Guardian*, 8 June. Online. https://www.theguardian.com/uk/2002/jun/08/immigration.immigrationandpublicservices (accessed 24 March 2020).
Kushner, T. 1994. *The Holocaust and the Liberal Imagination: A social and cultural history*. Oxford: Blackwell.
Lawson, T. 2010. *Debates on the Holocaust*. Manchester: Manchester University Press.
Lawson, T. 2017. 'Britain's promise to forget: Some historiographical reflections on *What do students know and understand about the Holocaust?*' *Holocaust Studies* 23 (3): 345–63.
London, L. 2000. *Whitehall and the Jews 1933–48: British immigration policy and the Holocaust*. Cambridge: Cambridge University Press.
Mbembe, A. 2001. *On the Postcolony*. Berkeley: University of California Press.
Mirzoeff, N. 2009. *An Introduction to Visual Culture*. 2nd ed. London: Routledge.
Prime Minister's Holocaust Commission Report. 2015. *Britain's Promise to Remember*. Online. https://assets.publishing.service.gov.uk/government/uploads/system/uploads/attachment_data/file/398645/Holocaust_Commission_Report_Britains_promise_to_remember.pdf
Prime Minister's Office press release. 2016. 'PM: Holocaust memorial will stand beside Parliament as permanent statement of our British values'. Online.https://www.gov.uk/government/news/pm-holocaust-memorial-will-stand-beside-parliament-as-permanent-statement-of-our-british-values
Reilly, J., Cesarani, D., Kushner, T. and Richmond, C. (eds) 1997. *Belsen in History and Memory*. London: Frank Cass.
Rieff, D. 2016. *In Praise of Forgetting: Historical memory and its ironies*. New Haven, CT: Yale University Press.
Sharf, A. 1964. *The British Press and Jews Under Nazi Rule*. London: Oxford University Press.
Seixas, P. 2000. 'Schweigen! die Kinder! Or, does postmodern history have a place in the schools?'In *Knowing Teaching and Learning History: National and international perspectives*, edited by Peter Stearns, Peter Seixas and Sam Wineburg. New York: New York. University Press.
Tollerton, D. 2017. 'The Problem with London's new Holocaust memorial', *The Conversation*. Online. http://theconversation.com/the-problem-with-londons-new-holocaust-memorial-86411 (accessed 15 February 2020).
Wasserstein, B. 1988. *Britain and the Jews of Europe, 1939–1945*. Oxford: Oxford University Press.

7

'I know it's not really true, but it might just tell us . . .': The troubled relationship between *The Boy in the Striped Pyjamas* and understanding about the Holocaust

Darius Jackson

Introduction

It is hard to overstate the popularity of John Boyne's novel for young adults *The Boy in the Striped Pyjamas*, not just as an English language novel, but as an international phenomenon. The book, which tells the story of a friendship between two boys, one the German son of a Nazi camp commandant and the other a Jewish inmate, has sold over 9 million copies globally. It has been translated into over 39 languages and in 2007 and 2008 it was the bestselling novel in Spain. The novel has won awards in Ireland and Spain as well as being shortlisted for awards in Great Britain, Italy, Belgium and Germany. In 2008 it was made into a very successful feature film, distributed by Miramax, with screenplay and directing by Mark Herman. The film was released in Britain on 12 September 2008 and went on to be nominated for awards in Great Britain, Spain, Ireland and the USA, earning 44.1 million US dollars over the next three years. As Pearce describes it, this novel, and film was 'a cultural and educational phenomenon . . . popular with young and old . . . [which] found its way into school departments and classrooms' (Pearce 2014, 228). As such, it has introduced a whole generation of children worldwide to the

Holocaust. Yet the novel has a troubled relationship with many historians and educators who share concern regarding its impact on readers' knowledge and understanding of this history.

The Boy in the Striped Pyjamas is the most commonly read book, of any type, about the Holocaust amongst school children in England. In the UCL Centre for Holocaust Education's student study (Foster *et al.* 2016), 43 per cent of students said they had read books about the Holocaust, and of this number 74.8 per cent said they had read *The Boy in the Striped Pyjamas*. Figures for the film were even higher: 76.2 per cent of students said they had watched a film about the Holocaust, and of them a staggering 84.4 per cent had seen the film (Foster *et al.* 2016, 90). The horizontal striped imagery of the book cover is so well known that it also appears on some editions of Boyne's later book *The Boy at the Top of the Mountain* (Boyne 2015). It is there as a small reproduction of the striped cover of the book and the words 'From the author of '*The Boy in the Striped Pyjamas*'.

The Boy in the Striped Pyjamas also seems to be quite a simple tale, a quality which is emphasised as it is also written from the perspective of a child. Bruno, the nine-year-old German boy, meets Shmuel, a Polish Jewish boy who coincidently shares the same birthday. They become friends and agree to go on an adventure together. They set out to discover what has happened to Shmuel's father. Bruno, now disguised as an inmate of the camp, which is run by his father, goes to help his friend. However, they are driven into a gas chamber and murdered by the camp guards. Bruno's family mourn for him as their glittering life unravels around them.

The novel is not an attempt at Gillian Rose's famous thought experiment in which she asks could we make a film 'which follows the life story of a member of the SS in all its pathos, so that we empathise with him, identify with his hopes and fears, disappointments and rage, so that when it comes to killing . . . wanting him to get what he wants' (Rose 1996, 50). In Boyne's book we do not revel in the career or status of Bruno's father nor approve of his role in running a camp during the Second World War. Boyne is writing a story that is intended to show us that genocide is wrong. The book apparently has a simple moral message and a commitment to remembering the victims of the Holocaust.

Yet despite these good intentions, its popularity, and commercial success, the novel has been dogged by controversy. David Cesarani has been critical of the historical inaccuracies in the book (Cesarani 2008) whilst in Austria, Breit and Hilmar are critical of Bruno's innocence and his total lack of real interest in the world (Breit and Hilmar n.d.). The

Holocaust Educational Trust, a major Holocaust education organisation in Britain, goes so far as to accuse the novel of inauthenticity, arguing that authentic works are 'informed by some knowledge and understanding of the Holocaust and attempt to be relatively faithful to the historical reality. For these reasons, the Trust does not recommend the use of John Boyne's *The Boy in the Striped Pyjamas*, despite its popularity in schools' (Holocaust Educational Trust n.d., 12).

That a controversy surrounds a novel about the Holocaust really should come as no surprise to us; literature about the Holocaust is invariably the subject of controversy (Bernstein 1994; Budick 2015; Eaglestone 2004; Franklin 2011; Vice 2000). The actual controversies about particular Holocaust-based novels do vary (Vice 2000), but for *The Boy in the Striped Pyjamas* the focus is around the inaccuracies within the narrative and the implausibility of the major storyline.

Why is literature about the Holocaust prone to controversy?

Aside from the content of *The Boy in the Striped Pyjamas*, the very idea of a work of art being based on the Holocaust is controversial. Theodor Adorno set out the argument clearly when discussing Arnold Schoenberg's composition *Survivor of Warsaw*, and it is worth quoting him at length:

> [B]y turning suffering into images, harsh and uncompromising though they are . . . these victims are used to create something, works of art, that are thrown to the consumption of a world which destroyed them. The so-called artistic representation of the sheer physical pain of people beaten to the ground by rifle-butts contains, however remotely, the power to elicit enjoyment out of it. The moral of this art, not to forget for a single instant, slithers into the abyss of its opposite [as] an unthinkable fate appear[s] to have had some meaning; it is transfigured, something of its horror is removed. This alone does an injustice to the victims; yet no art which tried to evade them could confront the claim of justice. . . . Works of less than the highest rank are also willingly absorbed as contributions to clearing up the past. When genocide becomes part of the cultural heritage in the themes of committed literature, it becomes easier to play along with the culture which gave birth to murder.
>
> (Adorno 1977, 189)

Adorno sees the danger as the normalising of the events of the Holocaust through works of art. In this way the events become merely the context of a work produced to entertain or, at best, to be, in Bernstein's phrase, part of a 'culture of redemption' (1994, 43), suggesting some form of closure along the lines of 'we have learnt from this atrocity and now we will remember it'.

Bernstein (1994) is unconvinced by Adorno's arguments and suggests that it is wrong of Adorno to set himself the role of saying what counts as an injustice towards the victims of the Holocaust. He goes on to point out that if the stories of the Holocaust are not told then the victims of the Holocaust will become forgotten. He also considers that reliance upon the oral testimony of survivors itself creates an injustice in the prioritising of one voice, one experience over the majority of Holocaust victims who did not survive. This idea is also present in Primo Levi (1988) and is a central theme in the introduction to Cesarani's last book *Final Solution* (2016). There are subtle differences, though. Bernstein confronts the issue of the way testimony is mediated both by novelistic conventions as well as the individual's own personal context, whilst Cesarani is frustrated by the use of personal testimony to trump scholarship about the Holocaust and to tell redemptive stories of people getting over their trauma to live ordinary lives. What Bernstein does not appreciate is that the choice is not necessarily between choosing to write about the Holocaust and choosing to be silent. A more important contrast could be between scholarship that attempts to reveal the nature of the Holocaust, in an effort to reveal the alethic truth about the Holocaust by constructing an historical narrative of the events (Porpora 2015), as against writing that exploits the Holocaust as a backdrop for the narrative and message of the story, which in turn may popularise myths and misunderstandings of the actual events of the Holocaust.

Langer points out that as the Holocaust moves further into history, less knowledge about it can be taken for granted, suggesting that in the future we may need to ask 'how will readers react to the news that in a place called Auschwitz (footnote), garments are being deloused (another footnote) with Cyclon B (yet another footnote) which kills lice in clothing – and humans in gas chambers (will that one day require a footnote, too)?' (Langer 1995, 235). Langer is clearly emphasising the need for literature about the Holocaust to be historically accurate.

Sue Vice in *Holocaust Fiction* (2000) points out that where there is an expressed preference for testimony over literature this is a choice based on non-literary criteria, in this case a desire for the truth, rather than for original and innovative storytelling. This desire to read eyewitness testimony can lead readers to 'extinguish the critical faculty and retreat to a position of all accepting deference' (Franklin 2011, 11). Franklin refers to the Wilkomirski controversy, but could equally refer to the Demidenko case in Australia too. In the former, a piece of writing was published that claimed to be a memoir, and in the latter a family history, but in reality both were works of fiction (Jost *et al.* 1996). Vice goes on to consider why Holocaust fiction is so controversial: 'Holocaust fictions are scandalous: they invariably provoke controversy by inspiring repulsion and acclaim in equal measure. To judge by what many critics have to say, to write Holocaust fictions is tantamount to making a fiction of the Holocaust' (Vice 2000, 1).

Vice sets out a series of areas where controversy over Holocaust fictions seems to occur. The first relates to the extent the author uses other historical accounts of the Holocaust to give the novel accuracy and realism. If the author sticks too closely to historical accounts there can be accusations of plagiarism and the simple question 'where is the fiction?' Vice's second area of controversy is over the use of time and plot. We know the outcome of the story. We know that the European Jewish population were the victims of genocide, we know that 90 per cent of European Jewish children were murdered during the Holocaust and that in 1945 the Allies defeated the Nazis. Consequently we must beware back-shadowing this knowledge into the characters in the story. Whilst we know the outcome for the characters in a novel, for the victims of the Holocaust the events were almost incomprehensible, and this must be acknowledged within Holocaust fiction. Bernstein (1994), making a similar point, is devastating in his criticism of Appelfeld. In his novel *Badenheim 1939* Appelfeld (2005) wrote about the Jewish inhabitants of the spa town as if they should have seen what was coming, leaving the reader 'at least as angry at, as we are grieved by, the blindness of the characters' (Bernstein 1994, 62).

Historical fiction and historical understanding

One of the major reasons for criticisms of *The Boy in the Striped Pyjamas* is the series of historical errors in the book and (as explored below) the implausibility of key aspects of the plot. Some authors have written Holocaust-related novels that have little relation to the real events of history, such as Philip K Dick (1962) in *The Man in the High Castle* and Philip Roth (2004) in *The Plot against America.* Both novels deal with the events in an explicitly counterfactual way; the former in a post-war world where the Axis powers are victorious and the latter in an America where Franklin Delano Roosevelt was defeated by the fascist sympathiser Charles Lindbergh in the 1940 presidential elections. Neither of these books claims, or pretends, to be realist in their approach to the events, and this non-realist approach suggests support for Jenni Adams's claim that magic realism is a valid genre for writing about the Holocaust, as a 'strategy in attempts to continue the project of Holocaust representation into the post-testimonial era' (Adams 2011, 1).

The Boy in the Striped Pyjamas does not, however, offer a magic realist account, nor is it set in a parallel history. The last two sentences of the novel are clear that, 'Of course all this happened a long time ago and nothing like that could ever happen again. Not in this day and age' (Boyne 2006, 216). These lines could be read ironically; any reader with knowledge of post-war history would know that genocides and persecution continue to this day. The words also highlight that the events of the Holocaust actually did happen.

Of course people are not expected to read a novel and treat it as if it were a reliable, eyewitness account of historical events. Though novels can and do explore social and political issues, they are, as Budick argues eloquently in *The Subject of Holocaust Fiction* (2015), a form of entertainment. Consequently she is critical of writers who do not look upon Holocaust literature as first and foremost literature which 'cannot but prompt us to question our knowledge of the events, in a way that documentary and historical accounts do not and perhaps cannot, fiction also highlights the centrality of subjectivity . . . ' (Budick 2015, 3).

The relationship between historical understanding and literatures set in a specific historical context is complicated. Arthur Marwick is quick to point out 'Right off we can make one obvious point: a novel or a poem, if it is a source at all, is a source for the period in which it was written, not for the period about which it was written. In other words the novels of Sir Walter Scott may tell us a great deal about the early nineteenth century [but] . . . a novel such as Ivanhoe will not tell us much about the twelfth century' (Marwick 1981, 147). This suggests that Boyne's novel tells us more about the state of Holocaust awareness in Ireland at the start of the twenty-first century than it does about the Holocaust itself.

However, as Marwick accepts, historical literature seeps into historical understanding. An example of this is the 1978 television miniseries *The Holocaust*. Within Holocaust studies it is a commonplace to say that it triggered interest in the Holocaust as an event, and according to Levy and Sznaider it represented a 'major turning point in the media representation . . . of the Holocaust' (Gray 2014).

These popular cultural events are not simple bridgeheads into history, however. The ideas can and do provide the frameworks through which we construct our understanding of the past. Understanding of English history is also framed by ideas carried over from literature. This cross-fertilising of the past and fiction is a well-established phenomenon. For example the dynastic conflict between the House of Lancaster and the House of York between 1455 and 1487 is referred to as the War of the Roses, and has been called that for the last two centuries after Sir Walter Scott popularised the scene from Shakespeare's *Henry V Part I* in which a nobleman and a solicitor select different roses from the Inns of Court Temple Garden to show their support for different houses in the coming civil war. Such an event never took place outside of Shakespeare's play, but the dramatic power of the event has seared it into national consciousness and it has become a 'real' event. So here we have a case where the fiction is actually framing the period and at times being treated as a real event. Consequently we need to see how the readers interpret the events outlined in *The Boy in the Striped Pyjamas*, as fictional narrative or as something like historical reality, and ask how are themes from the novel informing the interpretations students make.

The Boy in the Striped Pyjamas

As part of the UCL Centre for Holocaust Education's 2016 study of student knowledge and understanding (discussed in fuller detail in earlier chapters), 44 students aged between 12 and 17 were invited to take part in a series of focus groups specifically designed to explore the impact of *The Boy in the Striped Pyjamas* film (Foster *et al.* 2016). Those chosen to take part had indicated that they had watched the film and thought they had a good memory of it.

The research showed that virtually all the students were aware this was a work of fiction, with 'only one participant believing that the film was based on a true story' (Foster *et al.* 2016, 91). However this does not fit with Gray's findings, albeit with a much smaller sample size. When he asked students whether the story was true, 'the majority of interviewees believed that it was based on a true story' (Gray 2014, 116). Gray goes on to describe an exchange where a boy comments that he was upset by watching the film when he was younger as he had thought it true, to which another replies 'It is true!' (Gray 2014, 116).

Where Gray's research and the UCL student study do coincide is in the way that students refer to the story as if it were true, so that the ideas of the film become tools used to construct meaning from studying the Holocaust. This can happen where students reference a scene in the film or a part of the book to support their understanding of the Holocaust or where ideas that have their genesis in the book are used to explain or organise the information. This acceptance that fictional narratives do tell us about the past clearly goes against Marwick's injunction but chimes with our experience of reading elements of history through the lenses of Shakespeare or Sir Walter Scott. It also means that any errors in the book are of real importance.

In *The Boy in the Striped Pyjamas* there are historical inaccuracies such as on page 73, where Bruno is planning to make a swing and he suggests to Lieutenant Kotler that he use a spare tyre 'from one of the jeeps'. Though this may seem perfectly reasonable, the reality is that the Wehrmacht did not use jeeps in the Second World War.[1] Whilst this may seem a simple mistake, it is also a simple mistake to avoid. More seriously there are mistakes about the level of security in the camp and weaknesses in plotting. The story relies on there being a single strand of barbed wire that a child could dig under and that Jewish children in the camp would be unsupervised and free to walk around. These errors are so obvious that Year 8 students, who had yet to study the Holocaust, pointed out that 'if Bruno can get under the fence, why can't the boy, the Jewish boy get under the fence as well?' (Foster *et al.* 2016, 91).

It is unclear what sort of camp it is where Bruno's father is commandant. The name used in the novel, 'Out-with', clearly implies Auschwitz, a death camp in occupied Poland, but the description of Jews seemingly unsupervised as they go about their lives suggests something closer to a prison camp whilst the work details suggest a slave labour camp. The commandant's house at the real Auschwitz is situated close to the camp rather than so far away it is difficult to work out what the buildings are. When Gretel and Bruno first see the camp, they are unsure whether it is a farm or some 'modern types of houses' or 'the countryside . . . this is where the people live and work and send all the food to feed us' (Boyne 2006, 33). However, Boyne denies that Out-with is modelled on any specific camp: 'I decided very early on that I did not want to write a novel specifically about Auschwitz or Dachau or any of the camps during that time; I wanted the camp that I created to represent the many death camps which the criminals created around Europe in the early 1940s' (Davies-Edwards 2007, 3). So this is a generic camp, even though the description of the camp has similarities with a labour camp (Boyne 2006, 36), but that only makes things complicated. By placing Shmuel in the hybrid camp the story is deeply inaccurate. The vast majority of

Jews were shot near to their homes, with public knowledge, or sent to specific killing sites to be murdered on arrival. They were not sent to concentration camps. Small boys were not given licence to wander about; they were murdered soon after arrival.

In a world where Holocaust denial is present, do writers have a heavier than usual responsibility to make the history accurate? Kokkola (2003) is emphatic that it does, but this is because of the need for the Holocaust to be seen as a real event in history rather than a general statement about the nature of literature written about the past. It must be borne in mind that a literary reconstruction as against an historical reconstruction of the Holocaust are made for very different purposes. The latter must remain faithful to the evidence and produce an accurate and plausible explanation, whilst the former can mould reality to fit the needs of their narrative or the author's own aims.

Following Vice's advice we need to consider the role of the narrator in the novel. Again this becomes a contentious area. Boyne writes that he 'felt close to my main character, Bruno. I liked his innocence, his charm, his naiveté, his friendliness' (Davies-Edwards 2007, 3). Ostensibly the book is written from Bruno's perspective. Vice (2005) makes a more general point about the child's voice in Holocaust literature when she argues that even though a child's voice can be used to narrate, it cannot be unmediated by other voices, 'particularly those of an adult narrator, editor, or even reader' (Vice 2005, 22). Such unmediated presentation of a child's voice can diminish it.

Bruno's naiveté, dear to Boyne, causes tensions within the story. His sister finds him frustrating when she tries to explain who Jews are and what the Jews are doing in the camp. The word 'Jew' is so new to Bruno he practises pronouncing the word and wonders if they are themselves Jews (Boyne 2006, 182). However the naïve view only works because the narrator knows better and leaves enough clues for an adult reader to infer deeper meanings from the text. One such point is about the relationship between Bruno's mother and Lieutenant Kotler. The paragraph in question is: 'whenever father was called away to Berlin on an overnight trip the lieutenant hung around the house as if he were in charge: he would be there when Bruno was going to bed and be back again in the morning before he even woke up' (Boyne 2006, 163). The relationship is implied later in the book when Kotler is transferred elsewhere 'very suddenly and there had been a lot of shouting between Father and Mother about it [Kotler's transfer] late at night' (Boyne 2006, 178).

Whilst it would be quite reasonable to accept the child might not spot that his mother has a younger lover, it is harder to accept some of the other tricks the narrator is given in the body of the story all highlighting Bruno's innocence, such as Bruno not knowing what his father actually did as a job but knowing 'he had a fantastic uniform' (Boyne 2006, 5). Bruno's inability to recognise the word Führer (German for leader) is unlikely even though the error works perfectly in English as the term Bruno uses, Fury, is similar in sound, a classic malapropism. However Bruno did not speak English; he was a German-speaking child and the German word for fury is *wut* whilst furious is *wutend*. It could work if the term were referring to the classical Greek deities who persecute wrong-doers as *Griechische Furien* is the term for the Greek Furies. However the idea that a nine year old would mishear the word for leader and replace it with the word for a group of classical Greek deities is implausible to say the least. This situation is further exacerbated when in the German translation (Boyne 2007) the word *Furor* is used when referring to the Führer.

At least as implausible is the idea that Shmuel does not know why his father has disappeared. His father was with him on the Monday, then went to carry out his 'work duty with some other men and none of them have come back' (Boyne 2006, 194). Neither boy seems to know about the world they inhabit, but the narrator allows us to back-shadow our knowledge into the narrative. The adult reader will spot the infidelities of Bruno's mother, mentally correct him when he says fury not Führer and will be all too aware of the likely fate of Shmuel's father. Similarly an adult reader will appreciate that his mother 'storming out in search of a medicinal sherry' (Boyne 2006, 187) suggests an increasing alcohol dependency.

All this suggests that Boyne is writing for a knowing reader who wants to believe that a child can maintain their innocence in the face of great evil. Consequently the novel is less to do with the Holocaust and more about a belief in childhood innocence. Bruno, as the hero of the tale, is an innocent but adventurous soul who is dissatisfied with living in occupied Poland. He is loyal to his friend, though the loyalty is tested when Shmuel is brought to polish the glasses in the kitchen. Bruno gives him some chicken, then denies their friendship when Kotler accuses Shmuel of stealing it (Boyne 2006, 172). It is this very innocence that leads to his murder. Bruno has no idea what his father's job entails and when his sister tries to explain Nazi ideas about Jews to him he is not really listening or cannot understand what she says. His loyalty and curiosity lead him to break into the camp to help his friend Shmuel seek out his father. He has been so sheltered by his parents that even when he is confronted by reality it makes no sense to him. Even at the moment the doors to the gas chamber are shut, he still prefers the shadows of reality, as he believes 'that it had something to do with keeping the rain out and stopping people from catching colds' (Boyne 2006, 213). Since so many, though by no means all, of the errors within the narrative are there to show the innocence of the hero in the face of unspeakable evil, Bruno is an unreliable witness and the narrative contains his misunderstandings. Boyne is clear that he does not think Bruno's lack of awareness is in any way anachronistic when he argues that 'Bruno's innocence and ignorance are not only crucial to the story, but appropriate to the times . . . when the war ended and the camps were liberated the world was shocked by what they learned' (Davies-Edwards 2007, 6). However this is not true of German citizens during the Second World War. Research since the 1970s has highlighted the extent of knowledge about the fate of the Jews in occupied Europe (Aly 2016; Gellately 2002; Kershaw 2008; Lacquer 1980). Whether this knowledge was met by the German population with indifference, enthusiasm, or as a means of enriching themselves is less important than that the knowledge was there. The German population were not 'shocked by what they learned'.

Vice (2000) highlights the need to be aware of plot devices within literary texts based on the Holocaust. Within *The Boy in the Striped Pyjamas* there are a number of plot devices that tell the reader that things will not end happily. When Bruno is complaining to the housemaid that he doesn't like living in Poland she admonishes him, suggesting his ideas would 'worry your mother and father half to death' (Vice 2000, 65). Later in the book Gretel and Bruno get head lice and as part of the treatment Bruno has all his hair shaved off. Though his father assures him it will grow back, this lack of hair leads him to comment to Shmuel, 'I look just like you now' (Boyne 2008, 185). Both of these moments in the book point forward to Bruno's murder alongside Shmuel when he is mistaken for a Jewish boy, and his parents' breakdowns as they mourn for their lost son.

How *The Boy in the Striped Pyjamas* impacts upon students' understanding of the Holocaust

If we are to consider whether these 'errors' or plot devices are important, we need to see how they impact upon the readers of the story. One conclusion from the UCL student study is that students had difficulty distinguishing 'between camps established for work, imprisonment, punishment or "re-education", and the death camps created for the purpose of extermination' (Foster *et al.* 2016, 196). As noted earlier 'Outwith' appears to be a concentration camp, with elements of a labour camp and a gas chamber into which the bewildered boys are marched. The researchers suggest that Boyne's use of a hybrid camp with a name that sounds similar to Auschwitz could reinforce this confusion.

An even more troubling conclusion was about the impact of the film upon students' understanding of who the victims were. 'In almost all the schools where the film was discussed, students revealed a strong tendency to want to extend their concern to the German population' (Foster *et al.* 2016, 93). The concept of victim stretched to include everyone from Eva Braun to Shmuel. This leads Erica, one of the students, to say 'I feel sorry for practically everybody who was under Hitler's control . . . they were all still victims of Hitler's control in some shape or form' (Foster *et al.* 2016, 93). This suggests that for many students the victims were not just the Jews of Europe murdered as part of the German government's plan to destroy the 'Jewish race', but anybody under the control of Hitler, including the German population.

Throughout the book 'The Fury' is the all-powerful presence. It is he who sends Bruno's father to Outwith (Boyne 2006, 4) as he has big things in mind for Bruno's father (5), he invites himself to dinner (116) and brings a beautiful blonde woman along too (121) and finally he refuses to relieve Bruno's father of his command in Outwith (190). This reinforces a totally Hitler-centred explanation of the events of the Holocaust and coincides with the findings of the UCL student study. When asked 'Who was responsible for the Holocaust?' 50.7 per cent of students across all year groups answered simply 'Hitler'. A further 20.6 per cent suggested that Hitler was responsible along with the Nazis. The Holocaust was therefore 'seen as a top down process, with Hitler as executive director and others blindly following his will' (Foster *et al.* 2016, 150; see also related discussions in Foster, this volume).

So within the story the causes of the Holocaust are straightforward: Hitler willed it. In *The Boy in the Striped Pyjamas* Hitler becomes a real person in chapter 11 when he comes for dinner. He appears short and ill-tempered with a 'tiny moustache so tiny in fact that Bruno wondered . . . whether he had simply forgotten a piece when he was shaving' (Boyne 2006, 121). Eva Braun on the other hand enchants the young Bruno with her beauty, the consideration she shows him and his sister Gretel, and her ability to speak French. From the way Hitler summons her to the table he and Braun are clearly in an abusive relationship, emphasising the capacity of 'the fury' to exercise power over people and Germany too. The beautiful blonde is a metaphor for Germany as it is under the oppression of Hitler and treated like a puppy (Boyne 2006, 123). From this all-powerful Führer's personal dictatorship it is an easy step to seeing everybody, from Eva Braun all the way to Shmuel and his family in Poland, as his potential victims.

How is this blurring of the distinction between Nazi perpetrators and Jewish victims of the Holocaust achieved? Crucially we are sympathetic to Bruno, because he is innocent, brave and unaware of what is going on. In fact on the eve of the ill-fated adventure his nobility is emphasised: 'Bruno imagined a great adventure ahead and finally an opportunity to see what was really on the other side of the fence. . . . Shmuel saw a chance to get someone to help him in the search for his papa' (Boyne 2006, 199), making Shmuel in some way responsible for the death of the hero, Bruno. This responsibility is reinforced as he did suggest looking for his own father and suggested that Bruno should look like someone in the camp. He also pleaded with Bruno when Bruno wanted to go home. So in this world the Jewish child becomes, to a degree, indirectly responsible for the death of the Nazi's child (Majaro 2014, 11).

We are called upon to feel for the parents simply because they are parents. With Bruno's disappearance his family are literally worried 'half to death'. We no longer see them as a privileged family within the Nazi Party and part of the genocidal German occupation of Poland during the Second World War. They become parents who care for their children, one of whom has gone missing. Bruno's mother returns to the house in Berlin half expecting Bruno to be there, his sister Gretel cries because she misses him and his father stays on at Outwith until he is arrested, having lost the will to live. We do not need to identify with the commandant, as a character, to feel a sympathy for him as a parent. This is made all the more powerful because he is not a likable man; he is a committed Nazi, the Commandant of a death camp and a perpetrator of genocide. Despite all this he is still a father and as such cares about the loss of his only son; he shows a pain we all can understand. Boyne has not made us identify with Bruno's father as a Nazi or a camp commandant, as in Rose's thought experiment (Rose 1996); instead Boyne has made the perpetrators of the Holocaust and the victims of the Holocaust indistinguishable, or as the school student Jack put it, 'it is too easy to feel sorry for the Jews in the film. I don't mean that in a rude way . . . everyone . . . is going to sympathise with the Jews in the camp, but when you see it from like Bruno or the mother's perspective it seems a bit different' (Foster *et al.* 2016, 93). At this point it becomes impossible to distinguish between the victims and the perpetrators of the Holocaust, as they both suffered. The ability to identify the victim and to name the ill treatment is the first step towards justice. Whilst nine-year-old Bruno is clearly not a perpetrator, within the story his father is guilty of mass murder and yet it is he who gains victim status as we empathise with him over the loss of his son.

Conclusion

The Boy in the Striped Pyjamas is a problematic text. The blurring of the distinction between perpetrator and victim makes any discussion of justice impossible. When everyone becomes a victim, who is committing the crimes? By writing a novel in which the perpetrator of genocide becomes the object of sympathy, how can we discuss the atrocities he is responsible for committing? As students read this book the evidence shows they become more sympathetic to the plight of Germans and see everyone as victims of Hitler.

The historical inaccuracies and anachronisms are less to do with mistakes than the need to show Bruno to be an absolute innocent in the harshest of realities. This is in direct contrast to his other Second World War children's novel *The Boy at the Top of the Mountain* where Pierrot becomes corrupted by his life with Hitler at Berchtesgaden. Both novels are about innocence in the face of horror, and the context is there to help carry the message.

Note

1. The original jeep was designed by Karl Probst in 1941 and built by two American companies, Willis Overland and Ford, for use by the American military from 1942 onwards. The Wehrmacht had the VW Type 82 Kubelwagon, designed by Ferdinand Porsche, based on the VW Beetle; between 1940 and 1945 50,435 of these vehicles were built. There were also similar vehicles built by Daimler Benz and Tatra.

References

Adams, J. 2011. *Magic Realism in Holocaust Literature: Troping the traumatic real*. Basingstoke: Palgrave Macmillan.

Adorno, T. 1977. 'Commitment'. In Adorno, T., *Aesthetics and Politics*. London: New Left Books.

Aly, G. 2016. *Hitler's Beneficiaries: Plunder, racial war and the Nazi welfare state*. London: Verso.

Appelfeld, A. 2005 [1980]. *Badenhein 1939*. London: Penguin Classics.

Bernstein, M.A. 1994. *Foregone Conclusions: Against apocalyptic history*. Berkeley: University of California Press.

Boyne, J. 2006. *The Boy in the Striped Pyjamas*. London: David Fickling Books.

Boyne, J. 2007. *Der Junge im gestreiften Pyjama*. Frankfurt am Main: Fischer Verlag.

Boyne, J. 2015. *The Boy at the Top of the Mountain*. London: Penguin Random House.

Breit, J. and Hilmar, T. 'Die starrenden blauen Augen der Unschuld'. Online. https://tinyurl.com/vqftgjm (accessed 15 February 2020).

Budick, E.M. 2015. *The Subject of Holocaust Fiction*. Bloomington: Indiana University Press.

Cesarani, D. 2008. 'Striped Pyjamas', *Literary Review* 359 (Oct.).

Cesarani, D. 2016. *Final Solution: The fate of the Jews, 1933–1949*. London: Macmillan.

Davies-Edwards, H. 2007. *Reading Guide: The Boy in the Striped Pyjamas*. Oxford: Oxford University Press.

Dick, P.K. 1962. *The Man in the High Castle*. New York: G.P. Putnam's Sons.

Eaglestone, R. 2004. *The Holocaust and the Postmodern*. Oxford: Oxford University Press.

Foster, S.J., Pettigrew, A., Pearce, A., Hale, R., Burgess, A., Salmons, P. and Lenga, R.-A. 2016. *What Do Students Know and Understand about the Holocaust? Evidence from English secondary schools*. London: UCL Institute of Education.

Franklin, R. 2011. *A Thousand Darknesses: Lies and truth in Holocaust fiction*. Oxford: Oxford University Press.

Gellately, R. 2002. *Backing Hitler: Consent and coercion in Nazi Germany*. Oxford: Oxford University Press.

Gray, M. 2014. '*The Boy in the Striped Pyjamas*: A blessing or a curse for Holocaust education?' *Holocaust Studies* 20 (3): 109–36.

Holocaust Educational Trust (n.d.) Exploring the Holocaust: A cross-curricular scheme of work for key Stage 3 and S 2; teachers' guide. Online. https://www.het.org.uk/images/downloads/Resources/Exploring_the_Holocaust_Teachers_Guide.pdf (accessed 15 February 2020).

Jost, J., Totaro, G. and Tyshing, C. eds. 1996. *The Demidenko File*. Ringwood, Vic.: Penguin.

Kershaw, I. 2008. *Hitler, the Germans, and the Final Solution*. New Haven, CT: Yale University Press.

Kokkola, L. 2003. *Representing the Holocaust in Children's Literature*. London: Routledge.

Lacquer, W. 1980. *The Terrible Secret: Suppression of the truth about Hitler's 'Final Solution'*. Boston: Little Brown.

Langer, L.L. ed. 1995. *Art from the Ashes: A Holocaust anthology*. Oxford: Oxford University Press.

Levi P. 1988. *The Drowned and the Saved*. London: Michael Joseph.

Majaro, N. 2014. 'Looking for ideology in children's fiction regarding the Holocaust', *New Review of Children's Literature and Librarianship* 20 (1): 1–14.

Marwick, A. 1981. *The Nature of History*. 2nd ed. London: Macmillan.

Pearce, A. 2014. *Holocaust Consciousness in Contemporary Britain*. New York: Routledge.

Porpora, D. 2015. *Reconstructing Sociology: The critical realistapproach*. Cambridge: Cambridge University Press.

Rose, G. 1996. *Mourning Becomes the Law: Philosophy and representation*. Cambridge: Cambridge University Press.

Roth, P. 2004. *The Plot Against America*. Boston: Houghton Mifflin.

Vice, S. 2000. *Holocaust Fiction*. Abingdon: Routledge.

Vice, S. 2005. 'Children's voices and viewpoints in Holocaust literature', Holocaust Studies 11 (2): 11–24.

8
Antisemitism and Holocaust education

Andy Pearce, Stuart Foster, Alice Pettigrew

Introduction

'Is It Time for the Jews to Leave Europe?' provokes the headline of an article written by American journalist Jeffrey Goldberg for *The Atlantic* magazine in April 2015. 'For half a century, memories of the Holocaust limited anti-Semitism on the continent', the article's synopsis goes on to explain. 'That period has ended – the recent fatal attacks in Paris and Copenhagen are merely the latest examples of rising violence against Jews. Renewed vitriol among right-wing fascists and new threats from radicalized Islamists have created a crisis, confronting Jews with an agonizing choice' (Goldberg 2015). Since 2015 a 12-nation study of perceptions and experiences of antisemitism conducted by the European Union Agency for Fundamental Rights appears to suggest that an overwhelming majority of European Jews share these apprehensions[1] (European Agency for Fundamental Rights 2018), while the murder of 11 worshippers at the Tree of Life synagogue in Pittsburgh in October 2018 and fatal shooting at another synagogue in Poway, San Diego in April 2019 indicate that antisemitic violence is not only a European concern. In the context of the United Kingdom, the number of antisemitic incidents reported to the Community Security Trust – a charity established in the early 1990s to provide protection to the country's Jewish community – reached its highest ever recorded total in 2018 (1,652 incidents); a number that had risen every year with only one exception since 2013 (Community Security Trust 2018). Meanwhile, since 2016, discussion of antisemitism has also featured increasingly prominently within national media and domestic political discourse. Repeated charges of 'institutional antisemitism' have also been levelled against the British Labour party, charges so serious they are now being formally investigated by the Equality and Human Rights Commission (EHRC) (Lerman 2019).

As this chapter will go on to detail, the data, experiences and/or understandings that lie behind these and other concerns regarding rising or resurgent antisemitism warrant close attention. At this juncture, however, it is significant to note how regularly the same curative measure is prescribed. According to Douglas Schoen and Arielle Confino, two pollsters involved in a Canadian survey commissioned by the Claims Conference in the United States, 'the answer is simple. The answer is education.' More boldly, they claim their work 'shows clearly and unambiguously . . . that comprehensive knowledge of the Holocaust, not just superficial awareness, is a critical tool in combatting antisemitism and neo-Nazism' (Schoen and Confino 2019). An almost identical sentiment has been expressed as the rationale behind the recent introduction of a 'Never Again Education Act' in the US Senate and House of Representatives: 'We are at a dangerous moment in time', warns Rep. Carolyn Maloney. 'Anti-Semitism is on the rise around the world and here at home, and the memory of the Holocaust is fading for far too many Americans. . . . We can combat this by making sure we teach our students, tomorrow's leaders, about the horrors of the Holocaust' (as reported in Richman 2019). Indeed, the underlying principle that teaching and learning about the Holocaust is a primary – even *the* primary – bulwark against antisemitism has become increasingly prominent in recent years. Despite warnings from the likes of UNESCO that such an approach risks being counter-productive (UNESCO and OSCE 2018; Daventry 2018; see also Wetzel 2010), this principle has also been embraced by the UK government (Wilson 2015; Pickles 2015), is reflected in recommendations made by the All-Party Parliamentary Group Against Antisemitism (2015) and is frequently used to legitimise educational initiatives, such as taking university staff and students to Auschwitz-Birkenau in a bid to address antisemitism at UK universities (UK Government 2018).

In this chapter, our aim certainly is not to negate the important contribution that teaching and learning about the Holocaust can potentially make to addressing antisemitism in society. However, we do wish to problematise the belief that Holocaust education automatically offers a way forward and a one-size-fits-all approach to countering all and any instance of prejudice and ignorance. Critically, we consider it important to work with a more complex and nuanced understanding of 'antisemitism' – and of 'the Holocaust' – than many of these more strident educational 'correctives' would imply. Moreover, the assumption that young people who have learned about the Holocaust will necessarily know and understand what antisemitism is overlooks some of the most troubling findings of our research into students' knowledge and understanding. In order for teaching and learning about the Holocaust to truly contribute to developing students' conceptions of antisemitism, we argue it is necessary for this research to inform key changes in pedagogical practice. We identify specific opportunities where we consider educational engagement with the Holocaust could instructively deepen students' understanding of – and critical reflection upon – contemporary antisemitism(s) but also emphasise the necessary limitations and potential pitfalls in exclusive reliance upon such an approach.

A contested concept

Before turning our attention to discussion of empirical classroom data, it is important to briefly revisit some of the claims and concerns which opened this chapter. For behind the seemingly unambiguous headlines reporting a resurgent antisemitism, the concept of 'antisemitism' itself inhabits complex, contested and regularly contentious terrain (Feldman 2018; Judaken 2018; Fine 2009). And while this is not always made readily apparent in much media coverage, political discourse or interest-group activism, it should matter in the context of education. For if education, and specifically education about the Holocaust, is presented as 'the answer', it is important to consider what, exactly, is the nature of the 'problem'.

In this context it is important to appreciate that several scholars from a variety of disciplines have recently emphasised that 'the boundaries of what constitutes antisemitism are themselves hotly disputed' (Attias-Donfut *et al.* 2012). Furthermore, others have argued that the concept of antisemitism is 'under-theorised' (Judaken 2018), 'poorly and inaccurately researched' or 'distorted' (Kushner 2013) and 'contemporary discussions . . . have become a battlefield with scholarship caught in the cross-fire' (Judaken 2018). Among the many and varied areas of dispute and contention, the following issues are perhaps most salient to our argument and discussions here:

- To what extent does 'antisemitism' denote a single, enduring phenomenon? Is it possible or instructive to trace a unitary, continuous 'essence' to antisemitism that stretches from antiquity, through the Nazi period to the present day? Or does the meaning of antisemitism fundamentally change in different places and at different times? What can – and can't – a study of the context-specific, racially infused 'modern' antisemitism of the Holocaust tell us about the articulations and experiences of antisemitism potentially encountered today? (Following Feldman 2018)

- To what extent should antisemitism be conceived of as a unique and exceptional phenomenon, fundamentally distinct from other forms of racism, xenophobia or Islamophobia, for example? Is it ever appropriate or instructive to approach our understanding of antisemitism through comparative and/or intersecting frames? (Following Cousin and Fine 2012; Rothberg 2009; Gilroy 1993)
- To what extent is it possible or important to distinguish between antisemitic beliefs, antisemitic actions, antisemitic individuals, antisemitic social or political structures, antisemitic tropes, imagery or stereotypes? (Following Judaken 2018)
- How far is any contemporary understanding of antisemitism framed, impacted or 'distorted' by the experience and memory of the Holocaust? (Following Kushner 2013) How loud should our present-day alarm bells be ringing in response to recent indicators that antisemitic incidents are on the increase? Does any contemporary articulation of anti-Jewish – or anti-Israeli – sentiment 'carry potential residues of the longest hatred'? (Following Fine 2009, 46) To paraphrase Tony Kushner, in a 'post-Holocaust' society, does any attempt to 'query . . . the growth and future potential of anti-Semitism' risk complacency – or 'accusations of complacency, even appeasement given the historical precedents of the 1930s and the warnings that were, with hindsight, ignored.' (2013, 435)
- Who should be able to determine what constitutes 'antisemitism' and how?

This list is by no means exhaustive, of course, but the very complexity of these questions underscores how the conceptual frameworks which individuals and organisations employ to make sense of antisemitism are charged and contested. Navigating ways through this terrain is not easy – especially for classroom practitioners and others who do not work solely in the field of Holocaust education. It is partly in response to this challenge that the International Holocaust Remembrance Alliance (IHRA) formulated its definition of antisemitism in 2016. According to this statement:

> Antisemitism is a certain perception of Jews, which may be expressed as hatred towards Jews. Rhetorical and physical manifestations of antisemitism are directed toward Jewish or non-Jewish individuals and/or their property, toward Jewish community institutions and religious facilities.
>
> (International Holocaust Remembrance Alliance 2016)

A definition which is supplemented by various exemplars and one that has been adopted by the governments of 31 nation-states, this formulation has been taken up in the UK by 130 local councils and the judicial system (Sugarman 2018). Within British politics the IHRA definition has also become a subject of considerable attention in light of issues around antisemitism within the Labour Party, while the strengths and weaknesses of the term have equally provoked discussion (see for instance Feldman 2016; Gould 2018; Sedley 2017; Sedley *et al.* 2018). Leaving these debates to one side, if it is possible to read the IHRA definition as an attempt to provide guidance to – amongst others – those engaged in Holocaust education, its transferability as a discrete learning outcome must be measured against the existing schemas and substantive knowledge that students possess. In this regard, research suggests that securing a robust conceptual understanding among students is far from straightforward.

Students' understanding of antisemitism, Jewish life and the Holocaust

As has been extensively reported elsewhere in this book, the 2016 study conducted by the UCL Centre for Holocaust Education and drawn on below provided a detailed national portrait of students' knowledge of the Holocaust. It was clear from this research that young people rarely arrive in the classroom as 'blank slates' with no knowledge, understanding or consciousness of the Holocaust. For example, more than 95 per cent of students surveyed recognised either the word 'Holocaust' or the history that it describes. Most students also referred to the Holocaust as deeply traumatic ('horrible', 'terrible', 'devastating') and 93 per cent understood that Jews (or Jews and others) were victims of the genocide. Students also demonstrated a common willingness to learn about the Holocaust. For example, 83 per cent thought that all students should learn about the Holocaust while at school; 81 per cent found learning about the Holocaust interesting and almost 70 per cent said they would like to learn more about it. Nevertheless, despite these potentially positive findings, the research revealed some significant limitations in students' knowledge and understanding of this history. In particular, as will be explored below, many students appeared unable to comprehend and explain how and why the Nazis and their collaborators targeted Jews and only a small minority appeared to appreciate the significance of the long history of anti-Jewish prejudice and discrimination and of Nazi antisemitism in the unfolding genocide.

One of the headline findings of the 2016 study was the startling proportion of students who appeared entirely unfamiliar with the term 'antisemitism' at all. In an initial attempt to appreciate their understanding of key terms, students were asked in the questionnaire, 'What does "antisemitism" mean?' They were then invited to select from five multiple choice responses: 'Prejudice against poor people'; 'Prejudice against Jews'; 'Prejudice against Hindus'; 'Prejudice against homeless people'; 'Not sure/don't know'. Only 31.8 per cent of students selected 'Prejudice against Jews'. By point of contrast, 89.5 per cent and 87 per cent of students identify the meanings of 'racism' and 'homophobia' as 'Prejudice against people because of ethnicity' and 'Prejudice against people because of their sexual orientation' respectively. Indeed, even more striking is that when A level students aged 17 and 18 are excluded from the total, only 25.9 per cent of students aged 11–16 selected the most appropriate response to the question on antisemitism. In order to understand how and why the vast majority of students of all ages (i.e., 68.2 per cent) did not appear to know about antisemitism – or certainly did not seem to recognise the term itself – a careful analysis of data from other survey questions and, more importantly, close scrutiny of interview responses from more than 244 students was undertaken. Based on this focused enquiry a series of key findings emerged.

To begin with it should be recognised that although it is troubling that even after studying the Holocaust in school a significant majority of students were unfamiliar with the term 'antisemitism', it does not mean that students were unaware that Jews were a key target of Nazi murder and persecution. As stated above, 93 per cent recognised Jews as key victims of the Holocaust and some students were able to offer legitimate, albeit tentative, explanations of why they were targeted. For example, a small number of students (particularly 17–18-year-olds) reasoned that Jews were made 'scapegoats' for Germany's defeat in the First World War and the associated acceptance of the terms of the Treaty of Versailles. Others also argued that Germany's devastating economic depression in the late 1920s and early 1930s was often blamed on Jews. Typically, however, student explanations of why Jews were specifically targeted for persecution and mass murder were somewhat thin and often underdeveloped. Indeed, the research revealed a very common struggle among many students to credibly explain why Jews were targeted.

This significant finding is borne out not only by examining survey and interview responses from students who took part in the main 2016 study, but also from the results of preliminary pilot studies. For example, in a pilot study involving a sample of 342 students who had studied the Holocaust in five secondary schools, participants were asked what questions they still had about the subject. Students were given no prompts or choices but simply asked to write any questions they wanted to pose in a free text response. Of note, 63 per cent of students wrote a response which amounted to 'Why the Jews?' For example:

> Why did Hitler and the Nazis particularly dislike the Jews? (Year 8 student)
> What does Hitler and the Nazi party have against Jews specifically? (Year 9 student)
> Why did they hate Jewish people more than other discriminated groups? (Year 10 student)
> Why did Adolf Hitler punish the Jewish people living in Germany? (Year 9 student)

Students' understanding of 'Why the Jews?' was therefore explored further during focus group interviews in the main student research. For the most part students appeared unable to confidently answer this question and where attempts were made to offer an explanation, responses typically were tentative and uncertain. They also often revealed the prevalence of common myths, misconception and stereotypes.

Perhaps one of the most influential of these was students' misconceptions about the size and influence of Jews in Germany. One survey question asked students to approximate the size of the Jewish population in Germany in 1933. From a selection of five multiple choice answers only 8.8 per cent selected the correct answer (that the pre-war Jewish population was less than 1 per cent of the total German population). Revealingly, most students grossly overestimated the size of the Jewish population. For example, 38.6 per cent indicated that 15 per cent of the total population of Germany was Jewish and a further 35.3 per cent reasoned that Jews accounted for more than 33.5 per cent of the German population. Rather than recognise that German Jews were a loyal but vulnerable German minority, many students appeared to regard their existence as problematic and a key cause of Nazi victimisation.

The erroneous belief that the Jewish population in Germany was considerable led some students to subsequently deduce that many Germans viewed Jews as an increasing threat. This sense that Jews were perceived as a burgeoning menace was volunteered by way of explanation by many students albeit in some cases somewhat tentatively:

> I think there was quite a lot of them [Jews] in Germany so maybe Hitler thought that because there is a lot of them they could be blamed for why Germany was like broke and stuff. (Year 9 student)
>
> I think that, I'm not sure, but I think that the Nazis believed that partly the cause of the problems was overcrowding in Germany, so they thought that by killing these people they would get like less crowded. (Year 10 student)
>
> Weren't a lot of Jews immigrating into Germany at the time? A lot were going into the country, so I think Hitler would probably have realised that and said 'why are they coming into the country, from Poland and things like that?' (Year 12 student)

Another student misconception commonly underpinned by a resort to myths and stereotypes was the notion that all Jews were wealthy and often benefitted when other Germans were suffering economic hardship. Accordingly, in often ill-informed and speculative attempts to explain attacks on Jews, some students made the following sorts of suggestions:

> I have an idea but I'm not very sure. Is it because like they were kind of rich, so maybe they thought that that was kind of in some way evil, like the money didn't belong to them it belonged to the Germans and the Jewish people had kind of taken that away from them. (Year 8 student)
>
> I think Jews were rich at the time I think they had a lot of money and things like that. They invented jewellery or something like that, I'm just guessing. And I think because they invented a lot of stuff and they had lots of money and they were quite wealthy . . . other Germans weren't as wealthy as them. I don't know – jealousy maybe. I don't know. (Year 9 student)
>
> They were the odd ones out, they were the ones that were doing well when the rest of Germany was doing badly and I think

> that made people like jealous of them and so angry that they were doing well. (Year 9 student)
>
> The Germans, when they saw the Jews were better off than them, kind of, I don't know, it kind of pissed them off a bit. (Year 10 student)
>
> Jews had a reputation for being stingy, for not spending. (Year 13 student)
>
> Historically Jews are quite rich and have a lot of money. (Year 12 student)

In many respects, therefore, a significant number of students appeared to tacitly accept some of the egregious claims once circulated by Nazi propaganda. Many students also appeared to categorise Jews as separate from Germans, as if one could be either but not both. Another key finding identified in the national study was that, in an effort to try and explain why Jews were persecuted and murdered, students often sought not to understand the irrational world view of the perpetrator but rather to focus on the potential failings of the victims. This disturbing recourse to potentially apportion blame to the victim was particularly common among younger students and is exemplified by questions such as 'What's wrong with Jewish people?' (Year 9 student), 'Why did the Germans hate the Jewish, did they ever do anything wrong?' (Year 7 student), 'What happened that aggravated everyone and made them hate Jewish people?' (Year 8 student) and 'What did the Jews do to make the Germans hate them?' (Year 9 student).

During student interviews comments such as these were further explored. As a result of follow-up questions and analysis of additional student commentary, it became apparent that young people typically did not make such comments because they overtly harboured antisemitic beliefs or were being intentionally provocative. Rather, these comments appeared to have arisen in the absence of key contextual historical information and a widespread misunderstanding of who Jews were and of the Jewish experience during the Nazi period.

The UCL study further revealed that only a few students had even an elementary appreciation of the long history of anti-Judaism and antisemitism. In one interview, for example, a Year 10 student referred to the 'deep history of antisemitism' and a small minority of students appeared aware that Jews had experienced animosity prior to the Nazi period. However, only a small minority of 11–16-year-olds appeared to have any understanding that Jews had been victims of persecution in Europe for two millennia or that Nazi racial ideology had deeply rooted origins in the Western social, cultural and political traditions of the eighteenth and nineteenth centuries. Typically, therefore – even among those who used the term 'antisemitism' – students mistakenly saw aggressive antisemitism and the persecution of Jews in the 1930s as originating with Hitler. For example, students variously referred to Hitler as 'the man who began antisemitism' or who 'created antisemitic views'. For the most part the vast majority of students appeared unfamiliar with the centuries-old Christian hatred of Jews and the myths, stereotypes and misconceptions borne out of this relationship. Indeed, this lack of knowledge and understanding is perfectly exemplified in the comment of one Year 7 student who asked, 'Why did they [the Nazis] start this out of the blue?'

Survey data and interview responses also revealed that most students did not appear to have much if any understanding of the specific racial/biological characteristics of Nazi antisemitism. Few appeared to understand, for example, that the Nazis and their collaborators targeted Jews because they incorrectly saw them as a distinctive and existential threat to the advancement of the German nation and *volk*. Furthermore, few appreciated that Nazi ideology was propelled by a virulent antisemitism founded on the belief 'that Jews have common repellent and/or ruinous qualities that set them apart from non-Jews' (Hayes 2017, 13).

Accordingly, when asked to explain why Jews were targeted, rather than focus on explanations centred on the distinctive experience of Jews, students typically referenced vague notions of cultural or religious 'difference'. Few referred to the irrational nature of Nazi racial or biological determinism. Nevertheless, despite these apparent limitations in students' conceptual and substantive understandings, it was notable that many students referred to the Nazi 'Aryan' ideal of a people with 'blue eyes and blonde hair'. Thus, when asked, 'Why the Jews?', one Year 8 student reasoned, 'Is it because they don't have blonde hair and blue eyes that he [Hitler] mistreated them?' In a similar vein, a Year 12 student argued that Jews 'couldn't have been Aryan, as you had to be like tall, [with] blonde hair, blue eyes and broad shoulders'. Unfortunately, however, although reference to the Aryan race was not uncommon, very few students went beyond a simplistic understanding and often drew on imprecise references to racism, difference and intolerance. Most students appeared to lack sufficient understanding of the racial and biological Nazi world view and the specific reasons why Jews in particular were targeted across Europe.

Without an understanding of the distinctiveness of the Jewish experience and the impact of Nazi antisemitism, students appeared limited in their ability to fully understand how and why the Holocaust happened. This was entwined with other myths, misconceptions and misunderstandings exposed by the research. These include the failure to appreciate the long history of antisemitism and the distinctive characteristics of Nazi antisemitism; the diversity and vibrancy of pre-war Jewish life across Europe; that Jews typically were a small, integrated and loyal part of German society; and the irrationality of Nazi propaganda that presented Jews as an existential threat.

It is potentially worth repeating that, almost without exception, students did not appear to present any overtly antisemitic prejudices or harbour explicitly racist views. However, what the research revealed was the common absence of important contextual, conceptual and substantive knowledge which clearly inhibited students' ability to make sense of the Holocaust and offer even a rudimentary explanation of how and why it occurred.

Implications

This absence of knowledge and lack of understanding of antisemitism as a historical phenomenon, and of antisemitism as it manifested itself during the 1930s and 1940s, has significant implications for how young people view and understand antisemitism in the present day. In this context, it is worth considering how students' knowledge and understanding relates to why teachers teach about the Holocaust and what they seek to achieve in doing so.

On these matters, the Institute of Education's research into teaching practices in 2009 reported an overwhelming consensus among teachers about their aims in teaching the Holocaust. From a list of 13 possible aims, the majority of teachers – irrespective of subject discipline – indicated they were attempting 'to develop an understanding of the roots and ramifications of prejudice, racism and stereotyping in any society' (71 per cent) and 'to learn the lessons of the Holocaust and to ensure that a similar human atrocity never happens again' (55.9 per cent) (Pettigrew *et al.* 2009).

The generalised, universal dimensions of these aims shed some potential light on students' absent knowledge and misunderstandings about antisemitism. Equally, they indicate no small degree of confusion and/or contradiction, for if the Holocaust is viewed in this exemplary fashion then one might reasonably expect that learning about antisemitism would be a key part of 'develop[ing] an understanding of prejudice, racism and stereotyping' and even a foundational 'lesson' to ensuring 'never again'. This sense of paradox and peculiarity is further surfaced by teachers' content selection. When teachers in 2009 were presented with a list of 35 possible topics to include within a study of the Holocaust and asked to indicate the likelihood they would cover them, the topic of 'the long history of antisemitism' came in at 15th place. In total, 524 teachers said they were more likely than not to include this content in their teaching, approximately 52 per cent of all those who answered this question. By point of comparison, 875 indicated they would try to include reference to Auschwitz-Birkenau (87 per cent) and 600 Hitler's rise to power (60 per cent) while 509 were more likely than not to include reference to other genocides (51 per cent). This does not mean of course that teachers saw antisemitism as unimportant or irrelevant, nor that it was wholly absent from their teaching. Indeed, it was quite possible that teachers were including the topic in their curricula, but doing so in a way which focused on antisemitism during the Nazi epoch. Of course evidence of the sorts of understandings such telescopic approaches can cultivate in students have been seen in some of the findings referenced above, as have examples of students' unfamiliarity with the longevity of Jewish hatred.

The risk of antisemitism being viewed by young people as discretely time-bound and interpreted as exclusively 'Nazi', or of the murder of Europe's Jews being disconnected from anti-Jewish discrimination before and after the Holocaust, is therefore real and palpable. With this in mind, it is worth noting that emerging findings from new research being conducted at UCL suggests that change may have occurred. Exploring the current landscape of Holocaust education, this new study – which at the time of writing is still in development – has produced early data which indicates a shift in curriculum content. From quantitative responses to a survey instrument, it now appears that an overwhelming number of teachers *are* including the topic of 'long history of antisemitism' in their curricula – with over 90 per cent of respondents indicating they cover it in their teaching. If this is the case then a significant shift has taken place over the past decade, whereby the vast majority of teachers have come to believe it is essential to cover the history of antisemitism when teaching the Holocaust. While that development may be welcomed in principle, it still begs intractable questions: why, then, do most students not seem to know what the term antisemitism refers to? And how is it that students fall back on cultural myths and misconceptions to construct explanations for the Holocaust?

The student research of 2016 suggests that despite the Holocaust being a mainstay of the National Curriculum for over 25 years, and in spite of successive governments making significant investment of public funds in student-centred resources and programmes, interventions centred on promoting Holocaust education may well have been less successful than one might presume or like to believe – particularly with regards to improving and developing student knowledge and understanding of antisemitism. Indeed, this was precisely the premise discussed by a panel of educators at a recent symposium in London and locally reported under the headline, 'Is Holocaust education failing if antisemitism is on the rise?' (Rocker 2019). In the face of such empirical research, educators and policymakers should be compelled to reconsider and re-evaluate current practice and many of the core ideas and principles that currently underpin Holocaust education. The conviction, for instance, that more Holocaust education is the antidote to contemporary antisemitism becomes more an article of faith than a verifiable claim.

If the time has indeed come for realism over rhetoric, then it is necessary to establish what contribution Holocaust education – when done effectively – can make to advancing knowledge and understanding of the Holocaust generally, and antisemitism specifically. Since antisemitism is a transhistorical phenomenon – and one which is renowned for its mutability – learning about the ways it manifested itself in Europe during the 1930s and 1940s is clearly an immensely valuable exercise.

Importantly, this is not simply because the period saw millions of Jews killed across the continent. For some, such a statement will sound facetious, and quite clearly that outcome – the murder of two-thirds of Europe's Jews – cannot be understood in separation from antisemitism. After all, in the words of James W. Parkes (1963, 104), 'antisemitism was the unifying cement of the Fascist and National Socialist anti-democratic parties which Hitler encouraged all through the world from 1933 onwards, and . . . it was their antisemitism which attracted a great deal of general support'. Moreover, state-sponsored antisemitism in Germany, its allies, and its proxy states 'created the atmosphere that made the crime possible' (Jäckel 2002, 24). And, as recent perpetrator research has revealed, 'pervasive antisemitism' in large parts of European society 'provided a framework that allowed heterogenous perpetrators and motives to come together' (Stone 2010, 109).

In these ways, and for these reasons, antisemitism was indeed 'a fundamental precondition' (Jäckel 2002, 25) for the murder of European Jewry. However, this recognition has to coexist with what, for some, is an uncomfortable truth: namely, that 'antisemitism plays a role in the process but does not serve as a full explanation for the events which unfolded' (Marrus 2002, 32). The critical point here is more than simply a matter of avoiding monocausality; clearly, an explanatory account of 'the Holocaust' which does not duly recognise the role of antisemitism risks being at best incomplete, and at worst a distortion of actuality. But the same also cuts the other way – as Eberhard Jäckel puts it, 'there is no direct line from antisemitism to the Holocaust for the very simple reason that antisemitism had existed for centuries and yet had never before led to such murderous destruction' (Jäckel 2002, 25).

In this respect, what can be learned from a study of the period of the Holocaust is the manner by which antisemitism commixed with multiple forces and factors in a historically contingent context to unleash misery and murder on a continent-wide population. This does not mean ignoring antisemitism as causal factor or relegating its importance. It instead means appreciating that it intersected with other long- and short-term developments – from large, overarching trends such as the transition to modernity, secularisation, and arrival of the scientific age; to the revolution in ideas and ideologies of the late eighteenth and nineteenth centuries; and the debilitating and destabilising effects of total warfare, mass politics, and worldwide economic depression in the opening decades of the globalised twentieth century. Moreover, all of these occurrences – like antisemitism – played out in different ways in different national settings. The various forms that antisemitism assumed across continental Europe during the Second World War were, in this way, reflective of local histories and regional contexts as much as – if not more than – some grand, Nazi-imposed vision.

A study of the Holocaust can, therefore, also provide insight into the multidimensionality of antisemitism itself. With regard to the German-speaking community, it is possible (and highly desirable) for students to come to recognise distinctions 'between the antisemitism of the party, of the true believers, and the general population' (Berenbaum and Peck 2002, 240). Similarly, if justice is being done to the multinational nature of the perpetrators, then students will encounter the crucial reality that antisemitism during the 1930s and 1940s was not solely constituted by the radical and rabid Nazi brand. Whilst deepening knowledge and understanding of the racist dynamics of Nazi antisemitism is indispensable, equally important is confronting the unavoidable truth that very different types and forms of antisemitism existed within Europe at this time. Of course Nazi antisemitism was able to find purchase precisely because of 'the echo' it encountered, but – as Robert Wistrich notes – 'there were elements in Nazi antisemitism that turned against the Christian doctrines which had incubated it for centuries'. Coming to understand, for instance, that 'in contrast to the traditional teachings of Christianity, no spiritual redemption of the Jews was possible' in the Nazi world view (Wistrich 1992, 67) not only advances students' understanding of Nazi antisemitism but also its antecedents.

This latter notion represents a further development that can occur through learning about the Holocaust and antisemitism during this epoch. In his most recent work, Peter Hayes (2017) provides a very useful schema for capturing what he calls 'the overlapping layers of antisemitism' through time. Significantly, Hayes explains how 'animosity' evolved and overlapped, and was interwoven with 'changing definitions of the problem Jews supposedly represented' and 'the shifting prescriptions for fixing the situation'. Hayes's emphasis that differing 'frameworks for criticising Jews' did not preclude the existence of each other is at once instructive and salutary: it can remind us, and by extension our students, that antisemitism during the 1930s and 1940s was not a uniform entity, nor one which necessarily warranted continental genocide. Understanding how different antisemitisms interfaced with one another is, in this sense, as invaluable as appreciating how antisemitism more broadly intersected with other causal factors and contingencies.

By way of overview, it is evident there is a reciprocal relationship between studying the Holocaust and its context and advancing students' knowledge and understanding of antisemitism during the 1930s and 1940s. And in this fashion, it is possible for students to emerge from such a study with a deeper and more nuanced awareness of antisemitism as a historical phenomenon. This does not mean, of course, that they are necessarily duly positioned to completely comprehend or combat antisemitism in the present. There are two potential reasons for this.

The first relates to the complex relationship between the past and the present. In the context of this discussion, we can note how in the fields of Holocaust studies and Holocaust education these deliberations have manifested in the form of assertions and critiques of the claim there are 'lessons' of the Holocaust which can be learned and transmitted. Whichever side of the divide one falls on, it nevertheless remains the case that manifestations of antisemitism throughout history have been, and continue to be, contextually contingent. This is not to deny the existence of continuities across time, but it is equally important to recognise the continuity of change and changing continuities. There is no doubt that certain antisemitic tropes and motifs in our contemporary world found expression during the period of the Holocaust and before. Yet, by the same token, there are also features of contemporary antisemitism – or potential antisemitism – which cannot be found in the 1930s and 1940s because they did not exist. This includes exercises in Holocaust denial or distortion, the occurrence of 'secondary antisemitism', invocations of events in the Middle East as a justification for antisemitic acts or beliefs, and the use of online platforms and technologies to disseminate antisemitism (UNESCO and OSCE 2018, 20–5; Jikeli and Allouche-Benayoun 2013). That a number of these enterprises are practised by highly organised, well-financed extremist groups presents educators with further challenges for which simply learning about the Holocaust offers little to no guide (Katz 2018).

The second reason why it is problematic to presume understanding antisemitism during the Holocaust can prevent its current manifestations – related to the first – concerns what this knowledge and understanding is being understood to constitute and enable. Often, the rationale for needing to learn about antisemitism is wrapped up with wider attempts to address prejudice and discrimination more broadly, particularly in the form of racism. On this, Franklin Bialystok has provocatively written about how certain conceptions of Holocaust education are underpinned by the connected notions that 'antisemitism is the European version of racism', that 'racism is the reason for the Holocaust', and that 'when racism is unchecked it leads to the crematoria'. Taking issue with this idea, Bialystok forcefully argues 'antisemitism was not racism', suggesting the submergence of the one into the other prohibits comprehension of either (Bialystok 1996, 126).

Bialystok's comments highlight how the relationship between antisemitism and racism is not as obvious as many would presume. They also have notability in light of how the IOE's research from 2009 indicates that the majority of teachers see the purpose of Holocaust education as being 'to develop an understanding of the roots and ramifications of prejudice, racism, and stereotyping in any society' (Pettigrew *et al.* 2009, 77). In a contemporary world where issues related to antisemitism and racism garner considerable attention, but can in the process paradoxically become all the more amorphous and amalgamated, it is essential that young people are able to appreciate the connections and distinctions between the two. This is especially true if they are to potentially confront these ills. Doing so, however, requires not a simplification but a sophistication of students' understanding: they need to be supported to see how the past and present relate and how they depart, and how real-world instances of prejudice and discrimination can be conceptualised.

Conclusion

Reviewing the acclaimed travelling exhibition 'Auschwitz. Not Long Ago. Not Far Away', Dara Horn (2019) recalled how the spate of Holocaust museums and public exhibits of the 1990s

> were imbued with a kind of optimism, a bedrock assumption that they were, for lack of a better word, effective. The idea was that people would come to these museums and learn what the world had done to the Jews, where hatred can lead. They would then *stop hating the Jews*. It wasn't a ridiculous idea, but it seems to have been proved wrong. A generation later, anti-Semitism is once again the new punk rock, and it is hard to go to these museums in 2019 without the feeling that something has shifted.

Horn is correct to note that the assumptions which underpinned Holocaust museology in the 1990s – the same ones that have underwritten much Holocaust remembrance and educational activity over the past generation – were understandable enough. Yet if they have been 'proved wrong' this may be as much because they naively presumed a straightforward relationship between transmission and reception as because 'something has shifted'. Whilst the idea that exposure to the Holocaust can act as a form of inoculation against antisemitism has a logic and may not be unreasonable in terms of a moral expectation, it nevertheless leaves much to chance. As an expected outcome, it also begins to fall apart at the seams when – as the UCL research reveals – students' historical knowledge and understanding of what actually happened to the Jews of Europe is generally perforated by holes and punctured with misconceptions.

Horn's review of the exhibition is also relevant for us because of her fundamental concern with what she sees as its 'ultimate message' of 'how people need to love one another'. On this, Horn writes

> that the Holocaust drives home the importance of love is an idea, like the idea that Holocaust education prevents anti-Semitism, that seems entirely unobjectionable. It is entirely objectionable. The Holocaust didn't happen because of a lack of love. It happened because entire societies abdicated responsibility for their own problems, and instead blamed them on the people who represented . . . the thing they were most afraid of: responsibility.
>
> (Horn 2019)

Horn's critique is withering, and her stridency will no doubt be intolerable to some. Nevertheless, the spotlight she shines on key messages that accompany much Holocaust education warrants contemplation. If we follow Horn and state that the Holocaust didn't happen because of antisemitism this is not to be mendacious, but to press against the monocausality embedded in that generalisation and the residual laziness present in such seemingly self-evident explanations. Clearly the presence of multifarious types of antisemitism across Europe in the 1930s and 1940s was a critical reason for what happened to Europe's Jews; for some directly involved in its perpetration and others who facilitated the genocide, antisemitism was their sole motivation. Yet antisemitism alone is an insufficient explanation, and can lead to distorted understandings. A failure – or a refusal – to recognise this does students no favours. Nor will it advance what they know and understand antisemitism to be.

Common to both of the above examples is the power and potency of simplicity. In the face of the excesses and exigencies that flood forth from the intentional murder of 6 million human beings, simple explanations are alluring, easy – comforting, even. The historical events that are taken to make up 'the Holocaust' were none of these of course, but the same also applies to the uses to which we can and cannot reasonably apply that history. Knowing and understanding how and why two-thirds of European Jewry were annihilated has worth and value: it can enable young people to make sense of the world they inhabit, and affords them insight into some of the basest, most ungratifying and yet most 'human' dimensions of our species. These are critical outcomes and provide a compelling rationale for teaching and learning about the Holocaust. Yet those same enterprises also have limits and limitations. They cannot, for example, explain why antisemitism still exists *in spite of* the destruction of European Jewry, and – though laudable as an ambition – they certainly cannot prevent it. To presume or to expect otherwise is to run the risk of not just 'asking too much of Holocaust education' (Stone 2019) but of the Holocaust itself.

The criticisms forwarded in this essay are done so with awareness that they run counter to prevailing winds in the field of Holocaust education and the sociocultural and political spheres that take interests in it. However, it would be disingenuous to read the arguments made on these pages as either a counsel of despair or as a refutation of the capacity for Holocaust education to contribute to students' conceptions and consciousness of antisemitism. As educators, scholars and researchers professionally engaged with teaching and learning about the Holocaust, the persistence of antisemitism is a matter of considerable concern to us – and its palpable upturn in recent years only intensifies our alarm further. Like many others, we believe this warrants serious attention and should provoke concerted efforts to identify ways in which educational interventions can help to address these developments. Yet it is precisely because this urgent task is not easy, that it is necessary to problematise what have become orthodox ideas and common axioms. Fundamentally, the notion that more antisemitism can be neutralised by more Holocaust education side-steps a raft of basic issues. These include, but are by no means limited to, what the relationship can and should be between Holocaust education, the history of antisemitism, and contemporary antisemitism. How – in tangible terms – may an understanding of the Holocaust alert young people to the challenges of antisemitism today? What else is needed beyond knowledge and understanding of the Holocaust, to enable students to identify and effectively respond to antisemitism in their real worlds? And how can students be best supported to arrive at an understanding of what antisemitism is and what it is not?

Though meeting such challenges is not easy, a starting point is to begin with what we know – in an empirical sense – about the knowledge, understandings and frameworks of meaning that our students are presently operating with. How historically accurate are these? What do they reveal to us about students' conceptualisations of antisemitism? In what ways are they aligned to the social, cultural, and political contexts surrounding young people? At the same time, it is essential that the answers which arise from these questions subsequently inform the training provisions made for developing teachers' competency to teach these charged and complicated issues. Learning about the Holocaust together with high-quality CPD in Holocaust education undoubtedly have key parts to play in all these processes, but they cannot alone provide a solution. Until this is duly acknowledged, finding the appropriate role(s) for Holocaust education cannot begin in earnest.

Note

1. For example, 89 per cent of the 16,395 European Jews who took part in the survey indicated that they believed antisemitism had increased within their country during the last 5 years, and 85 per cent considered antisemitism to be 'a serious problem' (European Agency for Fundamental Rights 2018, 9).

References

All online material last accessed 24 July 2019 unless indicated otherwise.

All-Party Parliamentary Group against Antisemitism. 2015. *Report of the All-Party Parliamentary Inquiry into Antisemitism in the UK*. London.

Attias-Donfut, C., Fine, R. and Achinger, C. 2012. 'Introduction to the special issue on racism, antisemitism, and Islamophobia', *European Societies* 14 (3): 467–9.

Berenbaum, M. and Peck, A.J. 2002. '"Ordinary Men": The socio-political background'. In *The Holocaust and History: The known, the unknown, the disputed and the reexamined*, edited by Michael Berenbaum and Abraham J. Peck, 239–42. Bloomington: Indiana University Press.

Bialystok, F. 1996. 'Americanizing the Holocaust: Beyond the limit of the universal'. In *New Perspectives on the Holocaust: A guide for teachers and scholars*, edited by Rochelle L. Millen, Timothy A. Bennett, Jack D. Mann, Joseph E. O'Connor and Robert P. Welker, 122–30. New York: New York University Press.

Community Security Trust. 2018. *Antisemitic Incidents Report 2018*. London: Community Security Trust. Online. https://tinyurl.com/sjxjy2p

Cousin, G. and Fine, R. 2012. 'A common cause: Reconnecting the study of racism and antisemitism', *European Societies* 14 (2): 166–85.

Daventry, M. (2018) 'Holocaust education "not enough" to tackle antisemitism, Unesco warns'. *Jewish Chronicle*. 4 June.

European Union Agency for Fundamental Rights (FRA). 2018. 'Experiences and perceptions of antisemitism: Second survey on discrimination and hate crimes against Jews in the EU'. Online. https://fra.europa.eu/en/news/2018/persistent-antisemitism-hangs-over-eu (accessed 15 February 2020).

Feldman, D. 2016. 'Will Britain's new definition of antisemitism help Jewish people? I'm sceptical', *The Guardian*, 28 December.

Feldman, D. 2018. 'AHR roundtable: Toward a history of the term "Anti-Semitism"', *American Historical Review* 123 (4): 1139–50.

Fine, R. 2009. 'Fighting with phantoms: A contribution to the debate on antisemitism in Europe', *Patterns of Prejudice* 43 (5): 459–79.

Gilroy, P. 1993. *The Black Atlantic: Modernity and double consciousness*. London: Verso.

Goldberg, J. 2015. 'Is it time for the Jews to leave Europe?' *The Atlantic*, April. https://www.theatlantic.com/magazine/archive/2015/04/is-it-time-for-the-jews-to-leave-europe/386279/

Gould, R. 2018. 'We need principles, not rules, to fight antisemitism: The IHRA definition and the politics of defining racism', *Open Democracy*. Online. https://www.opendemocracy.net/en/opendemocracyuk/we-need-principles-more-than-rules-in-fight-against-antisemitism-on-ihra-definiti/

Hayes, P. 2017. *Why? Explaining the Holocaust*. New York: Norton.

Horn, D. 2019. 'Auschwitz is not a metaphor', *The Atlantic*, 6 June. Online. https://www.theatlantic.com/ideas/archive/2019/06/auschwitz-not-long-ago-not-far-away/591082/

International Holocaust Remembrance Alliance. 2016. 'Working definition of antisemitism'. Online. https://www.holocaustremembrance.com/working-definition-antisemitism

Jäckel, E. 2002. 'The Holocaust: Where we are, where we need to go'. In *The Holocaust and History: The known, the unknown, the disputed and the reexamined*, edited by Michael Berenbaum and Abraham J. Peck, 23–9. Bloomington: Indiana University Press.

Jikeli, Günther and Allouche-Benayoun, J. 2013. 'Introduction'. In *Perceptions of the Holocaust in Europe and Muslim Communities: Sources, comparisons and educational challenges*, edited by Günther Jikeli and Joëlle Allouche-Benayoun, 1–12. London: Springer.

Judaken, J. 2018. 'AHR roundtable, rethinking Anti-Semitism: Introduction,' *American Historical Review* 123 (4): 1122–38.

Katz, R. 2018. 'Inside the online cesspool of Anti-Semitism that housed Robert Bowers', *Politico Magazine*, 29 October. Online. https://www.politico.com/magazine/story/2018/10/29/inside-the-online-cesspool-of-anti-semitism-that-housed-robert-bowers-221949

Kushner, T. 2013. 'Anti-Semitism in Britain: Continuity and the absence of a resurgence?' *Ethnic and Racial Studies* 36 (3): 434–49.

Lerman, A. 2019. 'The Labour Party, "institutional antisemitism" and irresponsible politics', *Open Democracy*, March 2019. Online. https://www.opendemocracy.net/en/opendemocracyuk/the-labour-party-institutional-antisemitism-and-irresponsible-politics/

Marrus, M. 2002. 'The Holocaust: Where we are, where we need to go – a comment'. In *The Holocaust and History: The known, the unknown, the disputed and the reexamined*, edited by Michael Berenbaum and Abraham J. Peck, 30–4. Bloomington: Indiana University Press.

Parkes, J. 1963. *Antisemitism*. Chicago: Quadrangle Books.

Pettigrew, A., Foster, S., Howson, J., Salmons, P., Lenga, R.-A. and Andrews, K. 2009. *Teaching about the Holocaust in English Secondary Schools: An empirical study of national trends, perspectives and practice*. London: Institute of Education.

Pickles, E. 2015. 'We shall tackle anti-Semitism', speech, 21 January. Online. https://www.gov.uk/government/speeches/we-shall-tackle-anti-semitism

Richman, J. 2019. '"Never Again Education Act" to be introduced in US Senate', *Jewish News Syndicate*,10 July. Online. https://tinyurl.com/yc79b6jx

Rocker, S. 2019. 'Is Holocaust education failing if antisemitism is on the rise?' *The Jewish Chronicle*, 1 April. Online. https://www.thejc.com/education/education-features/is-holocaust-education-failing-if-antisemitism-is-on-the-rise-1.482360

Rothberg, M. 2009. *Multidirectional Memory: Remembering the Holocaust in the age of decolonization*. Stanford, CA: Stanford University Press.

Schoen, D. and Confino, A. 2019. 'Holocaust education is key in tackling global anti-Semitism', *The Hill*, 27 January. Online. https://thehill.com/opinion/international/427134-holocaust-education-is-key-in-tackling-global-anti-semitism

Sedley, S. 2017. 'Defining antisemitism', *London Review of Books* 39 (9): 8.

Sedley, S., Janner-Klausner, L., Bindman, G., Rose, J. and Kahn-Harris, K. 2018. 'How should antisemitism be defined?' *The Guardian*, 27 July.

Stone, D. 2010. *Histories of the Holocaust*. Oxford: Oxford University Press.

Stone, D. 2019. 'Asking too much of Holocaust education', *Centre for the Analysis of the Radical Right*, 9 February. Online. https://www.radicalrightanalysis.com/2019/02/09/asking-too-much-of-holocaust-education/

Sugarman, D. 2018. 'What is the IHRA definition of antisemitism? And why has Labour outraged Jews by rejecting it?' *Jewish Chronicle*, 20 July.

UK Government 2018. 'Government announces £144,000 of new funding to help universities tackle antisemitism on campus', 16 January. Online. https://www.gov.uk/government/news/government-announces-144000-of-new-funding-to-help-universities-tackle-antisemitism-on-campus

Wetzel, J. 2010. 'Speech delivered at OSCE Review Conference 2010, Working Session 8 "Tolerance and Non-Discrimination"', Warsaw, 6 October.

Wilson, P. 2015. 'The UK supports education and projects that address anti-Semitism and all other forms of hatred: Statement by Ambassador Peter Wilson of the UK Mission to the UN, to the General Assembly Informal Meeting on Anti-Semitism', 22 January. Online. https://www.gov.uk/government/speeches/the-uk-supports-education-and-projects-that-address-anti-semitism-and-all-other-forms-of-hatred

Wistrich, R.S. 1992. *Antisemitism: The longest hatred*. London: Thames Mandarin.

UNESCO and OSCE. 2018. *Addressing Antisemitism through Education: Guidelines for policymakers*. Paris, UNESCO.

9

Muslim students and the Holocaust in England's secondary schools: 'Reluctant learners' or constructed controversies?

Alice Pettigrew

Introduction

The theme 'challenges and controversies' is particularly pertinent to the current chapter since Muslim student responses to learning about the Holocaust are regularly presented as 'a challenge' and often framed in terms of 'controversy'. The central provocation of this chapter, however, is a critical examination of why this should be so.

The chapter traces the construction of a controversy. It examines existing empirical research in relation to wider popular and political discourses which have positioned both 'Muslim students' and 'the Holocaust' in powerful and often problematic ways. The chapter draws on the author's own data and analysis from two important research studies: a national examination of teachers' practice and perspectives when teaching about the Holocaust in England's secondary schools (Pettigrew *et al.* 2009); and an extensive investigation of English secondary school students' knowledge, understanding and experience of learning about this history (Foster *et al.* 2016). The second study included detailed survey responses from more than 1,000 young people who identified as Muslim and focus group interviews with 26 students from two, predominantly Muslim, secondary schools. This represents an unprecedented and important data-set within which to explore the chapter's central themes. While the author's primary research was conducted within the specific context of secondary-level education in England, the chapter locates its arguments within both national and international discursive frames.

Constructing a controversy? Reporting and misreporting the Historical Association's TEACH research

> TEACHERS DROP THE HOLOCAUST TO AVOID OFFENDING MUSLIMS, *The Daily Mail,* 2 April 2007 (see Clark 2007)
>
> UK SCHOOL'S SICKENING SILENCE, *The New York Post,* 8 April 2007 (see Rubenstein 2007)
>
> These agencies must be understood as actively and continuously part of the whole process to which, also, they are 'reacting'. They are active in defining situations, in selecting targets, in initiating 'campaigns', in structuring these campaigns, in selectively signifying their actions to the public at large, in legitimating their actions through the accounts of situations which they produce. They do not simply respond to 'moral panics'. They form part of the circle out of which 'moral panics' develop. It is part of the paradox that they also, advertently and inadvertently, *amplify* the deviancy they seem so absolutely committed to controlling.
>
> (Hall *et al.* 1978, 52; emphasis in original)

In April 2007, the United Kingdom's Historical Association (HA) published a report entitled 'Teaching Emotive and Controversial History 3–19'. Across more than 40 pages, the TEACH report shared examples of effective practice and provided several detailed case studies. These referred to varied areas of the history curriculum including, for example, British colonialism, the transatlantic slave trade, the Bolshevik Revolution and the War on Terror (Historical Association 2007).

The report received significant interest from the British press but just two paragraphs attracted most of this attention. Those paragraphs were drawn from a short chapter listing eight possible teaching constraints. One in particular – 'teacher avoidance of emotive and controversial history' – appears especially to have caught the imagination of journalists, and both are worth reproducing in full here:

> Teachers and schools avoid emotive and controversial history for a variety of reasons, some of which are well-intentioned. Some

> feel that certain issues are inappropriate for particular age groups or decide in advance that pupils lack the maturity to grasp them. Where teachers lack confidence in their subject knowledge or subject-specific pedagogy, this can also be a reason for avoiding certain content. Staff may wish to avoid causing offence or appearing insensitive to individuals or groups in their classes. In particular settings, teachers of history are unwilling to challenge highly contentious or charged versions of history in which pupils are steeped at home, in their community or in a place of worship. Some teachers also feel that the issues are best avoided in history, believing them to be taught elsewhere in the curriculum such as in citizenship or religious education.
>
> For example, a history department in a northern city recently avoided selecting the Holocaust as a topic for GCSE coursework for fear of confronting anti-Semitic sentiment and Holocaust denial among some Muslim pupils. In another department, teachers were strongly challenged by some Christian parents for their treatment of the Arab-Israeli conflict and the history of the state of Israel that did not accord with the teachings of their denomination. In another history department, the Holocaust was taught despite anti-Semitic sentiment among some pupils, but the same department deliberately avoided teaching the Crusades at Key Stage 3 because their balanced treatment of the topic would have directly challenged what was taught in some local mosques.
>
> (Historical Association 2007, 15)

Most of this detail was lost or entirely ignored, however, in newspaper stories which led with the misleadingly simplified contention schools were 'dropping the Holocaust' to avoid causing 'Muslims' offence. And this resulted in outrage. As Brian Whitaker notes in his account of 'The Birth of a Myth', coverage of the story in *The Times* newspaper alone quickly attracted some 450 alarmed or indignant readers' comments. 'From there, Chinese whispers took over . . . and suddenly the whole of Britain had apparently caved in to pressure from Muslims' (Whitaker 2007). On the other side of the Atlantic, *The New York Post's* reporting of the story under the headline 'UK's Sickening Silence' attracted similarly strident criticism. 'That a once-mighty nation should capitulate to a group of people whose fundamentalist beliefs are the antithesis of the culture that made that country great is an indictment of the present government of Great Britain', insisted one comments page contributor: 'What's next?

The adoption of Arabic as the official language of Great Britain?' Another contributor contended that 'England's decision to teach lies rather than facts for the sake of not offending anti-Western Muslim racists, may mark a turning point in history'. 'This is another symptom of latent anti-Semitism by many Europeans', concluded a third (Eckstein *et al.* 2007).

Within days, the 'story' began to circulate even more widely by way of an anonymously written email although the unknown author did not directly cite the TEACH report, nor any other empirical 'evidence', to support their hyperbolic claims:

> Recently, this week, the UK removed the Holocaust from its school curriculum because it 'offended' the Moslem population which claims it never occurred.
>
> This is a frightening portent of the fear that is gripping the world and how easily each country is giving into it!
>
> (Reproduced in Whitaker 2007)

Recipients were urged to forward the email, acting as links in a 'memorial chain'. Although its content was quickly and resoundingly debunked on numerous fact-checking websites (see, for example, Mikkelson 2007), it continued to circulate widely. So much so, in fact, that some ten months later, Britain's Minister for Schools was compelled to write directly to embassies and media agencies around the world to formally refute its message and clarify official departmental policy (BBC 2008).

The whole affair was a source of embarrassment and concern to the UK government. Britain, as one of the original signatories of the Stockholm Declaration on Holocaust education, remembrance and research, had, in 2000, formally pledged its commitment to promoting teaching and learning about the Holocaust in all its schools. As the Minister was very keen to reassure an international audience, this commitment was and continues to be reflected in England's statutory national curriculum. The Holocaust remains a compulsory component of history teaching at Key Stage 3 (for 11–14-year-olds). In the school at the epicentre of the TEACH report controversy, teachers had described their reticence to pursue an *additional* unit of Holocaust-related coursework for older students taking *post*-compulsory, GCSE level history. There was no indication that this or any other school were failing to meet their statutory duty and certainly no suggestion of a change in government policy here.

I did not choose to begin this chapter with an extended retelling of this episode to defend the potentially damaged international reputation of the British government, however. Rather, I conceived it as an opportunity to reflect upon the readiness with which the flimsiest of pretexts was seized upon as evidence of a 'turning point in history', 'capitulation' to 'anti-Western Muslim racists', or the 'latent antisemitism' of 'many Europeans' (Eckstein *et al.* 2007). It is also intended as an invitation to critically consider some of the other forms of damage that such problematic framings may entail: damage to our conceptualisations and expectations of 'Muslim' pupils, for example, or to the potential effectiveness of our pedagogical practice when teaching about the Holocaust in schools.

Contemporary 'folk devils' and 'moral panic': A social constructivist approach

Newspaper stories and their headlines are not commissioned, crafted or published in a vacuum. It is a central tenet of cultural studies that the media does not simply 'report' reality but, rather, helps construct it. The arguments offered in seminal studies by Cohen (1972) and Hall *et al.* (1978) have salience to the current chapter. Together they show how the media can help construct a heightened, disproportionate sense of public concern – or 'moral panic' – over the behaviour of certain groups in society (after Goode and Ben-Yehuda 1994, 33). Such groups are cast as 'folk devils'. Upon them wider social, cultural and political fears are projected and blame for both real and perceived threats to 'traditional way of life' is placed.

In recent decades, a growing number of scholars have argued convincingly that since the mid-1980s at least, 'Muslim' communities – and in particular 'Muslim youth' – through numerous instances of exaggeration, distortion, bias and/or sensationalism in large swathes of the British media, have increasingly been positioned as the pre-eminent contemporary 'folk-devil' within the UK (Baker *et al.* 2013; Poole 2009; Ameli *et al.* 2007). The 'moral panic' they engender is constructed as twofold: as both a physical threat to national security, and as an existential threat to the notion of a unitary British national identity, 'British values' or 'the British way of life'. The first is reflected in those popular and political discourses which repeatedly obscure important distinctions between Islam and Islamist terrorism and which focus on potential radicalisation and/or extremism. These have garnered significant momentum since the September 11th attacks of 2001. The second is reflected in discourses which emphasise obstacles to integration. Such discourses invoke notions of 'culture clash' or 'self-segregation' and regularly position all Muslims as foreign outsiders, irreducibly apart from – and often oppositional to – the dominant national 'we'.

It is in this context that the misreporting of the TEACH research – and, this chapter will argue, that any other serious exploration of the (potential) 'problem' of Muslim students' educational engagement with the Holocaust – must be understood. As both Cohen and Hall *et al.* emphasise, the media are not the only agencies complicit in the creation of moral panics. In *Policing the Crisis*, Hall *et al.* also documented the role of both the police and the judiciary in co-constructing a heightened, disproportionate and ultimately damaging societal anxiety around black youth and criminality. Following Cohen, more recent proponents of the moral panic thesis have also drawn attention to the collusion of parties such as politicians or religious representatives, relevant professionals and pressure groups (see, for example, Critcher 2008, after Cohen 1972). It is a central contention of the current chapter that, without considerable and consistent care and critical reflexivity, educational researchers, commentators, policymakers and practitioners concerned with Muslim student responses to the Holocaust might also risk contributing to (or in Hall *et al.*'s formulation, 'amplifying') the problem (or 'deviancy') they ostensibly seek to address. While the chapter is motivated by a desire to promote robust and potentially transformative educational encounters with the Holocaust for *all* British school students, it does so with a keen awareness of those wider discursive framings that can so readily position 'Muslims' – and here 'Muslim students' – in reductionist, problem-oriented and oppositional terms.

But perhaps the notion of a '*constructed* controversy' through which I have framed this chapter is itself a provocation. It could be interpreted by some as an act of cowardice, or as sophistry employed to avoid a knotty and perhaps uncomfortable problem in English schools and further afield.[1] It is therefore important to clarify that it is not the intention of the chapter to reject outright the reality that in some classrooms and in some contexts, students identified as Muslim may express antipathy, resentment or hostility towards learning about the Holocaust. Nor is it to deny that this reality, where encountered, warrants attention. Taking a broadly social constructivist perspective, I emphasise instead the need for reflexivity in considering how this 'problem' is identified, interpreted and ultimately framed (Goode and Ben-Yehuda 1994; Berger and Luckman 1966) in order that we may better understand – and ultimately better address – any actual experiences of student resistance or opposition if they arise.

In practice, this means asking the kinds of questions that inform my discussion in what remains of the chapter: How, by whom and on what basis was the phenomena of Muslim school students' responses to learning about the Holocaust first conceptualised and communicated as a 'problem'? To what extent has or can this conceptualisation be challenged? How widely is it shared? How is the signifier 'Muslim' employed and/or understood in the framing and discussion of this issue? What work is that word doing (either wittingly or unwittingly)? Which Muslim school students are we talking about? How many? And how have they been identified? In what – if any – specific contexts have encounters interpreted as problematic been most or least likely to occur? Crucially, what may be the consequence of constructing, and of empirically examining, this 'problem' in these ways? Wherever possible, I have considered questions such as these with reference to existing available data and published empirical research. Some prove easier to consider than others. All are complex and 'answered' only very tentatively and incompletely here.

'Reluctant learners?'

Following the TEACH report, the first empirical exploration of specifically Muslim students' responses to learning about the Holocaust in the UK appears in an article written by Geoffrey Short in 2008, 'Teaching the Holocaust in Predominantly Muslim Schools'. Explaining the rationale for this focus, Short notes the absence of existing studies able to examine 'how aspects of the student body, such as its ethno-religious identity, might frustrate the efforts of teachers' (Short 2008, 95). Short considers this absence 'troubling':

> For if, as has been claimed, antisemitism is spreading among the UK's Muslim population, there has to be concern over the way the Holocaust is taught in predominantly Muslim schools.
>
> (Short 2008, 95)

The nature of this concern, Short continues, is 'the possibility that such students will respond inappropriately'. Speculation as to a *potential* problem rather than an encountered reality motivates the research.

Short spends much of his opening four pages offering various illustrations to substantiate the first proposition, that 'antisemitism is spreading among the UK's Muslim population'. He also suggests potential sources for antisemitic sentiment including: individual and community-based political perspectives vis-à-vis international conflicts; the availability of 'imported' Middle Eastern and Arabic propaganda via satellite television and the internet; and potential interpretations of passages from the Koran. On this basis, he then reiterates that 'it might reasonably be assumed that *a significant proportion* of Muslim students will respond to lessons on the Holocaust in ways likely to cause their teachers some anxieties' (Short 2008, 97; emphasis added). He concedes, however, that, at the point of writing, there was little evidence to support such an assumption. As Short himself explains, the little 'evidence' he *was* able to examine was largely anecdotal and almost entirely related to contexts other than British schools. It is perhaps of little surprise, then, that based on his own research as reported in the 2008 paper, Short's overwhelming conclusion is that this was a largely unwarranted concern.

Short's research comprised in-depth interviews with teachers from 15 schools where Muslim students constituted the single largest ethnic group. As he reports, these teachers 'showed no reluctance to engage with the Holocaust'. Far from appearing tempted to avoid or reduce teaching time on the topic, on average they spent a comparatively large number of history lessons relative to teachers in previous studies (Short 2008, 101). 'Just over half' of the teachers that Short interviewed 'claimed that working in a predominantly Muslim environment had influenced their approach to teaching the Holocaust' but they also reported that, 'for the most part', their students seemed 'to respond very positively', were 'really interested' and 'very receptive' (Short 2008, 102):

> There was no opposition of any kind from parents and roughly half the teachers reported no antisemitism at all when discussing the subject with students, even though, in a couple of schools, negative stereotyping of Jews was said to be rife . . . .
>
> Three teachers stated that a minority of Muslim students made antisemitic remarks when starting work on the Holocaust, but that they stopped doing so as the work progressed. For a couple of teachers, however, their students' attitude towards Jews posed a major problem and, in the words of one them, the Holocaust had, at one stage, proved a 'hugely difficult topic to teach'.
>
> (Short 2008, 104–5)

Again, the experience of the small number of teachers who encountered 'major problems' among students or for whom the Holocaust proved 'a hugely difficult topic to teach' warrants further attention. However, the clear majority of those who took part in Short's small study did not appear to conceive of or experience the responses of Muslim students as a 'problem' or impediment to teaching about the Holocaust at all. As Short reflects in the conclusion to his 2008 paper, 'the fact that students in most schools responded enthusiastically has to be seen as a positive development' (Short 2008, 108). It is therefore perhaps surprising to note that when Short returned to this same data in a second paper five years later, this positive development was far from the forefront of his framing.

Under the revised title, 'Reluctant learners? Muslim youth confront the Holocaust', the later paper follows a similar format to the first but is updated with reference to additional international studies. Short concludes his 2013 paper on a rather more cautious note than the first, summarising that 'while many [Muslim students] have a positive attitude and behave appropriately, others are antagonistic and disruptive'. It is this second group – whom Short characterises as 'reluctant learners' '*confront[ing]* the Holocaust' (Short 2013, 121; emphasis added) – that frame and become the implicit focus of this second paper.

While Short's own empirical data did not change between the 2008 and 2013 papers, one can perhaps presume that his perspective was altered in relation to the additional studies cited. One particular paper, by Suzanne Rutland, shared a series of troubling accounts given in interview by eight teachers from Sydney schools with a 'very high proportion' of students with 'Arabic-speaking and Muslim backgrounds'. Rutland's teachers 'consistently testified to a pattern of anti-Semitic beliefs among their Muslim students' (Rutland 2010, 81; cited in Short 2013, 127). As Short acknowledges, Rutland's research was very small-scale. Importantly its conclusions were at odds, not only with Short's own initial empirical data, but also with most of the other studies referenced in his 2013 paper (for example, Carr 2012; Gryglewski, 2010; Cohen 2005; Reed and Novogrodsky 2000). Arguably, 'Enthusiastic learners: Muslim students engage with the Holocaust' might have been a more representative title under which to summarise the paper's empirical content. However, Short's paper also includes a number of practical suggestions for engaging the minority of 'reluctant' learners in the classroom, and the somewhat more provocative paper title may have been chosen in order to signpost this instructive content.

Teacher perspectives on the significance of cultural diversity in the classroom

In 2009, I was also presented with an opportunity to gauge the extent to which classroom teachers in England perceived or experienced Muslim students' engagement with lessons about the Holocaust as a 'problem'.

I worked as one of the small team of researchers on the Institute of Education's national study documenting practice in teaching about the Holocaust in England's secondary schools (Pettigrew *et al.* 2009). This study combined survey responses from a nationally representative sample of more than 2,000 teachers with focus-group interviews with a further 64.

Neither the survey-instrument nor interview-guide directly asked participants about teaching Muslim students as this was not an explicit focus of the research. However, both did invite teachers to share their perspectives on the rather more open question of cultural diversity in the classroom. One survey question asked respondents to what extent they agreed with the statement, 'I find having students from diverse cultural backgrounds influences the way that I teach about the Holocaust'. Of those who answered this question, 23.3 per cent agreed or strongly agreed. A free-text box accompanying the question invited those teachers to share further details.

In fact, a sizeable proportion of the 179 responses given here suggested that cultural diversity in the classroom did *not* – and moreover *should* not – influence teaching about the Holocaust. For example, one teacher's response read:

> I do not teach [about the Holocaust] to draw explicit moral lessons or sermons and so even in a school that is 70% Muslim with strong links to Palestine, I still take a historical disciplinary perspective and so [the salience of] the cultural background of the class is the same as for all other enquiries.
>
> (Extract from survey response)

This teacher's unprompted qualification, '*even* in a school that is 70% Muslim', denotes an awareness of the proposition large numbers of Muslim students in a classroom could pose specific challenges to teaching about the Holocaust. In this case, however, this is a premise that they themselves appear to reject.

Other teachers responding to the same question described diverse backgrounds and experiences among students as a resource that could be drawn upon in lessons. A small minority expressed an appreciation – or perhaps apprehension – that some students may perhaps feel a closer, personal or community-based connection to historical events other than the Holocaust. Some of these teachers appeared to share a concern that such students might believe their 'own' stories were being overlooked or that their personal and/or familial histories of persecution or prejudice were being ignored. This was almost entirely presented, however, as teacher interpretation and/or informed speculation and not made with reference to specific experience. None of these teachers described cultural diversity as a 'problem' to be overcome.

During interview, participating teachers were invited to reflect at length on *any* challenges encountered while teaching about the Holocaust in school. Given this invitation, very few teachers raised issues related to cultural diversity of their own volition. A follow-up prompt asked more directly, 'how might the particular group of students that you are teaching influence the approach you take?' Here teachers were much more likely to talk about variation in student ability or maturity than to raise cultural diversity as an area of concern. Even when asked more directly still, 'What about the cultural background of your students? Could that make a difference to how you teach? In what way?' few teachers responded in terms of challenges or problems they had encountered. Among those who did, the most common suggestion was that the presence of German or Polish heritage students during specific classroom discussions might require consideration and sensitivity. By and large, however, the cultural *homogeneity* of predominantly white, ethnic majority classrooms was more often framed as a challenge than cultural diversity; some teachers argued that where students had limited exposure to people from different cultural backgrounds, it could lead to problematic misunderstandings, insensitive attitudes and/or prejudice through ignorance and naiveté.

Contra the most contentious 'finding' of the TEACH report, not a single teacher within the survey or interviews gave any suggestion that they had ever even considered avoiding teaching the Holocaust. Moreover, while a small number of teachers suggested that they felt antisemitism and/or Holocaust denial *might* be a potential issue among certain groups of students, very few reported having any first-hand experience of this. Once again teachers were more likely to report this as a problem that they anticipated encountering among 'white', ethnic majority students than among those identified as Muslim (Pettigrew *et al.* 2009, 98–100).

Reluctance to remember? The Holocaust, 'new' antisemitism and Europe's Others

If research with teachers in the UK context gives only very limited support to the proposition that the responses of Muslim students can constitute a significant problem for Holocaust education, an alternative perspective is offered by international, and in particular, European scholars working in this and related fields. In 2013, an edited collection of papers was published entitled *Perceptions of the Holocaust in Europe and Muslim Communities: Sources, Comparisons and Educational Challenges*. In the book's introduction, its editors explain:

> The history of the Shoah remains challenging for humanity and for European societies in particular. However, a new challenge has been discussed in recent years. Some migrant communities which are now part of European societies although they do not share the history of the Shoah, seem to be reluctant to remember the murder of European Jewry as one of the greatest crimes of humanity. Teachers have reported difficulties teaching about the Holocaust, particularly with Muslim students.
>
> (Allouche-Benayoun and Jikeli 2013, 3)

While some of the illustrations of student disruption and/or outright hostility provided within the volume are compelling and certainly warrant further attention, it is perhaps instructive to note that one of the sources initially offered to substantiate the authors' opening framing is the much misreported TEACH report (Allouche-Benayoun and Jikeli 2013, footnote 4).

In order fully to understand the salience of this edited collection and of related publications and symposia (see, for example, Jikeli *et al.* 2007), it is important that we recognise not only national, but also international discursive frames. While earlier sections of this chapter made significant reference to the construction of a Muslim 'folk devil' as both a physical and existential threat to an imagined-as-unitary British national community, a related set of powerful discourses operate at the level of a larger, European 'we'. Within such discourses, the Holocaust performs a centrally important role. As Esra Özyürek describes:

> Since the turn of the twenty-first century, remembering the Holocaust and fighting against anti-Semitism have emerged as the connected centrepieces of European identity.
>
> (Özyürek 2016, 40; see also Romeyn 2014; Assmann 2007)

Özyürek describes how, through the 2000 Stockholm declaration and two later conferences convened by the Organization for Security and Cooperation in Europe (OSCE) in Vienna (2003) and Berlin (2004), 'fighting antisemitism' came to be 'defined as a central value of the recently enlarged Europe' (Özyürek 2016, 43). But as she continues, the price of galvanising a shared European identity on the basis of ostensibly very positive, democratic values was the creation of a necessary 'other' against and in relation to whom the virtues of post-war 'Europeanness' could be defined. Özyürek is not alone in locating this process at least in part within what she and others have characterised as an 'alarmist' discourse which closely associates Muslims and other 'immigrants' to Europe with what has, increasingly commonly, been framed as a 'new antisemitism'[2] (see also Rothberg and Yildiz 2011; Silverstein 2008; Bunzl 2005).

David Feldman outlines a similar argument while framing a recent research study of the relationship between antisemitism and immigration in five different European societies, including the UK:

> The prospects for absorbing and integrating a predominantly Muslim population of refugees has become a flashpoint for conflict between the proponents and opponents of liberal policies on immigration and cultural pluralism.
>
> The theme of 'Muslim antisemitism' plays a key role in these debates. In part this is because of the experience and impact of jihadist terror which on some occasions has been aimed specifically at Jewish targets. In part, too, it is a consequence of the role played by Holocaust memory, and the related commitment to overcoming antisemitism in the construction of European identity after the end of the Cold War. In this context, the commitment of Muslims to expunge antisemitism is regarded as not only good in itself but also as a marker of Muslims' capacity to integrate within European society.
>
> (Feldman 2018, 15, 16)

A related proposition, that any Muslim's ability to claim a right to belong within contemporary European society is contingent upon the 'appropriateness' or otherwise of their engagement with the Holocaust, is articulated clearly in one of the contributions to Jikeli and Allouche-Benayoun's edited collection:

> The reality is that however much Muslims may not wish to participate in Holocaust commemoration it is a defining aspect of European history, and *they will have to participate if they wish to live in, and be considered Europeans*.
>
> (Whine 2013, 38, emphasis added)

Although none of the other contributors state the case quite so baldly as Whine above, this appears to be a sentiment shared at least to some degree and articulated in various ways throughout many other chapters of the book.

Whose problem? Which Muslim students?

To avoid any possible confusion here, let me emphasise once more that it is by no means my intention to undermine very real concerns over – and very real recent experiences of – antisemitism as reported in Britain and across Europe. I do however believe that it is both possible and necessary to do so while at the same time advocating caution against the most alarmist and/or reductionist interpretations of existing available data. Again, this also means exercising critical reflexivity over how the specific issue of antisemitism – and, relatedly, potential opposition to learning about the Holocaust – among 'Muslim communities' is regularly framed.

This would also appear to be the position adopted by both Feldman and colleagues in the 2018 study already cited and in the 2017 report on antisemitism in Great Britain issued by the Institute for Jewish Policy Research (JPR) (Staetsky 2017). Both studies identify and acknowledge the apparent empirical reality of heightened levels of antisemitic attitudes as captured by survey instruments among respondents who identify as Muslim. At the same time however, both also emphasise three key points which bear relevance to the arguments explored in this chapter. Firstly, while levels of antisemitism as measured in the JPR's UK study, for example, were higher among Muslim respondents than among the general population as a whole, this still reflected only a minority of the total number of Muslim people surveyed. As Staetsky helpfully summarises, 'significant proportions of Muslims reject all such prejudice', 'thus the broad stigmatisation of all Muslims is neither accurate no[r] helpful' (Staetsky 2017, 58).

Secondly, in the UK study, as in all five nations reviewed in Feldman *et al.*'s comparative research, the relative size of the Muslim population is small and thus 'the degree to which Muslims are responsible for the total levels of antisemitism in these societies is low':

> The findings from the Muslim population, therefore, should not deflect from the fact that, for the most part, antisemitic attitudes stem from the majority population, not from minorities.
>
> (Feldman 2018, 23)

As Feldman warns,

> the focus on Muslim antisemitism can promote a process of 'externalisation': the projection of antisemitism in the majority society on to Muslim and immigrant minorities.
>
> (Feldman 2018, 16)

Indeed, Lentin and others would argue that this process of 'externalisation' extends further still, with the focus on 'new', Muslim antisemitism obscuring not only enduring European antisemitisms but also all other continuing forms of European racism (Lentin 2017; see also Benbassa 2007).

Thirdly, and as both Feldman and Staetsky are quick to remind us,

> Muslims encompass a very diverse population which contains distinctions of class, education, sex, ethnic background, generation, religious practice and belief. Surveys of attitudes [or indeed any enquiry] that are unable to take into account these potential sources of variation may prove blunt instruments.
>
> (Feldman 2018, 23)

As Feldman has written elsewhere, it is both misleading and damaging to think of 'the Muslim community' – or indeed any community – as a singular, homogenous or discrete entity, not least because 'the *similarities across* and *differences within* such communities are often at least as significant' (Feldman and Gidley 2014, 12; emphasis in original). Moreover,

> failing to recognise the diversity and range of voices and positions within such populations, also fail[s] to address the real structures of disadvantage that shape their experiences.
>
> (Feldman and Gidley 2014, 12)

In essence, the danger that we are being warned of here is of overdetermining what, if anything, the signifier 'Muslim' means in this context and how much explanatory power we might wittingly or unwittingly be awarding the term. This is perhaps the most resonant criticism that could be levelled against existing attempts to address or explore the 'problem' of Muslim student responses to the Holocaust.

Authors such as Short and Jikeli – who has conducted his own extensive qualitative research with young Muslim men in the UK, France and Germany and who reports significantly worrying articulations of antisemitism (Jikeli 2015) – invariably acknowledge that 'Muslim youth are not a monolithic entity' (Short 2013, 130) and/or that 'Muslim communities . . . are diverse, and individual's attitudes even more so' (Jikeli 2015, 4). However, they seldom appear to question whether, and to what extent, Muslim students' (rare) reluctance to learn about the Holocaust, or their expressions of antisemitism, are in fact attributable to their 'Muslimness'. Nor do they very significantly engage with the important argument that 'Muslimness' itself is a contingent and context-dependent, constructed phenomena. Critically, they minimise the role potentially played by 'majority' societies (and majority governments) who, as we have seen, can stand to gain from the identification of 'Muslims' in oppositional, pejorative and/or variously 'Othered' terms. They may also significantly contribute to the structural marginalisation and material disadvantage of minority communities (Kundnani 2007).

Julia Eksner makes a closely related argument in her 2014 study which examines how '(some) German Muslim youths come to position themselves against the State of Israel today' (Eksner 2014, 3). Eksner resists and is ultimately critical of the explanatory frame of '*Muslim* antisemitism' in Jikeli's and other German-language studies concluding, 'the assumed transmission of antisemitic stereotypes and attitudes via ethnocultural "Muslim" group membership as primary process pathway is currently not clearly supported by the empirical evidence' (Eksner 2014, 11). Instead, as she argues in a 2015 paper, that 'Muslim youth's positioning against Israel is by no means a "natural" or "cultural" given; rather, Muslim youth's responses are structured by pre-existing discursive relations in Germany'; 'in order to understand the anti-Israeli posture found among some German Muslim youths, one needs to understand less obvious discursive and structural conditions that fuel and encourage such attitudes' (Eksner 2015, 208).

Crucially, Eksner also suggests such discourses can become self-fulfilling. She cites a German study by Stender and Follert (2010):

> In the face of contradicting data about the attitudes of their Muslim students (which were not antisemitic), the mostly autochthonous German teachers of these students defined antisemitism as the problem of 'Muslim students,' influenced by the widespread mass media discourse on 'Muslim antisemtitism' in the phrasing of their words. . . . Most importantly, students who are ascribed with stigmatized identities that position them as Muslim, anti-Western, anti-Israeli, and antisemitic respond to these positionings.
>
> (Eksner 2014, 32, citing Stender and Follert 2010)

This is not to suggest that expectations of antisemitism – or of opposition to learning about the Holocaust – in any sense simply *create* antisemitism, or opposition, from nought. On the contrary, Eksner highlights that the experience of marginalisation and pejorative 'Othering' concomitant with precisely such expectations can contribute to the feelings of disengagement, resistance and/or antagonism which *may* in turn spark or fuel antisemitic or oppositional sentiment.

With this in mind, it is prudent to return to the conclusion reached in Short's 2013 paper. Short draws his paper to a close with the reflection, 'No matter how amenable some Muslim students might be to learning about the Holocaust, teachers ought to be prepared for a hostile reaction from others' (Short 2013, 130). There is a sound pedagogical rationale for such a reflection likely made in all good faith. However, if we are to take seriously the warning offered by Eksner and others, that Muslim students' identifications as Muslim are at least in part dependent on other people's expectations and wider discursive constructions, there is perhaps a danger that a 'prepared' but otherwise unreflexive teacher might exacerbate precisely the situation they were intending to address. At the very least, we could argue that this same teacher's preparation could more instructively be spent ensuring that their pedagogy encourages and enables students to respond to taught content from emergent and flexible rather than predetermined positions. More pragmatically, it is also important to offer alternative 'evidence' to counter any potential dominance of those narratives that position an essentialised notion of 'Muslim students' as an obstacle to teaching and learning about the Holocaust. Such 'evidence' is important not only for teachers but also for their students, especially those who might otherwise bear the weight of such skewed representational discourses.

The 2016 UCL student study

To this end it is instructive to share analysis of a sub-sample of student responses drawn from the UCL Centre for Holocaust Education's 2016 study (Foster *et al.* 2016): survey responses from 1,016 11–18-year-olds who self-identified as Muslim and interview responses from a further 26. On the basis of this data-set, the largest of its kind internationally, 'Muslimness' appears to have very low explanatory power as to attitude towards learning about the Holocaust. The wider study from which this data was drawn has already been described in earlier chapters of this book, but it is worth noting that Muslim students comprised 12.8 per cent of the total cohort of 7,978 individuals who completed the detailed online survey (see also Foster *et al.* 2016). At the 2011 census, approximately 8 per cent of all school-aged children in England were Muslim. Of those that took part in the UCL survey, 70.5 per cent indicated that religion was 'very important' to them personally, 26.2 per cent that it was 'quite important' and 3.4 per cent that it was 'not important'; 49.6 per cent identified their ethnicity as Asian–Pakistani, 16.2 per cent as Asian–Bangladeshi, 7.5 per cent as Asian–other (including Indian). This is broadly consistent with data collected from the adult Muslim population in 2011 (Muslim Council of Britain 2015).

Within the survey, all participating students were invited to indicate to what extent they agreed with a series of statements designed to examine attitudes towards learning about the Holocaust in school. There were 11 statements in total including items such as: 'The Holocaust does not really interest me'; 'Too much time in school is spent learning about the Holocaust'; 'Young people should learn about the Holocaust so they understand where prejudice and racism can lead'; and 'The Holocaust is not related to my life because it happened in another country'. To enable statistical comparison across students, a single mean measure was calculated by combining individual students' responses to all 11 statements. The highest scores reflected those students who appeared most positive towards learning about the Holocaust. Across all 7,958 students, the average score was 34.6 (of a possible 44). This was interpreted to demonstrate very high levels of positive engagement with this history across survey respondents as a whole; a 'neutral' rating in response to all 11 statements combined would have scored 22. Responses for individual groups and cohorts of students were also examined but only very limited variation was found. Most significantly for our discussions here, the average score across all those students who self-identified as Muslim was 33.8. The average score for those who identified as having 'no religion' by way of comparison was 34.2. However, when analyses were run to take account of the potential influence of other demographic variables captured in the survey, such as socio-economic class or academic ability, even this very small distinction was found to be statistically insignificant (Foster *et al.* 2016, 81). Among the students who took part in the UCL study, gender, academic ability and socioeconomic class all appeared to have a more pronounced impact than 'Muslimness' on how positively or otherwise a student felt towards learning about the Holocaust.

Positivity also characterised the accounts given by the 26 Muslim students invited to take part in interviews. It is important to emphasise the limitations of the qualitative dimension of this study. In total, only 5 focus groups were conducted in just 2 different schools and female interviewees outnumbered males by 20 to 6 as one of the participating schools was a single-sex girl's school. Nonetheless, the two schools – one in central London, the other in a large urban area in the West Midlands – offered significant contrast in the approaches they adopted to teaching and learning about the Holocaust. In one school a large amount of curriculum time across all year groups was devoted to the subject and students who took part in interview appeared especially knowledgeable about this history. In the second, the Holocaust received limited attention spread over just one or two lessons in Year 9. The students at both schools were aged between 12 and 17.

As such, the study certainly does not claim to offer an exhaustive or authoritative account of *all* Muslim students' attitudes towards learning about the Holocaust in *all* of England's schools. However, the responses given in interview do further corroborate and inform the impression given by the much larger and more representative survey data-set already described. Together, they strongly suggest that the more contentious negativity captured in studies by Jikeli and Rutland, for example, as cited above, is unlikely to reflect a majority perspective and is less widespread than readers of only those studies might be inclined to believe. Moreover, although they are less likely to find their way into arresting newspaper headlines, the positive affirmations shared by Muslim students in the UCL study are no less important to document than the outright hostility that both Jikeli and Rutland share.

In the school with a well-established and extensive programme related to the Holocaust, students demonstrated considerable interest and engagement. For example, some reported that they had chosen their post-compulsory examination subjects to ensure they could learn more about this history. Others emphasised what they saw as the Holocaust's universal significance: 'No matter where you are in the world you should learn about that' (extract from interview with Chandni, Year 9). These students repeatedly explained their interest with reference to a notion of shared humanity transcending ethnic, religious or national identities:

> It was done against humans. I think it's just innate in us to feel emotions towards it, regardless of their race or religion or anything. (Extract from interview with Laboni, Year 12)
>
> I think if we are empathetic people then we will be interested to learn about it. Because even though they are not Muslims or they are not Bengali, they are Jews, they are still human beings. (Extract from interview with Yasmina, Year 7)

Although students from the second school tended to be less emphatic in their responses, they still expressed interest in the Holocaust, considered it to be an important subject to learn about and, in general, expressed the desire to learn more than they already knew. Interestingly, while, during interview, some students shared strongly held personal views regarding the Israel-Palestine conflict and acknowledged that this could in some contexts lead to tensions between Muslims and Jews, they gave no indication that such perspectives in any way impacted their attitude towards learning about the Holocaust.

The closest that any student in either school got to articulating a position of potential opposition echoed one of the concerns tentatively advanced by a small number of teachers who took part in UCL's 2009 study:

Laboni: Some students might want to learn about something a bit more closer to their identity and identify with it a bit more . . .

Samreen: It's like Eurocentric. Being Muslim, it is more than likely that you'll be from somewhere in Asia or Africa. I think learning about perhaps the Nationalist challenge in India would be a bit more interesting to us than what happened in Germany perhaps.

(Extract from interview with Year 12 students)

One group of Year 13 students were willing to challenge the prominence given to the Holocaust within the national curriculum a little further and ventured criticism of the celebratory British national narrative within which they felt this history was framed:

Marwa: It [the Holocaust] shows the British in a positive light.

Zarak: That's why they publicise it . . . When you are studying certain subjects you sort of inoculate the conflicting arguments so you don't really know much about them, so you can't really acknowledge them. So obviously by putting the Holocaust in, you see Britain, as like they are doing a good thing, so you don't really think about the bad things they might have done.

[...]

Rameesha: I think it's like last year we learned about how Hitler got into power and more about the Holocaust. That should be like the British Empire, how they attained the British Empire, find out what the British Empire did for them.

Wassim: All they really talk about is how our tiny island ruled this many countries, which shows its power. It doesn't tell you about all the people who died, and like India and how they lost their freedom. They don't display the debts, they don't show the debts.

(Extracts from interview with Year 13 students)

One possible framing of these students' voices could interpret their words as resentment towards learning about the Holocaust, or worse still, a disavowal or undermining of its significance relative to other historical events, which, in some commentators' analyses, is tantamount to emergent Holocaust denial (see, for example, Jikeli 2015). There is insufficient space here to grapple with the legitimacy or otherwise of claims that attention given to the Holocaust in English classrooms (or elsewhere) underscores the relative inattention given to, for example, the country's own colonial and slave-trading past, (though for relevant contributions to such discussions see, amongst others, Lawson 2014; Stone 2000; and Rothberg 2009). However, given the concerns of the current chapter it is especially important to emphasise that almost exactly the same sentiments and potential provocations were also raised by a number of other, non-Muslim, 'white' or 'majority ethnic' students during interview. It would therefore and once again be both misleading and potentially harmful to read even these, very tentative, potential criticisms as foremost a function of students' 'Muslimness' in any simplistic way.

Concluding thoughts and unanswered questions

This chapter volunteered the notions of 'constructed controversy', 'folk devils' and 'moral panics' as instructive lenses through which to consider recent popular, media, and even some academic discourses regarding the 'problem' of Muslim student responses to learning about the Holocaust. It did so, not to deny the existence of any such problematic or otherwise challenging encounters, but to insist on a sense of proportionality and to highlight the importance of reflexivity and care in how teachers, policy makers, researchers and other commentators approach such discourse. It emphasised that discussions of how *some* Muslim students engage with taught content on the Holocaust are themselves framed by – and can in turn contribute to – wider discursive frameworks currently operating at both a national and international level which powerfully position 'Muslim' communities as a 'problem', a 'threat' and/or a 'challenge', outside of and antithetical to British and/or European 'values' and identity. Some of these same discourses simultaneously position 'appropriate' engagement with – and reverence for – the memory of the Holocaust as a litmus test for 'insider' status, an indicator of whether those marked as 'other' truly belong.

In this context, the chapter suggests that it is of considerable importance that both teachers and educational researchers avoid alarmist overgeneralisations and resist essentialist 'explanations' that overdetermine the significance of 'Muslimness'. Drawing on prior empirical research and an unprecedentedly large dataset that allowed comparative examination of Muslim students' attitudes towards learning about the Holocaust, the chapter found very little evidence to suggest that this should be considered a significant area of concern.

That said, as other chapters in this collection have powerfully argued, educational exposure to the Holocaust can be a profoundly enriching and potentially transformative opportunity. If *any* students are less likely than others fully to engage with this opportunity – whether by virtue of their own prior understandings and expectations, individual or familial political perspectives, religious beliefs, their own perception or experience of marginalisation, or, for that matter, the prior judgements made about them by teachers – this warrants further attention. Of all the indicative questions I listed earlier in this chapter, one proved impossible to answer on the basis of existing literature and empirical data: In what – if any – specific contexts have encounters interpreted as problematic been most or least likely to occur? But, in terms of responsive pedagogy, this is arguably the most important. If we are to move beyond 'Muslimness' as an insufficient explanation for a particular type of (potential) opposition to learning about the Holocaust, further, more nuanced, reflexive and responsible research and classroom reflection is required.

Notes

1. See, as a point of comparison, some of the charges of 'burying ones head in the sand' levelled at David Feldman and colleagues, for example, in their recent analysis of the relationship between antisemitism and immigration into Western Europe (Baker 2018) or at the European Monitoring Centre on Racism and Xenophobia accused of suppressing research which appeared to provide evidence that 'Muslim youths' were the main source of rising antisemitism within Europe (as detailed in Bunzl 2005).
2. The notion of Muslims as 'immigrants' – that is, as relative newcomers or 'outsiders' – is itself somewhat contentious and rather problematic but is precisely one of the characteristic hallmarks of those discourses that serve to repeatedly position Muslims – irrespective of their country of birth – as temporary sojourners in distinction to the dominant and largely unquestioned national, or here European, 'we'. The notion of a distinctly 'new' antisemitism is similarly contentious and much debated (see, for example, Fine 2009 for an instructive overview of relevant debates).

References

Allouche-Benayoun, J. and Jikeli, G. 2013. 'Introduction'. In *Perceptions of the Holocaust in Europe and Muslim Communities: Sources, comparisons and educational challenges*, edited by Günther Jikeli and Joëlle Allouche-Benayoun, 1–12. London: Springer.

Ameli, S.R., Marandi, S.M., Ahmed, S., Kara, S. and Merali, A. 2007. *The British Media and Muslim Representation: The ideology of demonisation*. Wembley: Islamic Human Rights Commission.

Assmann, A. 2007. 'Europe: A community of memory?', *German Historical Institute Bulletin* 40: 11–25.

Baker, A. 2018. 'A recent study into rising antisemitism in Europe ignores the role of Muslim migrants', *The Jewish Chronicle*, 24 May. Online. https://www.thejc.com/comment/comment/recent-study-into-rising-antisemitism-in-europe-ignores-the-role-of-muslim-migrants-andrew-baker-ajc-1.464720 (accessed 12 February 2020).

Baker, P., Gabrielatos, C. and McEnery, T. 2013. *Discourse Analysis and Media Attitudes: The representation of Islam in the British press*. Cambridge: Cambridge University Press.

BBC. 2008. 'UK government acts on hoax email'. Online. http://news.bbc.co.uk/1/hi/education/7226778.stm (accessed 12 February 2020).

Benbassa, E. 2007. 'Xenophobia, anti-Semitism, and racism: Europe's recurring evils?' In *Anti-Semitism and Islamophobia: Hatreds old and new in Europe*, edited by Matti Bunzl, 77–89. Chicago: Prickly Paradigm.

Berger, P.L. and Luckmann, T. 1966. *The Social Construction of Reality: A treatise in the sociology of knowledge*. New York: Random House.

Bunzl, M. 2005. 'Between anti-Semitism and Islamophobia: Some thoughts on the new Europe', *American Ethnologist* 32 (4): 499–508.

Carr, H. 2012. 'How do children in an Egyptian international school respond to the teaching of the Holocaust?' M.Ed. thesis, University of Hull.

Clark, L. 2007. 'Teachers drop the Holocaust to avoid offending Muslims', *The Daily Mail*, 2 April. Online. https://www.dailymail.co.uk/news/article-445979/Teachers-drop-Holocaust-avoid-offending-Muslims.html (accessed 12 February 2020).

Cohen, S. 1972. *Folk Devils and Moral Panics: The creation of the Mods and Rockers*. London: MacGibbon and Kee.

Cohen, S.K. 2005. 'Courage to care: A first encounter between the Holocaust and Australian school students', *Australian Journal of Jewish Studies* 19: 121–33.

Critcher, C. 2008. 'Moral panic analysis: Past, present and future', *Sociology Compass* 2 (4): 1127–44.

Eckstein, C., Biddulph, R., Braman, C., Middlebrooks, D., Greenberger, J. and Leon, M. 2007. 'Holocaust hush-up: It won't make UK safe', Comment on Barry Rubin, 'U.K. schools' sickening silence', *New York Post*. Online. https://nypost.com/2007/04/11/holocaust-hush-up-it-wont-make-uk-safe/ (accessed 12 February 2020).

Eksner, H.J. 2014. *Muslim Youths in Germany and the Question of Israel-Directed Antisemitism: The developmental and discursive context of a phenomenon* (Working Paper 137). Jerusalem: European Forum at the Hebrew University.

Eksner, H.J. 2015. 'Thrice tied tales: Germany, Israel, and German Muslim youth'. In *Being Jewish in 21st-Century Germany* edited by H. Fireberg and O. Glöckner, 208–28. Berlin: De Gruyter.

Feldman, D. 2018. *Antisemitism and Immigration in Western Europe Today. Is there a connection? Findings and recommendations from a five-nation study*. Berlin: Foundation 'Remembrance, Responsibility and Future' (EVZ) and London: Pears Institute for the study of Antisemitism, University of London.

Feldman, D. and Gidley, B. 2014. 'Introduction'. In *Integration, Disadvantage and Extremism*, edited by David Feldman and Ben Gidley, 9–12. London: Pears Institute for the study of Antisemitism, Birkbeck, University of London, in association with Centre on Migration, Policy and Society (COMPAS), University of Oxford and the All-Party Parliamentary Group Against Antisemitism.

Fine, R. 2009. 'Fighting with phantoms: A contribution to the debate on antisemitism in Europe', *Patterns of Prejudice* 43 (5): 459–79.

Foster, S.J., Pettigrew, A., Pearce, A., Hale, R., Burgess, A., Salmons, P. and Lenga, R.-A. 2016. *What Do Students Know and Understand about the Holocaust? Evidence from English secondary schools*. London: UCL Institute of Education.

Goode, E. and Ben-Yehuda, N. 1994. *Moral Panics: The social construction of deviance*. Oxford: Blackwell.

Gryglewski, E. 2010. 'Teaching about the Holocaust in multicultural societies: Appreciating the learner', *Intercultural Education* 21 (1): S41–S50.

Hall, S., Critcher, C., Jefferson, T., Clarke, J. and Roberts, B. 1978. *Policing the Crisis: Mugging, the state and law and order.* Basingstoke: Palgrave Macmillan.

Historical Association. 2007. *T.E.A.C.H.: Teaching emotive and controversial history 3–19.* London: The Historical Association.

Jikeli, G. 2015. *European Muslim Antisemitism: Why young urban males say they don't like Jews.* Bloomington: Indiana University Press.

Jikeli, G., Stoller, R. and Thoma, H. (eds) (2007) *Proceedings: Strategies and effective practices for fighting antisemitism among people with a Muslim or Arab background in Europe.* Berlin: International Institute for Education and Research on Antisemitism.

Kundnani, A. 2007. *The End of Tolerance: Racism in 21st century Britain.* London: Pluto Press.

Lawson, T. 2014. 'Coming to terms with the past: Reading and writing colonial genocide as a Holocaust historian', *Holocaust Studies: A Journal of Culture and History* 20 (1–2): 129–56.

Lentin, A. 2017. '"Je Suis Juif": Charlie Hebdo and the remaking of antisemitism'. In *After Charlie Hebdo: Terror, racism and free speech*, edited by Gavan Titley, Des Freedman, Gholam Khiabany and Aurélien Mondon, 262–77. London: Zed Books.

Mikkelson, D. 2007. 'Holocaust teaching ban in the UK?' *Snopes*,15 April. Online. https://www.snopes.com/fact-check/holocaust-teaching-ban-uk/ (accessed 12 February 2020).

Muslim Council of Britain. 2015. *British Muslims in Numbers: A demographic, socio-economic and health profile of Muslims in Britain drawing on the 2011 Census.* Online. http://www.mcb.org.uk/wp-content/uploads/2015/02/MCBCensusReport_2015.pdf (accessed 12 February 2020).

Özyürek, E. 2016. 'Export-import theory and the racialization of anti-Semitism: Turkish- and Arab-only prevention programs in Germany', *Comparative Studies in Society and History* 58 (1): 40–65.

Pettigrew, A., Foster, S., Howson, J., Salmons, P., Lenga, R.-A. and Andrews, K. 2009. *Teaching about the Holocaust in English Secondary Schools: An empirical study of national trends, perspectives and practice*. London: Institute of Education.

Poole, E. 2009. *Reporting Islam: Media representations of British Muslims*. London: I.B. Tauris.

Reed, C.A. and Novogrodsky, M. 2000. 'Teaching the Holocaust in a multiracial, multicultural, urban environment in Canada'. In *The Holocaust's Ghost: Writings on Arts, Politics, Law and Education*, edited by F.C. DeCoste and Bernard Schwartz, 513–21. Edmonton: University of Alberta Press.

Romeyn, E. 2014. 'Anti-Semitism and Islamophobia: Spectropolitics and immigration', *Theory, Culture & Society* 31 (6): 77–101.

Rothberg, M. 2009. *Multidirectional Memory: Remembering the Holocaust in the age of decolonisation*. Stanford, CA: Stanford University Press.

Rothberg, M. and Yildiz, Y. 2011. 'Memory citizenship: Migrant archives of Holocaust remembrance in contemporary Germany', *Parallax* 17 (4): 32–48.

Rubenstein, B. 2007. 'UK schools' sickening silence', *The New York Post*, 8 April. Online. https://nypost.com/2007/04/08/u-k-schools-sickening-silence/ (accessed 12 February 2020).

Rutland, S. 2010. 'Creating effective Holocaust education programmes for government schools with large Muslim populations in Sydney', *Prospects* 40 (1): 75–91.

Short, G. 2008. 'Teaching the Holocaust in predominantly Muslim schools', *Holocaust Studies: A Journal of Culture and History* 14 (2): 95–110.

Short, G. 2013. 'Reluctant learners? Muslim youth confront the Holocaust', *Intercultural Education* 24 (1–2): 121–32.

Silverstein, P. 2008. 'The context of antisemitism and Islamophobia in France', *Patterns of Prejudice* 42 (1): 1–26.

Staetsky, L.D. 2017. *Antisemitism in Contemporary Great Britain: A study of attitudes towards Jews and Israel*. London: Institute for Jewish Policy Research.

Stender, W. and Follert, G. 2010. '"Das kommt jetzt wirklich nur aus der muslimischen Welt." Antisemitismus bei Schülern in der Wahrnehmung von Lehrern und Schulsozialarbeitern'. In *Konstellationen des Antisemitism: Antisemitismusforschung und sozialpädagogische Praxis*, edited by Wolfram Stender, Guido Follert, and Mihri Özdogan, 199–224. Wiesbaden: Springer.

Stone, D. 2000. 'Day of remembering or day of forgetting? Or, why Britain does not need a Holocaust Memorial Day', *Patterns of Prejudice* 34 (4): 53–9.

Whine, M. 2013. 'Participation of European Muslim organisations in Holocaust commemorations'. In *Perceptions of the Holocaust in Europe and Muslim Communities: Sources, comparisons and educational challenges*, edited by Günther Jikeli and Joëlle Allouche-Benayoun, 29–40. London: Springer.

Whitaker, B. 2007. 'The birth of a myth', *The Guardian*, 21 August. Online. https://www.theguardian.com/commentisfree/2007/aug/21/birthofamyth (accessed 12 February 2020).

10
Seeing things differently: The use of atrocity images in teaching about the Holocaust

Ruth-Anne Lenga

Introduction

Atrocity images of the Holocaust have been in circulation across Europe and further afield since the Soviet and Allied liberation of concentration and death camps such as Majdanek, in July 1944, and Bergen-Belsen, in April 1945 (Struk 1998).[1] However, with the digital turn of the late twentieth century and the rapid escalation of computer use, 'smartphone' technology and other internet-enabled electronic devices, such images have never been as widespread, familiar or readily accessible as they are today (Reading 2001; see also Walden 2015). Anyone, of any age, can search for 'The Holocaust' via the internet and quickly find images of atrocity without filter, context or careful pedagogic framing. Whether we like it or not, the images are out there, are pervasive, and, as Janina Struk and others have argued, now form the basis of much public consciousness of this history (Dean 2015; Struk 1998). Indeed, young people can also readily encounter atrocity images through many other common fora including the conventional textbook (Foster and Burgess 2013) or television documentary. It is against this reality that the question of whether images of atrocity should be included in secondary school teaching programmes about the Holocaust will be explored.

The chapter offers a disruptive perspective on the prevailing position among leading Holocaust education organisations: that atrocity images have very limited, if any, place in the classroom. In 2004, the International Holocaust Remembrance Alliance (IHRA, then the International Task Force for Holocaust Education, Remembrance and Research) published its 'Guidelines for Teachers'. This document, which has been shared extensively since, was clear:

> The Holocaust can be taught effectively without using any photographs of piles of naked bodies, and the overuse of such imagery can be harmful. Engendering shock and revulsion is unlikely to constitute a worthwhile learning experience.
>
> (International Holocaust Remembrance Alliance 2004, 7)

In a similar manner, guidelines produced by the United Kingdom's Holocaust Memorial Day Trust recommend that teachers 'avoid unnecessary, repeated or inappropriate images of dead bodies or open graves' or 'images of Holocaust or genocide victims which dehumanise individuals' (Holocaust Memorial Day Trust n.d., 3).

This chapter will consider these and other concerns that circulate within the field. Such concerns include anxiety that distressing images have the potential to harm students – both in terms of their emotional well-being and, relatedly, in terms of their capacity to learn. Critics also warn that atrocity photographs damage and distort the memory of the individual men, women and children depicted, imposing upon them an abstracted and dehumanising frame (see, for example, Crane 2008). However, the chapter will also explore a series of counterarguments which offer a challenge to the current consensus and suggest an important re-think in light of data drawn from the UCL student study (Foster *et al.* 2016).

Taking seriously young people's own views when invited to consider the potential value and potential danger of using such material, the chapter argues against a blanket classroom ban. Instead, it insists that educators first return to fundamental questions about the aims and rationales for teaching about the Holocaust and invites its readers to question their expectations of young people and their capacity to confront profoundly difficult realities. On this basis, the chapter warns that avoiding the use of atrocity images entails its own risk. Denying young people the opportunity to encounter images that depict the horror of the Holocaust within a carefully considered – and carefully prepared for – educational context risks leaving them ill-equipped to move meaningfully beyond shock, distress or revulsion if – or more likely, *when* – they encounter the same or similar images outside of the classroom. It also risks denying them an opportunity to begin to grapple with the actual horror – and full significance – of this history.

As indicated in the words above, if the educational potential of an atrocity image is to be realised, careful consideration and careful preparation on the part of teachers is key. The chapter therefore concludes with a number of suggestions for how such images could be used responsibly and with sound educational rationale. It advocates that teachers can ensure a duty of care, both to their students and to the historical record, by adequately preparing classes before they encounter potentially distressing imagery; offering young people autonomy as decision makers over what they feel is appropriate – or necessary – to view; providing adequate time for students to process their thoughts and responses; and presenting photographs in such a way that seeks to dignify the memory of the human beings captured within them. In doing so the chapter neither diminishes nor denies the concerns already raised but foregrounds the ultimate responsibility of educators to frame the use of any such image in a manner that enables rather than forecloses in-depth 'meaning-making' and 'historical truthfulness' (Crane 2008, 316).

'Powerful knowledge' and the exceptional educational importance of the Holocaust

Genocide and mass atrocity are by their very extremity exceptional, but the Holocaust is considered by many to be distinct and unprecedented. Not only is it set apart in public consciousness as the ultimate representation of unspeakable evil but on historical grounds too. Historian Yehuda Bauer argues this case not on the basis of a measure of suffering or degree of scale. Extreme forms of human suffering, he argues, are not comparable (Bauer 2002, 13). Rather, Bauer sets the Holocaust apart from the catalogue of mass violence that has befallen human history due to the intent of the perpetrators to annihilate every member of a single group for purely ideological reasons. He states:

> there is something unprecedented, frightening about the Holocaust of the Jewish people that should be taught: for the first time in the blood stained history of the human race, a decision developed, in a modern state in the midst of a civilized continent, to track down, register, mark, isolate from their surroundings, dispossess, humiliate, concentrate, transport and murder every single person

> of an ethnic group as defined not by them, but by the perpetrators; not just in the country where the monster arose, not just on the continent the monster first wished to control, but ultimately everywhere on earth, and for purely ideological reasons. There is no precedent for that.
>
> (Bauer 2000)

For Bauer, understanding why the Holocaust happened – how vast numbers of ordinary people throughout Europe participated directly and indirectly in the murder of their Jewish neighbours and how this took place while the rest of the world was silent – is of crucial importance for understanding the world today. It is a 'cornerstone of contemporary Western culture' (Jinks 2016, 1) and a central reference point for understanding twentieth century European history and identity (Diner 2003). As a 'paradigmatic genocide', our understandings of the Holocaust and its precedents offer the potential to help us better comprehend – and perhaps even spot the warning signs of – other genocides, mass atrocities or human rights violations (International Holocaust Remembrance Alliance, online, no pagination). In the contemporary context, the rise in violent crime, violent extremism, antisemitism and increasingly regular episodes of denial, distortion and trivialisation of the Holocaust in the UK, Europe and elsewhere, all highlight the importance of ensuring young people know where such things can lead (Community Security Trust 2019; UNESCO and ODIHR 2018; Mulhall 2018). The Holocaust is, therefore, considered to be an essential component of young people's compulsory education by several national governments and education departments across the globe (Eckmann *et al.* 2017).

However, in terms of its ultimate pedagogical power, the rationale for teaching school students about the Holocaust must quickly be accompanied by careful consideration, not only of *what* students should be taught about this history (as discussed, for example, by Foster in this volume), but also *how.* Michael Young and colleagues have written extensively about the transformative potential of what they characterise as 'powerful knowledge', that is knowledge 'that provides more reliable explanations and new ways of thinking about the world and [that] can provide learners with a language for engaging in political, moral, and other kinds of debates' (Young 2008, 14; see also Young *et al.* 2014; and, for a discussion of 'powerful knowledge' and the Holocaust, Pettigrew 2017). Perhaps the most contentious contribution of this chapter is in posing the question, how 'powerful' or potentially transformative can students' knowledge of the Holocaust ever really be if they are too carefully shielded from its full atrocity? The chapter suggests that it is against this compelling educational potential that arguments against the use of atrocity images in the classroom must be weighed.

Using atrocity images to teach about the Holocaust: Opposition, opportunity and mitigating risk

Opposition

Reticence towards the use of atrocity images for teaching centres on three main issues: that images may traumatise young viewers; that they objectify the photographed subjects; and they dull the senses to the human consequence of the Nazi crime, thereby impeding learning and sensitive engagement. In the United Kingdom, all teachers have a legal as well as moral or ethical duty of care towards their students. The Institute of Education's 2009 research with secondary school teachers in England reported that, 'teaching about the Holocaust appeared to cause teachers to consider their pastoral relationships with students in ways that some had not necessarily experienced before'. As one teacher interviewed within the study characterised it, 'you go into mother mode' (Pettigrew *et al.* 2009, 96). As a consequence, it is perhaps entirely understandable – and appropriate – that teachers are wary of distressing their students; the notion of burdening young people with material likely to shock or disturb may seem unduly risky or inappropriate in the classroom.

Other teachers suggested that, rather than cause upset, the graphic nature of some readily available footage of the Holocaust could in fact serve to numb young people to its horror. These are concerns shared by many prominent Holocaust educators and historians, such as Elaine Culbertson, Cornelia Brink and Susan Crane. For Culbertson (2016, 143), for example, there is 'no possible use for [atrocity images] in the classroom that can be justified'; while acknowledging that a picture is powerful in its ability to provide evidence, Culbertson nonetheless asserts that such images 'have the ability to "desensitise students" into feeling absolutely nothing about the victims'. Brink (2000) in turn argues that looking at such images 'paralyzes' us and makes us emotionally 'fall silent'.

Leading educator, Shulamit Imbar, of Yad Vashem – Israel's Museum of the Holocaust – develops this anxiety further. Imbar asserts that images of piles of dead bodies only serve to dehumanise the victim and generate negative responses in young people. She expresses concern for what the images do in relation to how the viewer sees the victims and argues that using the images in class does little to re-humanise them. She asks:

> What do I know about that person when I see him as a body? I believe we have to rescue the individual from the pile of bodies.
>
> (Interview conducted by the author with Shulamit Imbar in 2017)

Similarly, Hirsch suggests that images which capture death and suffering can 'rupture' the spirit and deaden the viewer's ability to see the life that was lived before or facilitate any sort of real understanding or sympathetic response (Hirsch 2001, 6). She states: 'They resist the work of mourning. They make it difficult to go back to a moment before death, or to recognize survival. They cannot be redeemed by irony, insight, or understanding' (Hirsch 2001).

The concern of Crane (2008) rests on a worry that the images objectify the people caught in the image. She argues that since the end of the Second World War atrocity images of the Holocaust have become 'atrocious objects of banal attention' and warns that their use may well inhibit rather than facilitate learning and understanding of this history (Crane 2008, 309). In addition, she sees the act of viewing atrocity images as a re-visiting of the dehumanisation of the individuals, and finds little to justify doing so. Crane also questions the ethics of public displays of atrocity images of the Holocaust in classrooms corridors, exhibitions, art galleries or such like. She states that few if any of the victims pictured in the images were willing subjects and almost all are taken by the victims' tormentors, save for those taken by the liberating forces and journalists (Crane 2008, 329). This certainly is an unsettling thought. The job of the Nazi photographers was to record the genocide of the Jews for a variety of reasons (see Figure 10.1). Often this was for propaganda purposes and was instructed on the orders of senior Nazi leaders. *The Auschwitz Album* found by Lilly Jacob at liberation contains photos taken at the end of May (or possibly June) 1944 and depicts scenes of the arrival, selection and final moments of thousands of Hungarian Jews (Yad Vashem, online). The album of photographs was the work of members of the SS whose main task was to take ID photos and fingerprints of the inmates who were selected for slave labour. From Crane's perspective, the imbalance of power between the photographer and the subject renders the image itself an object of abuse. For her, the dehumanisation that played into

Figure 10.1 German soldiers taking pictures during the Lvov pogrom of 30 June to 3 July 1941 (courtesy of the Wiener Library, London).

that abuse makes the actual photograph an instrument of genocide and therefore ethically too morally problematic to view (Crane 2008, 315).

Opportunity and risk

If the *only* images shown to young people took the form of those described with concern by Imbar, it would indeed seem very hard to 'rescue the individual from the pile of bodies' (Imbar, interview with author) or to restore any dignity and meaning to the lives once lived by the men, women and children pictured, for example, lying dead in a heap at Bergen-Belsen. For this we must engage with images, testimony, and footage, which speaks of the vibrancy and diversity of individuals before the Holocaust as well as their responses to the unfolding genocide (International Holocaust Remembrance Alliance 2004). But images of Nazi atrocity also do something else – they offer visual evidence (albeit mediated by the motivation of the photographer and the partial view of the lens) of what happened. The first images that circulated after the liberation of camps documented the discovery of thousands upon thousands of unburied dead and provided photographic evidence of a crime that had shaken the liberating forces and went on to shock a largely ignorant (at that time) wider public across Europe and beyond (Stone 2015).

Images on newsreels and newspaper front pages were instrumental in enabling the world to begin to bear witness to the truth and full horror of the Holocaust (Zelizer 1998). As such, they served an invaluable purpose but there were concerns even then that the scenes of brutality and mass murder depicted were too traumatic to be seen. The British Ministry of Information, for example, commissioned Sidney Bernstein to make a documentary that would provide indisputable evidence of the Nazis' crimes, yet when the reels were examined the film was shelved. It was considered too shocking and was only used in war crimes trials to corroborate survivors' eyewitness accounts. Yet the filmmakers had conceived of their project in broader educational terms and the film's script was to conclude with the words: 'Unless the world learns the lessons these pictures teach, night will fall. But, by God's grace, we who live will learn' (Stone 2015).

Some of the images were to become iconic, such as the disturbing image of a child's arrest during the Warsaw Ghetto Uprising or the British liberating soldier standing to attention beside a mass grave filled with a mangled heap of broken corpses. Through their familiarity, the power of images such as these has arguably become detached from their historical roots (Crane 2008). Because today's students, more than any previous generation, live in a world where such images circulate freely, there is an important educational argument that schools should provide opportunities to help them discern their authentic provenance and to judge if and when they have been 'used' or taken out of context for good or ill.

While some critics, perhaps most famously Susan Sontag, have argued that the widespread proliferation of images of atrocity risks diminishing their impact through 'densensitising' viewers (Sontag 2003; see also Möller 2009), others argue that, more than any other medium, iconic images of atrocity retain enormous power. Susie Linfield, for example, argues compellingly that 'photographs of grievous history', 'of defeat and atrocity' '[tell us things we] urgently need to know'. She insists, 'we need to respond to and learn from photographs' (Linfield 2010, xiv). Moreover, following Jean Amery, Hannah Arendt and Primo Levi, Linfield suggests that 'we cannot talk – at least in meaningful or realistic ways – about building a world of democracy, justice, and human rights without first understanding the experience of their negation': 'we need to look at, and look into what James Agee called "the cruel radiance of what is." Photographs help us to do that' (Linfield 2010, xv).

From this perspective, learning about this history without exposure to such images limits its educational potential and risks diminishing the 'power' of student knowledge of the Holocaust, shutting down opportunities for important, complex conversations (Young *et al.* 2014): conversations regarding our moral obligation to the memory of the past, for example, consideration of our responsibility to the individuals captured in the image, or questions relating to voyeurism and what the viewer brings of themselves when viewing any individual image. Ethical discourses like these, can, with the right teacher intervention, contribute to important learning experiences and help promote spiritual, moral and social awareness, arouse curiosity, and increase emotional literacy and awareness of self (Scribner 2019, 54). This fulfils the obligation to help young people witness suffering in the hope that it may, in a metaphorical sense if not a physical sense, prevent future crimes (Dean 2015).

Atrocity images of the Holocaust therefore provide a learning opportunity that, if mediated by informed teaching and guided questioning, can help students see the human suffering in the image rather than the nakedness and shame, the human tragedy rather than the lifeless corpses and inevitability of death. We have to help students encounter and 'read' these important photographs with empathy and emotional intelligence. For the reality is that the Holocaust is a profoundly 'difficult' history and learning about it must inevitably entail risk (Gross and Terra 2019, 4). The heinous Nazi crime and devastating void it created in all but entirely extinguishing Jewish life from Europe has to be 'seen' or otherwise confronted if young people are to know and comprehend the significance of what actually took place. When we teach about the Holocaust, we are teaching about the mass murder of innocent people on an unprecedented level. To take out or avoid that which evidences this risks leaving students struggling to make sense of what really happened. Shock and emotional pain are indeed a likely reaction and part of what makes the Holocaust such a challenging – and such an important – subject to teach.

But what of the concerns raised by teachers and others regarding distress potentially experienced by students? Here it is perhaps salutary to reflect upon our expectations of young people and their capacity to engage with difficult and complex realities. And while it is perhaps entirely understandable that teachers may want to protect their students from confronting trauma in their classrooms, it is important not to forget that young people arrive at school with their own life experiences and, for a significant number, these are far from trauma free. For example,

UNHCR, UNICEF and IOM estimates suggest that between January and June 2019, 94,040 children arrived in Europe seeking asylum from countries including Syria, Afghanistan and Iraq (UNHCR *et al.* 2019). While it is very hard to compile accurate cross-national data on school enrolment, all of these children have a right to education under European Union law (UNHCR 2019). Other students may come to class with difficult experiences borne of poverty, illness, fragmented or unstable home and family relationships or with caring responsibilities that exceed their years (see, for example, Mulkami 2017).

The insights offered by the Polish-Jewish writer, doctor and pedagogue Janusz Korczak are especially resonant here. Korczak is renowned for his wholesale and extraordinary commitment to and respect for children, especially the 200 Jewish orphans with whom he lived and worked and was ultimately murdered alongside in the Warsaw ghetto and death camp of Treblinka (Lifton 1988). Central to Korczak's pedagogy was an insistence that adults acknowledge and respect the rights and capabilities of all children for who they are as children, and not for who they will become: as 'people of today and not tomorrow'. While Korczak embodied the belief that care will always be an essential component of any relationship between educator and student, he warned against the misinterpretation of care as 'overprotection' and the underestimation of children's strength, judgement and resilience. As Gabriel Eichsteller summarises, for Korczak, 'over protection disregards . . . children's right to freedom, self-experience and self-determination' while 'protecting them from hazards means all too often that children are kept from learning' (Eichsteller 2009, 36). In the place of 'over protection' Korczak insisted on the importance of listening to the perspectives of young people themselves and respecting their own judgements. This makes the inclusion of school students' voices from the UCL study a vitally important contribution to the debate.

As discussed in further detail below, those students often appeared to struggle to come to terms with the reality of what happened during the Holocaust. For some, atrocity images served at least in part to satisfy a need for a concrete visual tool, enabling them to see the Holocaust as a real event. Through them they could begin to grasp, not merely what happened, where it happened or why it happened but the fact that it happened, that it was carried out by real people and real people were its victims. As such, the images offer an important educational opportunity, one that many of the young people who took part in interview argued strongly that they and their contemporaries should not be denied.

What is an atrocity image?

For those who remain uncertain that the educational potential in allowing students this opportunity outweighs the risks of causing trauma, a further consideration is worth our attention here. For the notion of omitting imagery on the basis of avoiding upset is not as straightforward as it may at first seem. The line between 'appropriate' and 'inappropriate' in classroom settings is not always easily determined and many images of the Holocaust have the potential to shock or distress students without depicting depravity. The atrocity element can be deceptive, its disturbing elements obscured. Horror may lurk beneath the surface, revealed only through contextual knowledge. For example, consider the image of Hungarian Jewish men, women and children gathered in a clearing at Auschwitz-Birkenau in 1944 (Figure 10.2). No one in this image is stripped naked, bloodied, or beaten down; there is nothing that will *obviously* upset. Only a sense of displacement appears visible on the faces of the crowd. Yet, unbeknown to individuals pictured, they are being held there awaiting their murder in the nearby gas chambers. The horrific nature of the image is revealed through access to this important provenance. This is compounded by our sense that the photographer likely

Figure 10.2 Hungarian Jews 1944 waiting in a clearing at Auschwitz Birkenau (United States Holocaust Memorial Museum, courtesy of Yad Vashem).

Figure 10.3 Nazi officers and female auxiliaries (*Helferinnen*) run down a wooden bridge in Solahuette. The man on the right carries an accordion (United States Holocaust Memorial Museum, courtesy of Anonymous donor).

knew perfectly well of the imminent fate of the Jews he or she was photographing and that *we* are now looking through their lens – so to speak.

Another example of an image where atrocity is not immediately obvious is a rarely exhibited photograph of German SS auxiliaries partying away with gusto (Figure 10.3). It is hardly 'atrocity' in the conventional sense until one discovers the location and timing of the image: it was taken at Auschwitz sometime between May and December 1944, a place and time in which thousands of Jews were murdered day after day. So the people having fun are also murderers. Far from officers conducting their work in the death camp under duress – a misconception that young people often assume was the case (Foster *et al.* 2016) – they appear to be happy in the environment. The image becomes more disturbing as the layers of contextual knowledge reveal reality.

Determining exactly what constitutes an atrocity image is complicated further by the fact that emotional pain and tolerance are subjective and vary greatly in terms of how they are expressed (Izard 1991, 187). Different individuals find different things upsetting for a variety of reasons and to different extents. The image of a mother clinging to her child in Miedzyrzec Podlaski in 1942 or 1943 as a German soldier aims his rifle in their direction, is arguably so repellent it is hard not to recoil. While most people would consider this particular photograph harrowingly graphic, some people may find it to be temporarily disturbing while, for others, emotions could be felt as 'real pain' (Izard 1991, 187). Sociologist Jack Mezirow, a pioneer of transformational learning theory, states that meaning is constructed through our perceptions of those experiences which are seen through the lens developed from past experiences (Taylor and Cranton 2012). Batchen warns that we bring so much of ourselves into the viewing of an image that it ceases to be a reliable historical record as what we see is partly what we construct (Batchen 2009). Thus, images that a teacher or a museum curator may not initially categorise as having the potential to emotionally disturb might in fact do so depending on who is viewing it, the life experience they bring and what of themselves they forge onto the image that they see. The connection is intuitive and the degree of the viewer's 'pain' is dependent on the individual, their experience and their own deeply rooted emotional triggers. Perhaps the viewer is a parent, or has lost someone close, has been abandoned or isolated. On encountering the image, that pain may well be revisited through the vicarious engagement with the different moment in time and context to the one that the image presents. In a classroom context, individual students' own personal biographies of forced travel or escape from conflict, for example, could likewise be 'triggered' in unanticipated ways.

This underlines again how far the selection of images for educational purposes is laden with complexity and risk. For example, is the photo of a teenager holding her head in her hands after arriving in the UK via *Kindertransport* (Figure 10.4) one that might cause distress to an individual who has endured displacement or fear? Perhaps the photograph of a Jewish woman in Germany in 1935 trying to hide her face from the unwelcome photographer who captures her as she sits on an isolated bench marked 'for Jews only' (Figure 10.5) might also arouse emotional pain?

There is also Crane's (2008) perplexing question regarding the nature of the person behind the camera and for what purpose that person shot the image. Does the fact that it was taken by the perpetrator – thereby adding further to the humiliation and degradation of the victims – render such an image a reflection of atrocity? Looking through the lens of the perpetrator creates a particular distortion and moral conflict. Images taken by Jews or other victim groups were inevitably rare – most images were taken by the Nazis or collaborators. One exception is the highly significant, out-of-focus, set of photos taken secretly in Auschwitz-Birkenau in 1944 with a smuggled camera by a Jewish Sonderkommando prisoner desperate to get word out of the

Figure 10.4 A Jewish youth, wearing a numbered tag, sits on a staircase with her head in her hands after her arrival in England with the second *Kindertransport* (United States Holocaust Memorial Museum, courtesy of National Archives and Records Administration, College Park).

Figure 10.5 Bench 'for Jews only' (courtesy of the Wiener Library, London).

annihilation of the Jewish people taking place. On first glance the images give little away, but deeper scrutiny reveals the disturbing reality. One image (Figure 10.6), for example, is framed by an irregular shape in which appear a number of figures in close proximity to one another. In fact, the framing comes from the photographer's position, stood within a doorway inside a gas chamber at Crematoria V. What is shown is the burning of bodies of recently murdered people. The photographer took this at considerable risk, never knowing if it would make the perilous journey to achieve the photographer's mission – to wake the world into action and bring an end to the suffering, which tragically it did not.

Historian Dan Stone describes the image as having 'an emergency' and 'an immediacy', which bears 'full frontal atrocity'. He states that to even theorise about its representation is almost offensive (Stone 2001, 131).

Figure 10.6 Burning bodies of recently murdered victims, in a photograph taken furtively through a doorway (State Museum of Auschwitz Birkenau, Oswiecim, Poland).

While acknowledging that the images are still only representations, upon which the viewer socially constructs a 'new reality' rather than seeing the truth of what is depicted, Stone argues that the photographs provide 'imprints of reality' bringing a 'closeness to the events' enabling the viewer to draw meaning through the visceral impact these photographs have on us (Stone 2001, 131).

The Sonderkommando photos are without question harrowing images of atrocity but the unique value of them in terms of their closeness to the events, and their distinct provenance makes them highly significant and educationally essential. Not only do they evidence the Holocaust but also give agency to the Jews who, despite a common misconception to the contrary, fought to sabotage the actions of their murderers when possible.

So, are atrocity images to be excluded from students' usage or not? On the one hand we have a duty of care towards student wellbeing and the need for respect toward the victims presented in the images. On the other hand, teachers have a responsibility to evidence what took place, with the best available sources, especially in a political and social climate of a rise in denial and antisemitism. Carolyn Dean states that this discourse 'pits important if recent concepts of ostensibly transformative, if vexed political function – to "bear witness", "never again" – against an aversion to the display of violated human dignity whose sources are psychic and cultural' (Dean 2015, 239). Ultimately the judgement lies with individual teachers who will have to call on deep knowledge of their students, their school, their community and indeed their own views and coping strategies when selecting material for use in their individual classrooms. The discussions throughout this chapter are offered with the intention of helping teachers make such judgements from a position of critical reflection, understanding and respect.

Student reflections on encountering atrocity images of the Holocaust: Findings from the UCL study

So far this chapter has presented some of the pervading arguments against using atrocity images and explored a number of competing theoretical and pedagogical approaches. But returning to the perspective reflected across the work of Janusz Korczak, it is important to also ask, what do young people *themselves* think the value of encountering atrocity images might be? How do they respond to some of the criticisms presented by educators as to the appropriateness of their use? During the UCL student study, described in further detail in earlier chapters, researchers conducted a number of focus group interviews with secondary school aged students. In 9 of these focus groups, students were explicitly invited to share their reflections on the use of atrocity images in school. In total, 35 students aged between 12 and 16 took part in such interviews – 23 girls and 12 boys from 4 different secondary schools (Foster *et al.* 2016). As this is a relatively small number of schools and students, any generalised claims can only be made with caution. However, some very consistent messages do emerge which provide important insight into the ways these particular students think about the use of atrocity images.

Students were in the main unwavering in their view that graphic images of the Holocaust have their place in helping them understand what happened in the Holocaust. Only 1 of the 72 students interviewed stated images need not be seen in order to comprehend the event but a number did suggest that much younger children might be disturbed by seeing them as these Year 9 students suggest:

> Some people might get like shocked by it, some people might get a little bit too shocked, too scared.
>
> I think that's why we study it in Year 9. You're starting to become more mature in how you act around certain aspects and topics so I think it is appropriate from a certain age.

Students recognised the traumatic nature of the images but felt that this would not bring about an unreasonable or detrimental effect on them considering the history they were trying to comprehend. In fact some students felt that to truly engage with this history and the plight of the victims, feelings of upset were a necessary part of the learning process particularly with regard to promoting civic action and learning from the past. For example Joanna, a Year 9 student, explains:

> I think it's important to be upset about these things and if you are not upset, you're not having empathy for the subject, and I think people should be upset about it because then you know what these people have experienced, it makes you want to stop it.

A Year 11 student went on to acknowledge that learning is not exclusively a cognitive activity but involves affective engagement: 'You understand by being upset'. So whilst concerns exist about emotions standing in the way of understanding, here students explain how emotional engagement is actually how they learn.

When discussing the possibility that some teachers may have concerns about the effects of drawing on graphic images on their students' emotional wellbeing, students revealed that they see the images outside class in any case through the internet, or while searching for material for a classroom homework project. They suggested that it was important to view such images in order to help them face the content.

> Yes, because if you see piles of dead bodies. You can't just ignore it.

In the discussion on whether they see it necessary for their teachers to use images as part of the classroom learning, Year 10 Saehna responded:

> you'd understand it more, you wouldn't be more scared of it, you'd be more understanding of it.

The idea was put to students that some teachers of the Holocaust *may* feel they have a duty to avoid using the images in class to protect students' emotional wellbeing. In response some voiced consternation. Sophie, a Year 9 student, stated:

> I feel like the school tries to shield the Holocaust in a way. Like they will tell us about it but they are not going to show you images that upset you. . . . So it's almost shielded in a way.

A Year 10 student replied:

> If you don't learn about this now and you are just shielded from it then for the rest of your life, you never will learn about it.

When the students are asked how they think teachers *should* present the images, one student suggested that students be prepared in advance of the lesson:

> Maybe ask the class how they feel about it before bringing them in, they could ask first, but I don't think they should shield you if you don't want to be shielded.

One student acknowledged that graphic images were inherently disturbing but were not the cause of unreasonable or inappropriate psychological discomfort, given the horrific nature of the past reality that they were attempting to encounter. The students remarked on a sense of significance through the witnessing of the images:

> If it was real enough to happen it's real enough for us to view it, I think. It's important for us to see it.

Others spoke of the role of the visual image in deepening their comprehension:

> I think it also adds to your own, like, it being realistic to you and seeing consequences of it because lots of us are visual learners and we learn by seeing it.

Interestingly, most students raised the difficulty of truly realising that the Holocaust actually happened and how the atrocity images helped them grasp the *reality* of it. Billie, Sophie (both Year 12) and John (Year 13) discuss this here:

Billie: Yeah, as awful as the photos are you see that . . . it's almost like . . . okay this is real: look this is it. I think people have to see it before even believing it and then it just hits you.

Sarah: Or you hear this was done and that was done, but without actually seeing the pictures you can't actually translate it into a real event that happened in history. And so when we actually see the pictures we can make that link and see that it was actually something that happened.

John: It stops the idea of a story and a legend . . . it stops being a story: it makes it real.

This is further explored by Year 9 and 10 students as they articulate why images help them absorb that which otherwise appears incredulous.

> You're shown something, you're being shown evidence and it just connects everything that you've heard about, read about; and you look at that picture and . . .
>
> That's true. It's proof to what actually happened. If you have pictures from the time it shows that this actually happened and it shows the true horrors of what happened.
>
> I think even though it's upsetting, it will give you like some . . . it's official.

Put to the interviewees the fact that some professionals argue that showing these images could denigrate the memory of those pictured, their responses pivoted between agreement and an overriding sense that the importance of witnessing them was important too.

> It's really sad that they are textbook pictures now, but I suppose . . . . If in a newspaper, I wouldn't agree with that. But if it's educating future generations and it could have an impact and make society better, if I was I'd . . . well I wouldn't get a choice on it; but I wouldn't have a problem if it might have a chance of improving society.
>
> Sarah (Year 13)

Daisy: I think it can be unrespectful, well it is. But it . . . if it helps some people understand the extent a bit more, then I feel that that . . .
Shannon: Yeah. The intentions are . . .
Daisy: The intention is good . . .
Stan: Not to be disrespectful . . .
Shannon: It's not disrespectful if using it almost to teach, educate.

(Year 13)

No suggestion was made that the images dehumanised the Jewish people captured in them but Year 9 student Chandni explains that the images did much to remind students that this happened to real human beings:

> It adds the human element to the teaching of history. You know when we look at the figures and it's like millions died, but you never actually think about the people.

In summary, many students voiced a need to witness the atrocity image in order to grasp the reality of the Holocaust. They thought that viewing such images, whilst upsetting and disturbing, was not the same as *experiencing* what was pictured; and whilst seeing the images caused them upset it was not going to leave lasting damage. They also demonstrated sensitivity and concern in their conversations regarding the question of a possible responsibility they and their teachers may have towards the memory of the individuals captured in the photos in their classroom use but felt that if used with 'good intent' the educational importance of witnessing the images was paramount. There was a clear sense of grievance from some of the young people who felt it possible that their teachers were trying to shield them from the facts. Whilst the responses from this small group of teenagers may be limited in number, the views and perspectives shown here help us to rethink and re-examine and re-open a conversation on the issue.

Atrocity images of the Holocaust and education: Looking forward

Are photographs of Nazi atrocity exceptional sources of information depicting a difficult history which can facilitate complex understanding? Or are they simply too much for the visual consumption of young people of secondary school age? I would argue that atrocity images of the Holocaust *do* have a place in students' education about this catastrophic history – but not unconditionally. It remains important to consider the duty of care that needs to be in place to safeguard students from potential traumatisation, and teachers also require a framework that can protect and guide them in doing so. The following recommendations are intended as a useful starting point towards such a framework, advocating an approach in schools which supports teachers to responsibly and creatively navigate risk.

1. Schools could introduce guidelines for the use of potentially disturbing images within their whole-school teaching and learning or safeguarding policies. Incorporating the new IHRA recommendations for Teaching and Learning about the Holocaust (described in further detail below) would be an excellent place to start.
2. An important aspect of any whole-school policy statement is the need for clear educational rationales whenever such images are introduced. It is insufficient and inappropriate, for example, to use such images only to engender shock.
3. In relation to the Holocaust, the policy may specify the type of images that an individual school believes should be avoided, if it wishes to determine them. 'Permitted images' could be further specified in terms of age appropriateness. Images of naked women and children, particularly those taken by the perpetrator, may fall into a 'not permitted' category, for example. Ideally, such decisions would be collectively formulated including input from teachers, senior leaders, parents, and crucially, following Korszak, should also include student voices. This strategy has the added strength of engaging students in questions relating to the emotional wellbeing of not just themselves but their wider school community.

4. Young people should be given adequate warning of teachers' intention to bring to class images that are particularly graphic. They should be given the choice to view the image or look away and supported to themselves consider what is important and appropriate for them to see and why. This could include reflection on students' potential sense of responsibility to the memory of the individuals depicted and the various forms this can take.
5. Students should be provided with adequate support in 'reading' graphic imagery, confidently ascertaining the provenance of photographs and coming to their own interpretations of their potential significance and poignancy. Historical contextualisation can enable students to better understand what is taking place in the image; what is known or unknown; what choices were or were not available to those depicted; and what actions taken could have changed the course of events that led to the moment caught in time. Helping young people to consider who is behind the lens and why the photo is being taken is also a valuable exploration. Juxtaposing, for example, the Jewish Sonderkommando photographs discussed earlier in this chapter – which depict the murder of Jews taken in an act of resistance – with a photo of a similar scene taken by a perpetrator in order to record the Nazis' triumphs or to send back home as a souvenir, could inspire pertinent conversation about the past and present status of an image and the role of the photographer.
6. Supporting students to express their responses to potentially disturbing images is a further important consideration. What is necessary, in educational terms, is to find sensitive ways of handling *all* sources that testify to the Holocaust. It is appropriate that students are helped to discuss their responses openly should they wish to and to ruminate on ethical questions regarding the use of such images in classrooms and other contexts. Working through disturbance of this nature is a necessary part of emotional development and connecting to the suffering of others is important to knowing oneself. Students may express their reactions in very different and unexpected ways. It is important to be open and to support students' emotional literacy. On seeing such images there is also a risk that the experience might reawaken emotional wounds unrelated to the image or subject being studied. Thoroughly knowing one's individual students well – their particular strengths and vulnerabilities – is of paramount importance, whilst remaining ever conscious that young people are, in the main, incredibly resilient.

7. In order to ensure that exposure to the images does not dehumanise the victims, care and thought needs to be paid to planning and timing. The point at which the atrocity image is introduced within a scheme of work is critical. It should not, for example, be offered as a student's first encounter with this history. Engagement with stories and visual encounters with individual Jewish men, women and children before the war is a necessary prerequisite. Only then, when students have had a chance to invest in the human story, can the images of what happened to individuals strike home the true tragedy of the Holocaust.
8. As part of a school's safeguarding policy, schools could usefully invest time on teaching students e-safety and specifically on accessing images relating to the Holocaust. These could include how to responsibly search for images outside the safety of the school environment. This process might connect to other interventions made by schools to address antisemitism as images of the Holocaust are often used as psychological weapons to intimidate Jews today.
9. Drawing students into ethical, moral and civic debate about the images and how they are to be viewed can take students to deeper levels of understanding. Sontag has suggested that if there is an ethical duty to witness there is also a duty to do something with what you now know. She says active learning is a first step (Sontag 2003, 42). Perhaps this proposition would make a valuable starting point for young people to consider what action, if any, they feel they need to take in the light of their encounters with Holocaust history and representation.

Conclusion

For those concerned with the way secondary students come to understand and make sense of the Holocaust, the common presence of atrocity images can be a deeply troubling matter. However, a blanket ban on their use is also problematic. This chapter has sought to invite those who feel reticent about their use to further consider the issue. It has proposed that with due care and sound professional forethought from teachers, their use can be justified. Many justifications were in fact offered by young people themselves, through the UCL researchers' focus group interviews. Alongside those students, the chapter suggests that there can be profound educational value in seeing the photos, carefully unpacking them, asking questions of them, discovering how to learn from them. Indeed, it suggests that these things are vital if young people are going to engage seriously with the reality of this genocide. At a time when Holocaust distortion and trivialisation is increasing, the importance of knowing what the Holocaust was and what actually happened is especially pronounced. Images are of course only one form of representation, but for many students they appear particularly compelling and can teach us a great deal.

The chapter acknowledges that the use of graphic imagery is not without risk within the classroom but it also recognises that education itself is an inherently risky endeavour. Indeed, following Biesta (2013, 1) one could argue that if we take risk out of education, there is a real chance that we take out education altogether, certainly in terms of its potentially transformative power. Korczak's inspiring belief in the underestimated capabilities and ultimate resilience of all children suggests that we should protect children without shielding them, safeguard them without overprotecting. And while such images remain so widespread and 'out there', surely it is better that young people are given the opportunity to encounter them – to make meaning of and from them – in a supportive school environment, mediated by a teacher capable of constructing a learning experience that respects both the individuals depicted as victims and the individual children in their class.

In December 2019, a new set of guidelines for teachers was published by the International Holocaust Remembrance Alliance to replace those discussed at the very beginning of this chapter (International Holocaust Remembrance Alliance 2019). It is instructive to note that, rather than take the more programmatic approach that characterises much of the 2004 document, these appear to place much more emphasis on the critical responsibility of teachers to make considered choices with clear educational rationales and with sensitivity to their students. In doing so it echoes one of the most important arguments of the chapter, that in seeking to 'protect' both the students in our classrooms and the memory of the 6 million individual men, women and children at the centre of this history, we risk undermining its most powerful educational potential. Susan Sontag warns us of the 'shame' of looking close up at real horror but crucially she reserves a caveat for those who do it in order to serve a greater purpose. She states:

> Perhaps the only people with the right to look at images of suffering of this extreme order are those who could do something to alleviate it . . . or those who can learn from it.
>
> (Sontag 2003, 42)

Note

1. As documentary photographer Janina Struk alerts us, 'a great number of photographs' had in fact 'been made available by official and unofficial sources in Nazi occupied Europe in the early years of the War'. For example, 'In 1942 a book published in Britain by the Polish government in exile provided graphic accounts and photographs of the Nazi atrocities in occupied Poland' (Struk 1998, 97). However, such images did not begin to reach a wider public audience until after the war.

References

Batchen, G. 2009. 'Seeing and saying: A response to "incongruous images"', *History and Theory* 48 (4): 26–33.

Bauer, Y. 2000. 'Speech at the ceremonial opening of the forum', Stockholm International Forum. Online. http://www.d.dccam.org/Projects/Affinity/SIF/DATA/2000/page898.html (accessed 12 February 2020).

Bauer, Y. 2002. *Rethinking the Holocaust*. New Haven, CT: Yale Nota Bene.

Biesta, G.J.J. 2013. *The Beautiful Risk of Education*. Boulder, CO: Paradigm.

Brink, C. 2000. 'Secular icons: Looking at photographs from Nazi concentration camps', *History and Memory* 12 (1): 135–50.

Community Security Trust. 2019. 'Antisemitic incidents: Report 2018'. London: Community Security Trust. Online. https://cst.org.uk/public/data/file/2/9/Incidents%20Report%20 2018%20-%20web.pdf (accessed 12 February 2020).

Crane, S.A. 2008. 'Choosing not to look: Representation, repatriation, and Holocaust atrocity photography', *History and Theory* 47 (3): 309–30.

Culbertson, E.A. 2016. 'A reflection on the use of iconic Holocaust resources'. In *Essentials of Holocaust Education: Fundamental issues and approaches*, edited by S. Totten and S. Feinberg. New York: Routledge.

Dean, C.J. 2015. 'Atrocity photographs, dignity, and human vulnerability', *Humanity: An International Journal of Human Rights, Humanitarianism, and Development* 6 (2): 239–64.

Diner, D. 2003. 'Restitution and memory: The Holocaust in European political cultures', *New German Critique* 90: 36–44.

Eckmann, M., Stevick, D. and Ambrosewicz-Jacobs, J. (eds) 2017. *Research in Teaching and Learning about the Holocaust: A dialogue beyond borders*. Berlin: Metropol Verlag.

Eichsteller, G. 2009. 'Janusz Korczak: His legacy and its relevance for children's rights today', *International Journal of Children's Rights* 17 (3): 377–91.

Foster, S. and Burgess, A. 2013. 'Problematic portrayals and contentious content: Representations of the Holocaust in English history textbooks', *Journal of Educational Media, Memory, and Society* 5 (2): 20–38. Online. https://doi.org/10.3167/jemms.2013.050202 (accessed 12 February 2020).

Foster, S.J., Pettigrew, A., Pearce, A., Hale, R., Burgess, A., Salmons, P. and Lenga, R.-A. 2016. *What Do Students Know and Understand about the Holocaust? Evidence from English secondary schools*. London: UCL Institute of Education.

Gross, M.H. and Terra, L. (eds) 2019. *Teaching and Learning The Difficult Past: Comparative perspectives*. New York: Routledge.

Hirsch, M. 2001. 'Surviving images: Holocaust photographs and the work of postmemory', *Yale Journal of Criticism* 14 (1): 5–37.

Holocaust Memorial Day Trust (HMDT). n.d. 'Guidelines for delivering Holocaust and genocide education on Holocaust Memorial Day'. Online. https://www.hmd.org.uk/wp-content/uploads/2019/09/HMD-education-guidelines.pdf (accessed 12 February 2020).

International Holocaust Remembrance Alliance. 2004. 'How to Teach about the Holocaust in Schools'. Accessed 21 July 2019. https://www.holocaustremembrance.com/resources/educational-materials/how-teach-about-holocaust-schools

International Holocaust Remembrance Alliance. n.d. 'The Holocaust and other genocides'. Online. https://www.holocaustremembrance.com/index.php/educational-materials/holocaust-and-other-genocides (accessed 12 February 2020).

International Holocaust Remembrance Alliance. 2019. 'Recommendations for teaching and learning about the Holocaust'. Online. https://holocaustremembrance.com/sites/default/files/inline-files/IHRA-Recommendations-Teaching-and-Learning-about-Holocaust.pdf (accessed 12 February 2020).

Izard, C.E. 1991. *The Psychology of Emotions*. New York: Plenum Press.

Jinks, R. 2016. *Representing Genocide: The Holocaust as paradigm?* London: Bloomsbury.

Lifton, B. 1988. *The King of Children: A biography of Janusz Korczak*. New York: Farrar, Straus and Giroux.

Linfield, S. 2010. *The Cruel Radiance: Photography and political violence*. Chicago: University of Chicago Press.

Möller, F. 2009. 'The looking/not looking dilemma', *Review of International Studies* 35 (4): 781–94.

Mulhall, J. 2018. 'Holocaust denial is changing: The fight against it must change too', *The Guardian*, 21 November. Online. https://www.theguardian.com/commentisfree/2018/nov/21/holocaust-denial-changing-antisemitism-far-right (accessed 12 February 2020).

Mulkami, G. 2017. 'The crisis of young carers: "Going to school is a break"', *The Guardian*, 26 January. Online. https://www.theguardian.com/society/2017/jan/26/crisis-young-carers-uk-child-schools-end-secrecy-stigma (accessed 12 February 2020).

Pettigrew, A. 2017. 'Why teach or learn about the Holocaust? Teaching aims and student knowledge in English secondary schools', *Holocaust Studies* 23 (3): 263–88.

Pettigrew, A., Foster, S., Howson, J., Salmons, P., Lenga, R.-A. and Andrews, K. 2009. *Teaching about the Holocaust in English Secondary Schools: An empirical study of national trends, perspectives and practice*. London: Institute of Education Online. https://tinyurl.com/ya46s4by.

Reading, A. 2001. 'Clicking on Hitler: The virtual Holocaust @Home'. In *Visual Culture and the Holocaust*, edited by B. Zelizer. London: Athlone.

Scribner, C.F. 2019. 'Sublime understanding: Cultivating the emotional past'. In *Teaching and Learning the Difficult Past: Comparative perspectives*, edited by M.H. Gross and L. Terra. New York: Routledge.

Sontag, S. 2003. *Regarding the Pain of Others*. New York: Picador.

Stone, D. 2001. 'The Sonderkommando photographs', *Jewish Social Studies* 7 (3): 132–48.

Stone, D. 2015. *The Liberation of the Camps: The end of the Holocaust and its aftermath*. New Haven, CT: Yale University Press.

Struk, J. 1998. 'Photographs from the Holocaust archive', *The Journal of Holocaust Education* 7 (3): 87–112.

Taylor, E. and Cranton, P. 2012. *Handbook of Transformative Learning: Theory, research, and practice*. San Francisco, CA: Jossey-Bass.

UNESCO, and ODIHR. 2018. 'Addressing Anti-Semitism through education: Guidelines for policymakers'. Paris: UNESCO. Online. http://unesdoc.unesco.org/images/0026/002637/263702e.pdf.

UNHCR, UNICEF and IOM. 2019. Refugee and Migrant Children in Europe Overview of Trends in January–June 2019. Online. https://tinyurl.com/u5j9tld (accessed November 2019).

UNHCR (2019) Access to Education for Refugee and Migrant Children in Europe. Online. https://data2.unhcr.org/en/documents/download/71202 (accessed November 2019).

Walden, V. G. 2015. 'New ethical questions and social media: Young people's construction of Holocaust memory online,' *Frames Cinema Journal*. Online. http://framescinemajournal.com/article/new-ethical-questions-and-social-media-young-peoples-construction-of-holocaust-memory-online/

Yad Vashem. *The Auschwitz Album*. Online. https://www.yadvashem.org/yv/en/exhibitions/album_auschwitz/index.asp

Young, M. 2008. 'From Constructivism to Realism in the sociology of the curriculum', *Review of Research in Education* 32: 1–28.

Young, M., Lambert, D., Roberts, C. and Roberts, M. 2014. *Knowledge and the Future School: Curriculum and social justice*. London: Bloomsbury.

Zelizer, B. 1998. *Remembering to Forget: Holocaust memory through the camera's eye*. Chicago: University of Chicago Press.

Index

www.ingramcontent.com/pod-product-compliance
Lightning Source LLC
LaVergne TN
LVHW010731020926
846742LV00029B/41